Pope Benedict XVI

A REASON OPEN TO GOD

Pope Benedict XVI

A REASON
OPEN TO GOD

ON UNIVERSITIES, EDUCATION, AND CULTURE

With a foreword by John Garvey

Edited by J. Steven Brown

THE CATHOLIC UNIVERSITY OF AMERICA PRESS
WASHINGTON, D.C.

LIBRARY OF CONGRESS CATALOGING-IN-PUBLICATION DATA
Benedict XVI, Pope, 1927–
A reason open to God : on universities, education, and culture /
Pope Benedict XVI ; with a foreword by John Garvey ;
edited by J. Steven Brown.
pages cm
Includes bibliographical references and index.
ISBN 978-0-8132-2147-2 (pbk. : alk. paper)
1. Catholic Church—Doctrines.   2. Catholic universities and colleges.
3. Catholic Church—Education.   4. Christianity and culture.
I. Brown, J. Steven.   II. Title.
BX1378.6.B457 2013
261.8—dc22   2012049498

CONTENTS

PREFACE

The idea for this book was born out of a challenge laid before me by the president of the Catholic University of America in January 2011—namely, he asked me to respond publicly, together with five of my colleagues, to the question "What does faith have to do with the intellectual life?" For me this question was not a dry, abstract one, but a vital and existential one. I have taught engineering at the Catholic University of America since 1998, and President John Garvey's question touched the heart of the dramatic dialogue between faith and reason lived by me and by anyone engaged in university teaching and scholarship. Perhaps it will seem obvious to the reader that the question of relationship between faith and reason can and should be asked in a Catholic university. But is not the same question in play at all universities, and can it be asked at all universities—religiously affiliated or not? I believe that it can and must be. It is a crucial and dramatic one, and its challenge is urgent. In the words of Pope Benedict XVI, "A purely positivistic culture that tried to drive the question concerning God into the subjective realm, as being unscientific, would be the capitulation of reason, the renunciation of its highest possibilities, and hence a disaster for humanity, with very grave consequences."

This book gathers various speeches, homilies, and letters that Pope Benedict XVI has addressed to university audiences responding to today's situation. In addition to university addresses, I have included several key addresses on education and culture, since these themes are at the heart of the mission of a university and possess a value for society as a whole. As the reader will see, the pope's contribution presents two thousand years of lived tradition with a striking newness that is able to respond to our contemporary problems. It is my hope that, once these texts have been studied, the reader will see that the contribution made by Pope Benedict XVI to this crucial and dramatic question will have an enduring historical impact.

The speeches, homilies, and letters contained herein are taken from the official English texts prepared by the Libreria Editrice Vaticana and have been slightly edited, with permission, to aid the reader. In particular, greetings and concluding blessings in the spoken texts have been omitted, American English spellings have been adopted, and citations, excluding biblical references, have been moved to footnotes. For each text I include a source note below the title of the address that states the audience to whom the address was given and its location if some place other than the Vatican.

While Pope Benedict XVI never set out to produce a unified body of work as he addressed the various groups, certain key themes do emerge around which I have attempted to group the texts, although there is some overlap of several themes in many of the texts.

The biblical citations are taken from *The New American Bible* (Washington, D.C.: United States Conference of Catholic Bishops, 2002).

J. Steven Brown

FOREWORD

John Garvey

This is a collection of Pope Benedict XVI's addresses and writings about education and the university. During his papacy Benedict has devoted special attention to the "educational emergency" of recent years.[1] It is a subject about which he has a lot to say. Before his election he was a widely admired academic theologian. For twenty-five years he was prefect of the Congregation for the Doctrine of the Faith, the oldest congregation in the Roman Curia. The pieces in this book are the reflections of a finely tuned theological mind and a meditative disposition on that modern problem.

They also address another, and for us more important, question: How should a Catholic education differ from a secular one? What unique contributions might the schools born from the heart of the Church make to the solution of the modern educational emergency? Benedict's writing offers a response, which I want to highlight by way of introduction. At the center of a Catholic education, as at the center of Catholicism itself, is a friendship between God and man, mediated through the tradition of the Church. Benedict insists that Catholic education ceases to do its job when it ignores, sidelines, or alters this friendship.

Benedict's insistence on the centrality of friendship with God in Catholic education is not trite or sentimental rhetoric. It is a

1. Pope Benedict XVI, *Letter to the Faithful of the Diocese and City of Rome on the Urgent Task of Educating Young People,* January 21, 2008.

deeply held theological commitment that is evident throughout his career as a theologian and ecclesial authority. We see it in his work as a young man involved in the debates at Vatican II. We see it in the more mature writings found in this book. Benedict's reflections on education stress a distinctively Catholic formation of the intellect. But given the importance he attaches to friendship with God, it is natural that he should see more in Catholic education than just an intellectual component. He also emphasizes cultivating virtue and love of neighbor, since the relationship with God is never only vertical, but also always horizontal.[2] Friendship with God adds a moral dimension to Catholic education. However, nothing we do, no matter how intellectually rigorous or scientific, happens outside our relationship with God. To forget this is to forget who we are and for what and for Whom we are made. This is the main point of the pope's writings on this subject, and it is the reason we should pay attention to what he has said.

◆ ◆ ◆

I F WE LET Christ into our lives, we lose nothing, nothing, absolutely nothing of what makes life free, beautiful and great. No! Only in this friendship are the doors of life opened wide. Only in this friendship is the great potential of human existence truly revealed. Only in this friendship do we experience beauty and liberation ... open wide the doors to Christ—and you will find true life.

Pope Benedict XVI, *Homily for the Mass for the Inauguration of the Pontificate,* April 24, 2005

Late in the first session of Vatican II, Joseph Ratzinger was summoned to act as an advisor for the archbishop of Cologne, Joseph Cardinal Frings. By that time Ratzinger had written a doctoral dissertation on Augustine's ecclesiology and a postdoctoral dissertation on Bonaventure. Just in his mid-thirties, he had already spent a year teaching at Freising College and a few years at the University of Bonn. The Council, which sought to respond

2. Cf. Benedict XVI, *Address to Representatives from the World of Culture at the "Collège des Bernardins" in Paris,* Apostolic Journey to France, Paris, September 12, 2008.

to questions posed to the Church by the modern world, put an indelible mark on the young theologian.

In some ways Vatican II merely rephrased an old question about the Church's relation to other traditions. Since its earliest days the Church has engaged in a dialogue with other intellectual and moral currents. Many of the brightest lights in Church history made their mark by integrating insights from other traditions into Catholic thought. The early Church fathers married Greek philosophy with Christian theology. Medieval theologians like Thomas Aquinas synthesized the pagan wisdom of the Greeks and Romans with Christian thought. Those who succeeded in these endeavors used the wisdom of other traditions while preserving the central tenets of their faith.

The question facing the bishops and theologians who gathered at Vatican II appeared to be more complex. Many elements of modern thought seem inconsistent with a serious commitment to religion. Beginning with Descartes, modern philosophers have insisted that we doubt anything for which we lack rational certainty. Others have sought to offer universal accounts of knowledge and morality, accessible to any individual in any culture, which would do away with the need for stories about creation, Jesus, and the saints. Immanuel Kant demoted religion to the role of moral guide, not mediator of revealed truths. Devotees of the scientific method, committed to a philosophy of materialism, have insisted on the supremacy of empirical evidence. Influential modern economic and political thought emphasizes the role of the individual over that of the community.

None of these approaches is especially congenial to Catholicism. Some are outright hostile. The widespread skepticism fashionable in most intellectual circles has little in common with the ancient Greek philosophy on which Aquinas and the early Church fathers drew. Those who carve out a space for religion in general and Catholicism in particular do so with a view to minimizing their scope and relevance.

Some theologians at the Second Vatican Council nevertheless remained optimistic that the insights of modern philosophy
might be reconciled with Catholic theology. Joseph Ratzinger
was wary of these attempts. He feared that they conceded too
much to modern philosophy and felt that they paid too little attention to the unique revelation of the Christian faith.

Christ's life, death, and resurrection; his real presence in the
Eucharist; the teaching authority of the Church—these are not
dispensable myths or moral fables. They are essential elements
for cultivating friendship with God. Modes of theology that
sideline tradition and scripture lose sight of this point.

Ratzinger's reluctance to join these trends reflects a deeper
theological commitment. He believes that the love that gives
rise to friendship with God is the heart of the Christian religion. And friendship with God is made real and possible for us
through the historical Christ, scripture, the sacraments, and the
Church. Ratzinger makes the same point in his prolific treatment of the liturgy. "Liturgy," he says, "implies a real relationship with Another, who ... gives our existence a new direction."³
When we participate in the liturgy we draw on all the resources
God has used to reach out to us in love. In turn we find ourselves
in a friendship as universal as the Church and as personal as a
marriage. We discover God's response to Augustine's cry, "you
have made us for yourself, and our heart is restless until it rests
in you."⁴

Friendship with God through the mediation of the Church
remains the cornerstone of Ratzinger's theology today. He has
devoted two encyclicals to the topic of love and friendship with
God: *Deus Caritas Est* and *Caritas in Veritate*. In his remarks on
education, we will see, he gives the same priority to friendship
with God.

---

3. Joseph Cardinal Ratzinger, *Spirit of the Liturgy,* translated by John Saward (San
Francisco: Ignatius Press, 2000), 22.
4. Augustine, *Confessions,* translated by Henry Chadwick (New York: Oxford University Press, 2008), 3.

◆ ◆ ◆

Sᴛ. ᴛʜᴏᴍᴀs ᴀǫᴜɪɴᴀs's thought and witness suggest that we should study emerging problems with great attention in order to offer appropriate and creative responses. Confident in the possibilities of "human reason," in full fidelity to the immutable depositum fidei, we must as the "Doctor Communis" did always draw from the riches of Tradition, in the constant search for "the truth of things."

Pope Benedict XVI, *Address to Participants in the 14th Public Session of the Pontifical Academies,* January 28, 2010

When Pope John Paul II issued the apostolic constitution *Ex Corde Ecclesiae* in 1990, he sought to respond to the problem—which still exists—of a waning Catholic identity in higher education. Increasing specialization, a heightened emphasis on science and technology, and a widespread disinterest in the contributions of faith have marginalized the Catholic voice in higher education. Some colleges and universities seek to assure students and scholars of their academic stature by downplaying their Catholic identity. John Paul II reminded Catholic schools that

it is in the context of the impartial search for truth that the relationship between faith and reason is brought to light and meaning. The invitation of Saint Augustine, "Intellege ut credas; crede ut intellegas," is relevant to Catholic Universities that are called to explore courageously the riches of Revelation and of nature.[5]

Pope Benedict's writings on education and the university echo the concerns of John Paul II. He writes that Catholicism is an "intrinsic and essential dimension of education in the faith."[6] Like his predecessor, Benedict XVI holds that Catholic education is fundamentally different from its modern secular counterpart, which often attempts "to drive the question concerning God into the subjective realm, as being unscientific."[7] "The world is charged

5. Pope John Paul II, Apostolic Constitution *Ex Corde Ecclesiae* (August 15, 1990), n. 5.

6. Benedict VI, *Address to Participants in the Convention of the Diocese of Rome,* Rome, June 11, 2007.

7. Benedict XVI, *Address to Representatives from the World of Culture at the "Collège des Bernardins" in Paris,* Apostolic Journey to France, Paris, September 12, 2008.

with the grandeur of God,"[8] and, in a Catholic understanding, can be explored through faith and reason. The best secular education often only discovers part of that grandeur through careful philosophical, scientific, and artistic reflection, while stunting a fuller discovery by disregarding faith as a method of knowledge and by applying a reason closed to the transcendent. Catholic education adds the special revelation of God in scripture and tradition to the exercise of reason. As John Paul II put it, "Faith and reason are like two wings on which the human spirit rises to the contemplation of truth."[9]

Benedict goes on to make a more subtle, and more profound, point. Faith and reason are not just two essential, but independent ingredients in a Catholic education, as meat and potatoes are parts of a healthy meal. Faith transforms reason, imbuing it with the power to contemplate the highest truths. Faith likewise transforms education, enriching both the intellectual and moral pursuits of the university.

Let me illustrate these points by saying a few words about Catholic intellectual formation (specifically, what we study and how we study it) and the cultivation of virtue in Catholic education. I will return, then, to the centrality of friendship with God in Benedict's theology. This idea stands at the center not only of moral formation, but of the whole enterprise of Catholic education.

◆ ◆ ◆

THANKS TO THE teaching of the Catholic religion, school and society are enriched with true laboratories of culture and humanity in which, by deciphering the significant contribution of Christianity, the person is equipped to discover goodness and to grow in responsibility, to seek comparisons and to refine his or her critical sense, to draw from the gifts of the past to understand the present better and to be able to plan wisely for the future.

Pope Benedict XVI, *Address to Catholic Religion Teachers,* April 25, 2009

8. Gerard Manley Hopkins, "God's Grandeur," in *Poems,* edited by Robert Bridges (London: Humphrey Milford, 1918).

9. John Paul II, Encyclical Letter *Fides et Ratio* (September 15, 1998), n. 1.

In the last few decades many have noted, often with disappointment, the loss of a core liberal arts curriculum in American colleges and universities. Students no longer ask perennial questions, these critics charge, or take the time to meditate on the collective wisdom of Western civilization. How can our future scientists, composers, and authors do their jobs without asking fundamental questions about human existence? Where will they acquire the intellectual habits that will enable them to participate creatively and critically in their areas of specialization? Something similar happened in Catholic education. At one time all students were required to learn the basics of Christian theology, Church history, and ethics. Theology, like a core liberal arts curriculum, asks and answers fundamental questions. It is relevant to all courses of study for the Catholic student because it instills the vital intellectual habit of putting God before all else and teaches students to think about science and art, economics and literature, from a Catholic perspective. "[T]heology was the heart of the University," Benedict explains; it was "something that concerned everyone, in which all felt involved and somehow also knew that they were competent."[10]

Theology must resume its place at the center of a Catholic education, not only because it teaches students the story of their faith, but because it instills the intellectual habits that enable them to critically engage other subjects. The Platonist who studies *King Lear* analyzes the use of language and the symmetry of the plot, just like any other student. But she also asks whether Shakespeare's view of love converges with or diverges from Plato's philosophy. Our Catholic faith enables us to do something similar. The gospel narratives, the sacramentality of the Church, and the doctrine of original sin inform the way we view the world. They tell us something about love and its place in our lives. When we read *King Lear* we wonder whether he is like Christ or like Judas.

Consider another example. In her novel *To the Lighthouse* Vir-

---

10. Benedict XVI, *Address to a Delegation of the Theological Faculty of the University of Tübingen in Germany,* March 21, 2007.

ginia Woolf replaces religion with art as the source of sacred truth. Catholic students who read the novel might appreciate Woolf's use of stream of consciousness and her clever approach to characterization. But they will also consider how Woolf's vision of the world, in which art is sacred, differs from their own. The psalmist says of God

> For you formed my inward parts,
> you knitted me together in my mother's womb.
> I praise you, for I am wondrously made.
> Wonderful are your works!
> You know me right well. (Ps 139:13–14)

Can art replace this human longing for a deeply personal relationship with God? Do human beings really find satisfaction in worshipping their own creations? Catholic intellectual habits teach students to ask these questions of Virginia Woolf. Far from diminishing our capacity to think critically, Catholicism enriches it.

And just as we expect the Platonist to devote much of her time to the Platonic tradition, so also Catholic education should pay special attention to the voices of its tradition. We can appreciate the work of Virginia Woolf. But we will find perspectives more in line with our own in the writings of Paul Claudel and Francois Mauriac, J. R. R. Tolkien and Evelyn Waugh, Flannery O'Connor and Walker Percy.

There are obvious and not unimportant benefits to such acculturation. They include learning to speak the language of the Bible and the Church; discovering the uses of scripture, theology, and Church teaching in literature; and appreciating the inspiration that Catholic themes provided to generations of authors, poets, and playwrights.

But the most important effect of engaging Catholic voices in Catholic education may be the one illustrated by G. K. Chesterton in this story. An English yachtsman sailing abroad miscalculated his route and came ashore at his homeland, believing he had discovered a new land. Chesterton says,

His mistake was really a most enviable mistake; and he knew it, if he was the man I take him for. What could be more delightful than to have in the same few minutes all the fascinating terrors of going abroad combined with all the humane security of coming home again? ... How can we contrive to be at once astonished at the world and yet at home in it?[11]

Good Catholic literature does this for Catholicism: it creates a fictional world that feels new and yet has the familiarity of home. Fiction casts a new light on what we take for granted in Catholicism, and in so doing refreshes and preserves it.

Tolkien's epic tale *The Lord of the Rings* exemplifies the point. Though much too sophisticated to be an allegory, it relies for strength on a range of Catholic motifs. The character Gollum illustrates what it means to be enslaved to sin. Samwise Gamgee gently conveys the Christian meaning of friendship. Gandalf is like the holy monks of the medieval Church, cultivating intelligence and wisdom through intent study and practice of the virtues, while Frodo Baggins's mission to destroy the ring draws upon the Catholic meaning of vocation.

To appreciate the power of Tolkien's Catholic literature, consider that by the time the third installment of the film adaptation of *The Lord of the Rings* was released in 2004, the scourge of the 2002 sex scandals weighed heavy upon Catholics. Yet the films were a tremendous success, and together remain the highest-grossing motion-picture trilogy of all time. The genius of good Catholic literature is that it puts us far enough away from Catholicism that we leave aside our grievances, misconceptions, and sheer boredom. But when we probe the literature we find that we've fallen in love with something very like our own story.

Catholic education has a stake in teaching its students to appreciate and enjoy this power of Catholic literature. It helps them preserve an important part of Catholic tradition and love the story of their Catholic faith. Virginia Woolf's feminism

---

11. G. K. Chesterton, *Orthodoxy* (New York: Dodd, Mead, 1908), 3.

might resonate with some students' concerns and experiences. But her answers will never be the deeply satisfying ones told by the gospel.

◆ ◆ ◆

It's hard to dismiss out of hand this argument for the place of theology in literature. But the stuff of literature is myth and allegory, symbol and rhyme. What about the hard sciences, which deal with weights and measures, systems and laws? What contribution can faith make to the teaching and study of biology, chemistry, and physics? A class in biology covers the same material at a Catholic and a secular university. The mechanics of meiosis look the same; so does the taxonomy of the animal kingdom.

The Church is often accused of extending the reach of faith beyond its proper scope. Science can be guilty of the same kind of trespassing—or at least of an imperialism that assumes its answers are qualitatively superior to those of other modes of thought. Consider the way physicists approach the subject of cosmology. The current standard explanation for why the universe seems to be expanding in all directions is that it began with a big bang from a very small point about 13.7 billion years ago and has been going outward ever since. Theories about what happened before that do not seem like science in the usual sense of the word. One possibility physicists have suggested is that the matter that exploded appeared out of nothing, with no cause. Another is that it was always there. Or that it cycled in and out of existence—perhaps it popped out of another universe.

These speculations are not inherently different from the kind theologians offer. St. Augustine observed that God created the world out of nothing, and created time with it.[12] Aquinas believed that there could be only one universe; but his may have been a minority position among theologians of the time.[13] The

---

12. Augustine, *Confessions* Bk. 11.
13. Thomas Aquinas, *Summa Theologiae* I, q. 47, a. 3; Commentary on Aristotle's *De Caelo* bk 1, lectio 19.

bishop of Paris condemned as heretical the teaching "That the first cause cannot make more than one world."[14] The point is not that theology, much less scripture, should govern the creative instincts of astrophysicists. It is rather that the material world may not be all there is, and where it fits in the larger scheme of things is something they are not well-equipped to tell us about.

Nor are scientists better prepared than the rest of us to say how we should value the things we can see and measure. Food, drug, and cosmetic companies test their products on animals, a practice some people condemn as unethical. Some philosophers,[15] and even lawyers,[16] claim moral rights on behalf of plants, trees, and rivers. The Catholic Church teaches that the intentional destruction of a human embryo is gravely immoral. Science itself has no position on these questions, unless it might be, as it sometimes unfortunately is, that scientists should be allowed to pursue their research without the hindrance of ethical considerations.

Faith and science—both properly understood—are not inconsistent. They are answers to different kinds of questions. And the questions they deal with are frequently entangled with one another. Religious fundamentalism makes the mistake of ignoring what science can tell us about the age of rocks and the evolution of species. Scientific fundamentalism assumes that the only true answers are ones that science can give.

There is a nice illustration of this point in Walker Percy's novel *Love in the Ruins*. Thomas More, the book's main character, tries to explain to his doctor why he worries that he doesn't

14. Étienne Tempier, *Condemnation of 219 Propositions,* translated by Ernest Fortin and Peter O'Neill, in *Medieval Political Philosophy,* edited by Ralph Lerner and Muhsin Mahdi (New York: Free Press of Glencoe, 1963) 335, 340; P. Mandonnet, OP, *Siger de Brabant et l'averroïsme latin au XIIIme-siècle,* vol. 2, *Textes inédits,* 2nd ed. (Louvain: Institut Supérieur de Philosophie de l'Université, 1980), 175–91.

15. Graham Harvey, *Animism: Respecting the Living World* (New York: Columbia University Press, 2005); Freya Mathews, *For Love of Matter* (Albany: State University of New York Press, 2003).

16. *Sierra Club v. Morton,* 405 U.S. 727, 743 (1972) (*Douglas, J., dissenting:* "The river as plaintiff speaks for the ecological unit of life that is part of it").

feel guilty after having an affair. The doctor, a man of science, tries to persuade Thomas that the sin he imagines he committed is a myth, and that any feelings of guilt he suffers from might be conditioned away. More insists that it is not the guilt that worries him, but his lack of it.[17]

"Why does that worry you?"
"Because if I felt guilty, I could get rid of it."

Science can rid us of certain feelings, but it cannot give us the joy of faith or freedom from sin. In a 2008 conference on the changing identity of the person, Benedict cautioned, "no science can say who man is, where he comes from or where he is going."[18] One of the aims of Catholic education in the field of science is to open students' eyes to the many possibilities of enlightenment. Catholic education is one of the few places where the dignity of the human person is preserved against the tide of reductive materialism. That is a responsibility colleges and universities must take seriously.

❖ ❖ ❖

FAR FROM BEING JUST a communication of factual data— "informative"—the loving truth of the Gospel is creative and life-changing—"performative."

> Pope Benedict XVI, *Address to Catholic Educators at The Catholic University of America,* Apostolic Journey to the United States, Washington, April 17, 2008

It is a common misunderstanding to suppose that Christianity is a worldview or a theory of knowledge, like Marxism or empiricism, or a philosophy, like Platonism. The most casual acquaintance with Church tradition will dispel this idea. Many Catholics have known only the rudiments of their faith and could offer no

---

17. Walker Percy, *Love in the Ruins: The Adventures of a Bad Catholic at a Time Near the End of the World* (New York: Farrar, Straus, and Giroux, 1971), 116–17.

18. Benedict XVI, *Address to Participants in an Interacademic Conference on "The Changing Identity of the Individual": Organized by the "Académie Des Sciences" of Paris and by The Pontifical Academy of Sciences,* January 28, 2008.

more insight into theological doctrine than a child. Joseph Cupertino could barely read and write, but he was elevated to sainthood. That is because Christianity is as much about what we do as about what we know. Teaching students how to be Catholic, Benedict says, means instructing them to "perform" their faith well.

The theological reason for this is that love is the centripetal force of Christianity. "The human person … bears within himself, written in the most profound depths of being, the need for love, to be loved and in turn to love."[19] Because we are mere human beings and because we are fallen, loving God requires that he first give us grace. "Grace," the catechism tells us, "is a participation in the life of God" and comes through the sacraments of the Church.[20]

If receiving grace through the sacraments stands at the center of the Catholic moral life, it must also have a central place in Catholic education. Of course going to mass and confession should not be compulsory. God "did not will to save us without us," Augustine says.[21] But Catholic universities should encourage students to avail themselves of the sacraments, the visible signs of God's grace. It is a disservice when Catholic universities make them invisible to students.

Grace is about loving others as well as loving God. That is the message of the Gospel of John: "[E]ven as I have loved you, that you also love one another" (Jn 13:34). Christians extend their love of God to others, building up Christian communities by acting with patience, kindness, prudence, justice, temperance, and courage. Catholic universities help students to cultivate friendship with God by encouraging virtues that help them

19. Benedict XVI, *Address to the Participants in the Fourth National Ecclesial Convention,* Pastoral Visit to Verona, October 19, 2006.

20. *Catechism of the Catholic Church* (1993), n. 1997.

21. Augustine, *Sermon* 169.11.13, *Patrologia Cursus Completus, Series Latina (PL),* edited by Jacques P. Migne, 38:923 (Paris: 1844–1864): "Qui ergo te fecit sine te, non te justificat sine te."

to avoid the evils that rupture friendship. More positively, they teach students to live in ways that behoove a friend of God.

At the same time the virtues orient the intellectual life of the university. There is a scene in the movie *Apollo 13* where Jim Lovell has to steer the space craft manually because there is not enough power to operate the guidance system, and the ship has drifted off course. In order to get back on course, he aims to keep the sight of the earth in the craft's small window while he fires the engines. In steering the course of the intellectual life of a Catholic university, we need to keep God in the window. He is the point of the journey and what we need to keep in view if we want to stay on course. As Aristotle says in the *Nicomachean Ethics,* "virtue makes us aim at the right mark, and practical wisdom makes us take the right means."[22] Benedict puts it this way:

> In your Catholic schools, there is always a bigger picture over and above the individual subjects you study, the different skills you learn. All the work you do is placed in the context of growing in friendship with God, and all that flows from that friendship. So you learn not just to be good students, but good citizens, good people.[23]

Cultivating a life of virtue equips students to navigate the intellectual and cultural pitfalls that threaten to push God out of the picture on both fronts.

An academic setting has a special need for the virtues. Universities are places where research is done, where new discoveries are made, and where careers are built on hypotheses and arguments. For that reason they can also be contentious. Catholic universities must be places where knowledge and charity go hand in hand.

University professors, in particular, are called to embody the virtue of intellectual charity, recovering their primordial vocation to train future generations not only by imparting knowledge but by the prophetic wit-

---

22. Aristotle, *Nicomachean Ethics* 1144a.

23. Benedict XVI, *Address of the Holy Father to Pupils of St. Mary's University College,* Apostolic Journey to the United Kingdom, Twickenham, September 17, 2010.

ness of their own lives. The university, for its part, must never lose sight of its particular calling to be an "universitas" in which the various disciplines, each in its own way, are seen as part of a greater unum.[24]

So the virtues, especially love for God, keep the intellect oriented toward its goal. They also hold together the learning community. Just as knowing God through revelation allows the biologist to see the work of a Creator in a single cell, so too living the virtues changes the way we see the world. Pinning down exactly how it alters our vision is difficult, but it is like the difference that being in love makes. The virtues incline us to see the world as the Jesuit poet Gerard Manley Hopkins does in his poem "Pied Beauty." He writes,

> Glory be to God for dappled things—
> For skies of couple-colour as a brinded cow;
> For rose-moles all in stipple upon trout that swim;
> Fresh-firecoal chestnut-falls; finches' wings;
> Landscape plotted and pieced—fold, fallow, and plough;
> And áll trádes, their gear and tackle and trim.
>
> All things counter, original, spare, strange;
> Whatever is fickle, freckled (who knows how?)
> With swift, slow; sweet, sour; adazzle, dim;
> He fathers-forth whose beauty is past change:
> Praise him.[25]

Benedict XVI thinks that learning to love God is the central purpose of Catholic education. "Knowledge can never be limited to the purely intellectual realm; it also includes a renewed ability to look at things in a way free of prejudices and preconceptions, and to allow ourselves to be 'amazed' by reality, whose truth can be discovered by uniting understanding with love."[26] Hopkins's poem expresses amazement at a reality that we know

24. Benedict XVI, *Address to the Participants in the First European Meeting of University Lecturers,* June 23, 2007.

25. Hopkins, "Pied Beauty," in *Poems.*

26. Benedict XVI, *Address to the Participants in the First European Meeting of University Lecturers,* June 23, 2007.

not only with the mind, but with the heart as well. Catholic education, Benedict maintains, must teach us to see the world as Hopkins does, full of love and wonder.

◆ ◆ ◆

[T]RUTH IS NEVER purely theoretical: In drawing a parallel between the beatitudes of the Sermon on the Mount and the gifts of the Spirit listed in Isaiah 11, Saint Augustine argued that there is a reciprocity between scientia and tristitia: knowledge on its own, he said, causes sadness.

Pope Benedict XVI, *Address that the Holy Father Intended to Give During a Visit to La Sapienza University in Rome on Thursday, January 17, 2010*

If there is one thread that ties together Benedict's concern for theology after Vatican II, his encyclicals, and his reflections on the university and culture, it is this: love for God stands at the center of all. When he says that knowledge alone causes sadness, Benedict is making an empirical claim, not a theoretical one. We are a world in possession of a lot of knowledge. We can prolong the lives of people who suffer from diseases that were once devastating; we are developing genetic therapies that will prevent the diseases altogether. We save millions with medicines; we can wipe out as many with our weapons technology. But we have not been fulfilled by this knowledge. We are a sad, longing world that has an abundance of power and not enough wisdom.

Benedict's writing on the university is a prescription for that sadness. Our knowledge must be matched by love. Catholic universities must be places where students learn more than how to extract DNA or read a Marxist critique of Shakespeare. They need to be places where students learn to love God. If they do, then they will grow in the virtues they need to be good citizens of the world. They also stand a better chance of knowing something worthwhile.

It is into this context that the many pieces of the university fit. Study of the liberal arts, professional education, preparation for an academic career, and socialization are far more likely to fall into place if the community is ordered around the love of God. In 2008 Benedict addressed the diocese of Rome on the urgent task of educating the young. He said:

As opposed to what happens in the technical or financial fields, where today's advances can be added to those of the past, no similar accumulation is possible in the area of people's formation and moral growth, because the person's freedom is ever new.[27]

Throughout his career Pope Benedict has clung tenaciously to the Augustinian insistence that love for God is both the proximate and final end of all we do as Christians. Every student who enrolls in our institutions of higher education has a soul that, in the words of Joseph Ratzinger, is "nothing other than man's capacity for relatedness with truth, with love eternal."[28] Catholic universities that organize around another goal are bound to fail to give their students what is most important. They run the risk of trading the joy that comes from knowing and loving God for an empty knowledge that brings only sadness. Catholic education aims at nothing short of helping students to foster a friendship with God. "A good school provides a rounded education for the whole person," Benedict insists, "a good Catholic school, over and above this, should help all its students to become saints."[29]

27. Benedict XVI, *Letter to the Faithful of the Diocese and City of Rome on the Urgent Task of Educating Young People,* January 21, 2008.

28. Joseph Cardinal Ratzinger, *Eschatology: Death and Eternal Life,* translated by Michael Waldstein, translation editor Aidan Nichols (Washington D.C.: The Catholic University of America Press, 2007), xxi.

29. Benedict XVI, *Address of the Holy Father to Pupils of St. Mary's University College,* Apostolic Journey to the United Kingdom, Twickenham, September 17, 2010.

Pope Benedict XVI

A REASON OPEN TO GOD

INTRODUCTION

THE PROBLEM AND THE URGENT
TASK AHEAD

The Urgent Task of Education

From *Letter to the Faithful of the Diocese and City of Rome on the
Urgent Task of Educating Young People,* January 21, 2008

We all have at heart the good of the people we love, especially
our children, adolescents, and young people. Indeed, we know
that it is on them that the future of our city depends. Therefore,
it is impossible not to be concerned about the formation of the
new generations, about their ability to give their lives a direction
and to discern good from evil, and about their health, not only
physical, but also moral.

Educating, however, has never been an easy task, and today
seems to be becoming ever more difficult. Parents, teachers,
priests, and everyone who has direct educational responsibilities
are well aware of this. Hence, there is talk of a great "educational
emergency," confirmed by the failures we encounter all too often
in our efforts to form sound people who can cooperate with others and give their own lives meaning. Thus, it is natural to think
of laying the blame on the new generations, as though children
born today were different from those born in the past. There is
also talk of a "generation gap" that certainly exists and is making

itself felt, but is the effect rather than the cause of the failure to transmit certainties and values.

Must we therefore blame today's adults for no longer being able to educate? There is certainly a strong temptation among parents and teachers as well as educators in general to give up, since they run the risk of not even understanding what their role or rather the mission entrusted to them is.

In fact, it is not only the personal responsibilities of adults or young people, which nonetheless exist and must not be concealed, that are called into question, but also a widespread atmosphere, a mindset and form of culture that induce one to have doubt about the value of the human person, about the very meaning of truth and good, and ultimately about the goodness of life. It then becomes difficult to pass on from one generation to the next something that is valid and certain, rules of conduct, credible objectives around which to build life itself.

Dear brothers and sisters of Rome, at this point I would like to say some very simple words to you: Do not be afraid! In fact, none of these difficulties is insurmountable. They are, as it were, the other side of the coin of that great and precious gift that is our freedom, with the responsibility that rightly goes with it. As opposed to what happens in the technical or financial fields, where today's advances can be added to those of the past, no similar accumulation is possible in the area of people's formation and moral growth, because the person's freedom is ever new. As a result, each person and each generation must make his own decision anew, alone. Not even the greatest values of the past can be simply inherited; they must be claimed by us and renewed through an often anguishing personal option.

When the foundations are shaken, however, and essential certainties are lacking, the impelling need for those values once again makes itself felt: thus today, the request for an education that is truly such is in fact increasing. Parents, anxious and often anguished about the future of their children, are asking for it; a great many teachers going through the sorrowful experience of their schools' deterioration are asking for it; society overall, seeing doubts cast on the very foundations of coexistence, is asking for it; children and young people themselves who do not want to be left to face life's challenges on their own are also asking for it in their inmost being. Those who believe in Jesus Christ, moreover, have a further and stronger reason for not being afraid: they know in fact that God does not abandon us, that his love reaches us wherever we are and just as we are, in our wretchedness and weakness, in order to offer us a new possibility of good.

Dear brothers and sisters, to make my considerations more meaningful, it might be useful to identify several common requirements of an authentic education. It needs first of all that closeness and trust that are born from love: I am thinking of the first and fundamental experience of love that children have, or at least should have, from their parents. Yet every true teacher knows that if he is to educate he must give a part of himself, and that it is only in this way that he can help his pupils overcome selfishness and become in their turn capable of authentic love.

In a small child there is already a strong desire to know and to understand, which is expressed in his stream of questions and constant demands for explanations. Therefore, an education would be most impoverished if it were limited to providing notions and information and neglected the important question about the truth, especially that truth that can be a guide in life.

Suffering is also part of the truth of our life. So, by seeking to shield the youngest from every difficulty and experience of suffering, we risk raising brittle and ungenerous people, despite our good intentions: indeed, the capacity for loving corresponds to the capacity for suffering and for suffering together.

We thus arrive, dear friends of Rome, at what is perhaps the most delicate point in the task of education: finding the right balance between freedom and discipline. If no standard of behavior and rule of life are applied even in small daily matters, the character is not formed and the person will not be ready to face the trials that will come in the future. The educational relationship, however, is first of all the encounter of two kinds of freedom, and successful education means teaching the correct use of freedom. As the child gradually grows up, he becomes an adolescent and then a young person; we must therefore accept the risk of freedom and be constantly attentive in order to help him to correct wrong ideas and choices. However, what we must never do is to support him when he errs, to pretend we do not see the errors, or worse, that we share them as if they were the new boundaries of human progress.

Education cannot, therefore, dispense with that authoritativeness that makes the exercise of authority possible. It is the fruit of experience and competence, but is acquired above all with the coherence of one's own life and personal involvement, an expression of true love. The educator is thus a witness of truth and goodness. He, too, of course, is fragile and can be mistaken, but he will constantly endeavor to be in tune with his mission.

Dear faithful of Rome, from these simple observations it becomes clear that in education a sense of responsibility is crucial: the responsibility of the educator, of course, but also, as he grows up, the responsibility of the child, the student, the young person who enters the world of work. Those who can measure up to themselves and to others are responsible. Those who believe seek further; indeed, they seek to respond to God who loved them first.

Responsibility is in the first place personal, but there is also a responsibility that we share as citizens in the same city and of one nation, as members of the human family and, if we are believers, as children of the one God and members of the Church. Indeed, ideas, lifestyles, laws, the orientations in general of the society in which we live and the image it has of itself through the mass media exercise a great influence on the formation of the new generations, for good but often also for evil. However, society is not an abstraction; in the end we are ourselves all together, with the orientations, rules, and representatives we give one another, although the roles and responsibilities of each person are different. Thus, the contribution of each one of us, of each person, family, or social group, is necessary if society, starting with our city of Rome, is to become a more favorable context for education.

Lastly, I would like to offer you a thought that I developed in my recent encyclical letter *Spe Salvi* on Christian hope: the soul of education, as of the whole of life, can only be a dependable hope. Today, our hope is threatened on many sides, and we even risk becoming, like the ancient pagans, people "having no hope and without God in the world," as the Apostle Paul wrote to the Christians of Ephesus (Eph 2:12). What may be the deepest difficulty for a true educational endeavor consists precisely in this: the fact that at the root of the crisis of education lies a crisis of trust in life.

I cannot finish this letter, therefore, without a warm invitation to place our hope in God. He alone is the hope that withstands every disappointment; his love alone cannot be destroyed by death; his justice and mercy alone can heal injustices and recompense the suffering experienced. Hope that is addressed to God is never hope for oneself alone: it is always also hope for others; it does not isolate us, but renders us supportive in goodness and encourages us to educate one another in truth and in love.

I. THE RELATIONSHIP OF FAITH AND REASON

Faith, Reason, and the University

From *Meeting with Representatives of Science,* Apostolic Journey
to Germany, University of Regensburg, September 12, 2006

It is a moving experience for me to be back again at the university and to be able once again to give a lecture at this podium. I think back to those years when, after a pleasant period at the Freisinger Hochschule, I began teaching at the University of Bonn. That was in 1959, in the days of the old university made up of ordinary professors. The various chairs had neither assistants nor secretaries, but in recompense there was much direct contact with students, and in particular among the professors themselves. We would meet before and after lessons in the rooms of the teaching staff. There was a lively exchange with historians, philosophers, philologists, and, naturally, between the two theological faculties. Once a semester there was a *dies academicus,* when professors from every faculty appeared before the students of the entire university, making possible a genuine experience of *universitas*—something that you, too, magnificent rector, just mentioned—the experience, in other words, of the fact that despite our specializations, which at times make it difficult to communicate with each other, we made up a whole, working in everything on the basis of a single rationality with its various aspects and sharing

7

responsibility for the right use of reason—this reality became a lived experience. The university was also very proud of its two theological faculties. It was clear that, by inquiring about the reasonableness of faith, they too carried out a work that is necessarily part of the "whole" of the *universitas scientiarum,* even if not everyone could share the faith that theologians seek to correlate with reason as a whole. This profound sense of coherence within the universe of reason was not troubled, even when it was once reported that a colleague had said there was something odd about our university: it had two faculties devoted to something that did not exist: God. That even in the face of such radical skepticism it is still necessary and reasonable to raise the question of God through the use of reason, and to do so in the context of the tradition of the Christian faith: this, within the university as a whole, was accepted without question.

I was reminded of all this recently when I read the edition by Professor Theodore Khoury (Münster)[1] of part of the dialogue carried on—perhaps in 1391 in the winter barracks near Ankara—by the erudite Byzantine emperor Manuel II Paleologus and an educated Persian on the subject of Christianity and Islam, and the truth of both.[2] It was presumably the emperor himself who set down this dialogue during the siege of Constantinople

1. Khoury taught at Münster and retired from there in 1993 as professor and head of the theology department.

2. Of a total of twenty-six conversations (διάλεξις—Khoury translates this as "controversy") in the dialogue ("Entretien"), Theodor Khoury published the seventh controversy with footnotes and an extensive introduction on the origin of the text, the manuscript tradition, and the structure of the dialogue, together with brief summaries of the controversies not included in the edition; the Greek text is accompanied by a French translation: Manuel II Paléologue, "Manuel II Paléologue, Entretiens avec un Musulman: 7e Controverse," *Sources Chrétiennes* 115 (Paris: Éditions du Cerf, 1966); hereafter Khoury. In the meantime, Karl Förstel published an edition of the text in Greek and German with commentary; see Manuel II. Palaiologus, "Manuel II. Palaiologos, Dialoge mit einem Muslim," in *Corpus Islamico-Christianum,* 3 vols., Series Graeca, edited by Adel Theodor Khoury and Reinhold Glei (Würzburg-Altenberge: Echter Verlag, 1993–1996). As early as 1966, Erich Trapp had published the Greek text with an introduction as *Wiener byzantinische Studien,* vol. 2, *Manuel II Palaiologus: Dialog emit einem "Perser"* (Vienna: Böhlau, 1966). I shall be quoting from Khoury's edition.

between 1394 and 1402; and this would explain why his arguments are given in greater detail than those of his Persian interlocutor.[3] The dialogue ranges widely over the structures of faith contained in the Bible and the Qur'an, and deals especially with the image of God and of man, while necessarily returning repeatedly to the relationship between—as they were called—three "Laws" or "rules of life:" the Old Testament, the New Testament, and the Qur'an. It is not my intention to discuss this question in the present lecture; here I would like to discuss only one point—itself rather marginal to the dialogue as a whole—which, in the context of the issue of "faith and reason," I found interesting, and which can serve as the starting point for my reflections on this issue.

In the seventh conversation (διάλεξις—controversy) edited by Professor Khoury, the emperor touches on the theme of the holy war. The emperor must have known that surah 2:256 reads, "There is no compulsion in religion." According to some of the experts, this is probably one of the suras of the early period, when Mohammed was still powerless and under threat. But naturally the emperor also knew the instructions, developed later and recorded in the Qur'an, concerning holy war. Without descending into details, such as the difference in treatment accorded to those who have the "Book" and to the "infidels," he addresses his interlocutor with a startling brusqueness, a brusqueness that we find unacceptable, on the central question about the relationship between religion and violence in general, saying, "Show me just what Mohammed brought that was new, and there you will find things only evil and inhuman, such as his command to spread by the sword the faith he preached."[4] The emperor, after

3. On the origin and redaction of the dialogue, cf. Khoury, 22–29; extensive comments in this regard can also be found in the editions of Förstel and Trapp.

4. Khoury VII.2c, 142–43; Förstel, vol. 1, VII, Dialog 1.5:240–41. In the Muslim world this quotation has unfortunately been taken as an expression of my personal position, thus arousing understandable indignation. I hope that the reader of my text can see immediately that this sentence does not express my personal view of the Qur'an, for

having expressed himself so forcefully, goes on to explain in detail the reasons that spreading the faith through violence is something unreasonable. Violence is incompatible with the nature of God and the nature of the soul. "God," he says, "is not pleased by blood—and not acting reasonably (σὺν λόγω) is contrary to God's nature. Faith is born of the soul, not the body. Whoever would lead someone to faith needs the ability to speak well and to reason properly, without violence and threats.... To convince a reasonable soul, one does not need a strong arm, or weapons of any kind, or any other means of threatening a person with death."[5]

The decisive statement in this argument against violent conversion is this: not to act in accordance with reason is contrary to God's nature.[6] The editor, Theodore Khoury, observes, "For the emperor, as a Byzantine shaped by Greek philosophy, this statement is self-evident. But for Muslim teaching, God is absolutely transcendent. His will is not bound up with any of our categories, even that of rationality."[7] Here Khoury quotes a work of the noted French Islamist R. Arnaldez, who points out that Ibn Hazm went so far as to state that God is not bound even by his own word, and that nothing would oblige him to reveal the truth to us. Were it God's will, we would even have to practice idolatry.[8]

At this point, as far as an understanding of God and thus the concrete practice of religion is concerned, we are faced with an

---

which I have the respect due to the holy book of a great religion. In quoting the text of the Emperor Manuel II, I intended solely to draw out the essential relationship between faith and reason. On this point I am in agreement with Manuel II, but without endorsing his polemic.

5. Khoury VII, 3b–c, 144–45; Förstel, vol. 1, VII, Dialog 1.6, 240–43.

6. Cf. Khoury, 144n1.

7. It was purely for the sake of this statement that I quoted the dialogue between Manuel and his Persian interlocutor. In this statement the theme of my subsequent reflections emerges.

8. Roger Arnaldez, *Grammaire et théologie chez Ibn Hazm de Cordoue* (Paris: Librairie Philosophique J. Vrin, 1956), 13; cf. Khoury, 144. The fact that comparable positions exist in the theology of the late Middle Ages will appear later in my discourse.

unavoidable dilemma. Is the conviction that acting unreasonably contradicts God's nature merely a Greek idea, or is it always and intrinsically true? I believe that here we can see the profound harmony between what is Greek in the best sense of the word and the biblical understanding of faith in God. Modifying the first verse of the book of Genesis, the first verse of the whole Bible, John began the prologue of his gospel with the words, "In the beginning was the λόγος." This is the very word used by the emperor: God acts, σὺν λόγω, with *logos*. *Logos* means both reason and word—a reason that is creative and capable of self-communication, precisely as reason. John thus spoke the final word on the biblical concept of God, and in this word all the often toilsome and tortuous threads of biblical faith find their culmination and synthesis. In the beginning was the *logos,* and the *logos* is God, says the evangelist. The encounter between the biblical message and Greek thought did not happen by chance. The vision of St. Paul, who saw the roads to Asia barred and in a dream saw a Macedonian man plead with him, "Come over to Macedonia and help us!" (cf. Acts 16:6–10)—this vision can be interpreted as a "distillation" of the intrinsic necessity of a rapprochement between biblical faith and Greek inquiry.

In point of fact, this rapprochement had been going on for some time. The mysterious name of God, revealed from the burning bush, a name that separates this God from all other divinities with their many names and simply asserts being, "I am," already presents a challenge to the notion of myth, to which Socrates' attempt to vanquish and transcend myth stands in close analogy.[9] Within the Old Testament the process that started at the burning bush came to new maturity at the time of the exile,

9. Regarding the widely discussed interpretation of the episode of the burning bush, I refer to my book *Introduction to Christianity* (London: Burns and Oates, Ltd., 1969), 77–93 (originally published in German as *Einführung in das Christentum* [Munich: Kösel-Verlag GmbH, 1968]). N.B.: The pages quoted refer to the entire chapter entitled "The Biblical Belief in God"). I think that my statements in that book, despite later developments in the discussion, remain valid today.

when the God of Israel, an Israel now deprived of its land and worship, was proclaimed as the God of heaven and earth and described in a simple formula that echoes the words uttered at the burning bush: "I am." This new understanding of God is accompanied by a kind of enlightenment, which finds stark expression in the mockery of gods who are merely the work of human hands (cf. Ps 115). Thus, despite the bitter conflict with those Hellenistic rulers who sought to accommodate it forcibly to the customs and idolatrous cult of the Greeks, biblical faith, in the Hellenistic period, encountered the best of Greek thought at a deep level, resulting in a mutual enrichment evident especially in the later wisdom literature. Today we know that the Greek translation of the Old Testament produced at Alexandria—the Septuagint—is more than a simple (and in that sense really less than satisfactory) translation of the Hebrew text: it is an independent textual witness and a distinct and important step in the history of revelation, one that brought about this encounter in a way that was decisive for the birth and spread of Christianity.[10] A profound encounter of faith and reason is taking place here, an encounter between genuine enlightenment and religion. From the very heart of Christian faith and, at the same time, the heart of Greek thought now joined to faith, Manuel II was able to say that not to act "with *logos*" is contrary to God's nature.

In all honesty, one must observe that in the late Middle Ages we find trends in theology that would sunder this synthesis between the Greek spirit and the Christian spirit. In contrast with the so-called intellectualism of Augustine and Thomas, there arose with Duns Scotus a voluntarism that, in its later developments, led to the claim that we can only know God's *voluntas ordinata*. Beyond this is the realm of God's freedom, in virtue of which he could have done the opposite of everything he has

10. Cf. Adrien Schenker, "L'Écriture sainte subsiste en plusieurs formes canoniques simultanées," in *L'Interpretazione della Bibbia nella Chiesa: Atti del Simposio promosso dalla Congregazione per la Dottrina della Fede* (Vatican City: Libreria Editrice Vaticana, 2001), 178–86.

actually done. This gives rise to positions that clearly approach those of Ibn Hazm and might even lead to the image of a capricious God who is not even bound to truth and goodness. God's transcendence and otherness are so exalted that our reason, our sense of the true and good, are no longer an authentic mirror of God, whose deepest possibilities remain eternally unattainable and hidden behind his actual decisions. As opposed to this, the faith of the Church has always insisted that between God and us, between his eternal Creator Spirit and our created reason, there exists a real analogy, in which—as the Fourth Lateran Council in 1215 stated—unlikeness remains infinitely greater than likeness, yet not to the point of abolishing analogy and its language. God does not become more divine when we push him away from us in a sheer, impenetrable voluntarism; rather, the truly divine God is the God who has revealed himself as *logos* and, as *logos,* has acted and continues to act lovingly on our behalf. Certainly love, as St. Paul says, "transcends" knowledge and is thereby capable of perceiving more than thought alone (cf. Eph 3:19); nonetheless it continues to be love of the God who is *Logos.* Consequently Christian worship is, again to quote Paul—"λογικὴ λατρεία," worship in harmony with the eternal Word and with our reason (cf. Rom 12:1).[11]

This inner rapprochement between biblical faith and Greek philosophical inquiry was an event of decisive importance, not only from the standpoint of the history of religions, but also from that of world history—it is an event that concerns us even today. Given this convergence, it is not surprising that Christianity, despite its origins and some significant developments in the East, finally took on its historically decisive character in Europe. We can also express this the other way around: this convergence, with the subsequent addition of the Roman heritage, created Europe and remains the foundation of what can rightly be called Europe.

11. On this matter I expressed myself in greater detail in my book *The Spirit of the Liturgy* (San Francisco: Ignatius Press, 2000), 44–50.

The thesis that the critically purified Greek heritage forms an integral part of Christian faith has been countered by the call for a dehellenization of Christianity—a call that has more and more dominated theological discussions since the beginning of the modern age. Viewed more closely, three stages can be observed in the program of dehellenization; although interconnected, they are clearly distinct from one another in their motivations and objectives.[12]

Dehellenization first emerges in connection with the postulates of the Reformation in the sixteenth century. Looking at the tradition of scholastic theology, the Reformers thought they were confronted with a faith system totally conditioned by philosophy—that is to say, an articulation of the faith based on an alien system of thought. As a result, faith no longer appeared as a living historical Word, but as one element of an overarching philosophical system. The principle of *sola scriptura,* on the other hand, sought faith in its pure, primordial form, as originally found in the biblical Word. Metaphysics appeared as a premise derived from another source, from which faith had to be liberated in order to become once more fully itself. When Kant stated that he needed to set thinking aside in order to make room for faith, he carried this program forward with a radicalism that the Reformers could never have foreseen. He thus anchored faith exclusively in practical reason, denying it access to reality as a whole.

The liberal theology of the nineteenth and twentieth centuries ushered in a second stage in the process of dehellenization, with Adolf von Harnack as its outstanding representative. When I was a student, and in the early years of my teaching, this program was highly influential in Catholic theology, too. It took as its point of departure Pascal's distinction between the God

12. Of the vast literature on the theme of dehellenization, I would like to mention, above all, Alois Grillmeier, "Hellenisierung-Judaisierung des Christentums als Deuteprinzipien der Geschichte des kirchlichen Dogmas," in idem, *Mit ihm und in ihm: Christologische Forschungen und Perspektiven* (Freiburg: Herder, 1975), 423–88.

of the philosophers and the God of Abraham, Isaac, and Jacob. In my inaugural lecture at Bonn in 1959, I tried to address the issue,[13] and I do not intend to repeat here what I said on that occasion, but I would like to describe at least briefly what was new about this second stage of dehellenization. Harnack's central idea was to return simply to the man Jesus and to his simple message, underneath the accretions of theology and indeed of hellenization. This simple message was seen as the culmination of the religious development of humanity. Jesus was said to have put an end to worship in favor of morality. In the end he was presented as the father of a humanitarian moral message. Fundamentally, Harnack's goal was to bring Christianity back into harmony with modern reason, liberating it, that is to say, from seemingly philosophical and theological elements, such as faith in Christ's divinity and the triune God. In this sense, historical-critical exegesis of the New Testament, as he saw it, restored to theology its place within the university: theology, for Harnack, is something essentially historical and therefore strictly scientific. What it is able to say critically about Jesus is, so to speak, an expression of practical reason, and consequently it can take its rightful place within the university. Behind this thinking lies the modern self-limitation of reason, classically expressed in Kant's "Critiques," but in the meantime further radicalized by the impact of the natural sciences. This modern concept of reason is based, to put it briefly, on a synthesis between Platonism (Cartesianism) and empiricism, a synthesis confirmed by the success of technology. On the one hand, it presupposes the mathematical structure of matter, its intrinsic rationality, which makes it possible to understand how matter works and to use it efficiently; this basic premise is, so to speak, the Platonic element in the modern understanding of nature. On the other hand, there is nature's capacity to be exploited for our purposes, and here only the possibility of verification or falsification through experimentation can yield decisive certainty. The weight between the two poles can, depending on the circumstances, shift from one side to the other. As strongly positivistic a thinker as J. Monod has declared himself a convinced Platonist/Cartesian.

This gives rise to two principles that are crucial for the issue we have raised. First, only the kind of certainty resulting from the interplay of mathematical and empirical elements can be considered scientific. Anything that would claim to be science must be measured against this criterion. Hence the human sciences, such as history, psychology, sociology, and philosophy, attempt to conform themselves to this canon of scientificity. A second point, which is important for our reflections, is that by its very nature this method excludes the question of God, making it appear an unscientific or prescientific question. Consequently we are faced with a reduction of the radius of science and reason, one that needs to be questioned.

I will return to this problem later. In the meantime, it must be observed that from this standpoint any attempt to maintain theology's claim to be "scientific" would end up reducing Christianity to a mere fragment of its former self. But we must say more: if science as a whole is this and this alone, then it is man himself who ends up being reduced, for the specifically human questions about our origin and destiny, the questions raised by religion and ethics, have no place within the purview of collective reason as defined by "science," so understood, and must thus be relegated to the realm of the subjective. The subject then decides, on the basis of his experiences, what he considers tenable in matters of religion, and the subjective "conscience" becomes the sole arbiter of what is ethical. In this way, though, ethics and religion lose their power to create a community and become a completely personal matter. This is a dangerous state of affairs for humanity, as we see from the disturbing pathologies of religion and reason that necessarily erupt when reason is so reduced that questions of religion and ethics no longer concern it. Attempts to construct an ethic from the rules of evolution or from psychology and sociology end up being simply inadequate.

Before I draw the conclusions to which all this has been leading, I must briefly refer to the third stage of dehellenization, which is now in progress. In the light of our experience with cultural pluralism, it is often said nowadays that the synthesis with Hellenism achieved in the early Church was an initial inculturation that ought not to be binding on other cultures. The latter are said to have the right to return to the simple message of the New Testament prior to that inculturation in order to inculturate it anew in their own particular milieus. This thesis is not simply false, but it is coarse and lacking in precision. The New Testament was written in Greek and bears the imprint of the Greek spirit, which had already come to maturity as the Old Testament developed. True, there are elements in the evolution of the early Church that do not have to be integrated into all cultures. Nonetheless, the fundamental decisions made about the relationship between faith and the use of human reason are part of the faith itself; they are developments consonant with the nature of faith itself.

And so I come to my conclusion. This attempt, painted with broad strokes, at a critique of modern reason from within has nothing to do with putting the clock back to the time before the Enlightenment and rejecting the insights of the modern age. The positive aspects of modernity are to be acknowledged unreservedly: we are all grateful for the marvelous possibilities that it has opened up for mankind and for the progress in humanity that has been granted to us. The scientific ethos, moreover, is … the will to be obedient to the truth, and, as such, it embodies an attitude that belongs to the essential decisions of the Christian spirit. The intention here is not one of retrenchment or negative criticism, but of broadening our concept of reason and its appli-

cation. While we rejoice in the new possibilities open to humanity, we also see the dangers arising from these possibilities, and
we must ask ourselves how we can overcome them. We will succeed in doing so only if reason and faith come together in a new
way, if we overcome the self-imposed limitation of reason to the
empirically falsifiable, and if we once more disclose its vast horizons. In this sense theology rightly belongs in the university and
within the wide-ranging dialogue of sciences, not merely as a historical discipline and one of the human sciences, but precisely as
theology, as inquiry into the rationality of faith.

Only thus do we become capable of that genuine dialogue
of cultures and religions so urgently needed today. In the Western world it is widely held that only positivistic reason and the
forms of philosophy based on it are universally valid. Yet the
world's profoundly religious cultures see this exclusion of the divine from the universality of reason as an attack on their most
profound convictions. A reason that is deaf to the divine and
that relegates religion into the realm of subcultures is incapable of entering into the dialogue of cultures. At the same time,
as I have attempted to show, modern scientific reason with its
intrinsically Platonic element bears within itself a question that
points beyond itself and beyond the possibilities of its methodology. Modern scientific reason quite simply has to accept the rational structure of matter and the correspondence between our
spirit and the prevailing rational structures of nature as a given
on which its methodology has to be based. Yet the question of
why this has to be so is a real question, and one that has to be
remanded by the natural sciences to other modes and planes of
thought—to philosophy and theology. For philosophy and, albeit in a different way, for theology, listening to the great experiences and insights of the religious traditions of humanity, and
those of the Christian faith in particular, is a source of knowledge, and to ignore it would be an unacceptable restriction of
our listening and responding. Here I am reminded of something

Socrates said to Phaedo. In their earlier conversations, many false philosophical opinions had been raised, and so Socrates says, "It would be easily understandable if someone became so annoyed at all these false notions that for the rest of his life he despised and mocked all talk about being—but in this way he would be deprived of the truth of existence and would suffer a great loss."[14] The West has long been endangered by this aversion to the questions that underlie its rationality, and can only suffer great harm thereby. The courage to engage the whole breadth of reason, and not the denial of its grandeur—this is the program with which a theology grounded in biblical faith enters into the debates of our time. "Not to act reasonably, not to act with *logos,* is contrary to the nature of God," said Manuel II, according to his Christian understanding of God, in response to his Persian interlocutor. It is to this great *logos,* to this breadth of reason, that we invite our partners in the dialogue of cultures. To rediscover it constantly is the great task of the university.

Christian Faith Forms Reason to Be Itself

From *Address that the Holy Father Intended to Give During a Visit to La Sapienza University in Rome on Thursday, January 17, 2008*

It is a cause of deep joy for me to meet the community of *La Sapienza,* the University of Rome, on the occasion of the inauguration of the academic year. For centuries this university has been a part of the story and the life of the city of Rome, harvesting the fruits of the best intellects in every field of knowledge. Both in the past, when the institution depended directly on ecclesiastical authority (having been founded at the behest of Pope Boniface VIII), and in its more recent history, when the *Studium Urbis* became an institution of the Italian state, your academic com-

14. Cf. Plato, *Phaedo;* for this text, cf. also Romano Guardini, *Werke: Der Tod des Sokrates;* Eine Interpretation der platonischen Schriften Eutyphron, Apologie, Kriton und Phaidon, 5th ed. (Mainz-Paderborn: Matthias-Grünewald-Verlag, 1987), 218–21.

munity has maintained a high scientific and cultural standard that places it among the world's most prestigious universities. The Church of Rome has always looked with affection and admiration at this university center, recognizing its dedication, often arduous and demanding, to research and to the formation of generations of young people. There have been important instances of collaboration and dialogue in recent years. I would like to recall in particular the World Meeting of Rectors on the occasion of the Jubilee of Universities, when your community not only hosted and organized the event, but above all took responsibility for the prophetic and complex proposal to elaborate a "new humanism for the third millennium."

On this occasion I am happy to express my gratitude to you for your invitation to give a lecture at your university. With this prospect in view, I first of all asked myself the question: what can and should a pope say on such an occasion? In my lecture at Regensburg I did indeed speak as pope, but above all I spoke in my capacity as a former professor of my old university, seeking to link past memories with the present. However, it is as bishop of Rome that I am invited to *La Sapienza,* Rome's ancient university, so it is as such that I must speak. Of course, *La Sapienza* was once the university of the pope. Today, however, it is a secular university with that autonomy that, in keeping with the vision inspiring its foundation, has always been part of the nature of universities, which must be tied exclusively to the authority of the truth. It is in their freedom from political and ecclesiastical authorities that the particular function of universities lies—a function that serves modern society as well, which needs institutions of this kind.

To return to my initial question: what can and should the pope say at a meeting with the university in his city? As I pondered this question, it seemed to me that it included two others, and the answer should follow naturally from an exploration of these. We need to ask ourselves this: What is the nature and mission of the papacy? And what is the nature and mission of the university? I have no wish to detain you or myself with an extended discussion on the nature of the papacy. Let a brief comment suffice. The pope is first and foremost the bishop of Rome, and as such—as successor to the Apostle Peter—he has an episcopal responsibility for the whole of the Catholic Church. In the New Testament, the word "bishop"—*episkopos*—, the immediate meaning of which indicates an "overseer," had already been merged with the biblical concept of shepherd: the one who observes the whole landscape from above, ensuring that everything holds together and is moving in the right direction. Considered in such terms, this designation of the task focuses the attention first of all within the believing community. The bishop—the shepherd—is the one who cares for this community; he is the one who keeps it united on the way toward God, a way that, according to the Christian faith, has been indicated by Jesus—and not merely indicated: he himself is our way. Yet this community that the bishop looks after—be it large or small—lives in the world; its circumstances, its history, its example, and its message inevitably influence the entire human community. The larger it is, the greater the effect, for better or worse, on the rest of humanity. Today we see very clearly how the state of religions and the situation of the Church—her crises and her renewal—affect humanity in its entirety. Thus the pope, in his capacity as shepherd of his community, is also increasingly becoming a voice for the ethical reasoning of humanity.

Here, however, the objection immediately arises: surely the pope does not really base his pronouncements on ethical reasoning, but draws his judgments from faith, and hence cannot claim to speak on behalf of those who do not share this faith. We will have to return to this point later, because here the absolutely fundamental question must be asked: What is reason? How can one demonstrate that an assertion—especially a moral norm—is "reasonable"? At this point I would like to describe briefly how

John Rawls, while denying that comprehensive religious doctrines have the character of "public" reason, nonetheless at least sees their "non-public" reason as one that cannot simply be dismissed by those who maintain a rigidly secularized rationality. Rawls perceives a criterion of this reasonableness, among other things, in the fact that such doctrines derive from a responsible and well-thought-out tradition in which, over lengthy periods, satisfactory arguments have been developed in support of the doctrines concerned. The important thing in this assertion, it seems to me, is the acknowledgment that down through the centuries, experience and demonstration—the historical source of human wisdom—are also a sign of its reasonableness and enduring significance. Faced with an ahistorical form of reason that seeks to establish itself exclusively in terms of ahistorical rationality, humanity's wisdom—the wisdom of the great religious traditions—should be valued as a heritage that cannot be cast with impunity into the dustbin of the history of ideas.

Let us go back to our initial question. The pope speaks as the representative of a community of believers in which a particular wisdom about life has evolved in the course of the centuries of its existence. He speaks as the representative of a community that preserves within itself a treasury of ethical knowledge and experience important for all humanity: in this sense, he speaks as the representative of a form of ethical reasoning.

Now, however, we must ask ourselves, "What is the university? What is its task?" This is a vast question to which, once again, I can only endeavor to respond in an almost telegraphic style with one or two comments. I think one could say that at the most intimate level, the true origin of the university lies in the thirst for knowledge that is proper to man. The human being wants to know what everything around him is. He wants truth. In this perspective, one can see Socratic questioning as the impulse that gave birth to the Western university. I am thinking, for example—to mention only one text—of the dispute with

Euthyphro, who in debate with Socrates defended the mythical religion and cult. Socrates countered with a question: "Do you believe that the gods are really waging war against each other with terrible feuds and battles? ... Must we effectively say, Euthyphro, that all this is true?"[15] The Christians of the first centuries identified themselves and their journey with this question, which seems not particularly devout—but which in Socrates' case derived from a deeper and purer religious sensibility, from the search for the true God. They received their faith not in a positivistic manner, nor as a way of escape from unfulfilled wishes; rather, they understood it as dispelling the mist of mythological religion in order to make way for the discovery of the God who is creative Reason, God who is Reason-Love. This is why reasoned inquiry concerning the truly great God, and concerning the true nature and meaning of the human being, did not strike them as problematic, as a lack of due religious sentiment; rather, it was an essential part of their way of being religious. Hence they did not need to abandon or set aside Socratic inquiry, but they could, indeed, were bound to accept it, and recognize reason's laborious search to attain knowledge of the whole truth as part of their own identity. In this way, within the context of the Christian faith, in the Christian world, the university could come into being—indeed it was bound to do so.

Now it is necessary to take a further step. Man desires to know—he wants truth. Truth in the first instance is something discerned through seeing, understanding, what Greek tradition calls *theoria*. Yet truth is never purely theoretical. In drawing a parallel between the Beatitudes of the Sermon on the Mount and the gifts of the Spirit listed in Isaiah 11, St. Augustine argued that there is a reciprocity between *scientia* and *tristitia:* knowledge on its own, he said, causes sadness. And it is true to say that those who merely see and apprehend all that happens in the world end up being saddened. Yet truth means more than knowledge: the

15. Plato, *Euthyphro.*

purpose of knowing the truth is to know the good. This is also the meaning of Socratic inquiry: What is the good that makes us true? The truth makes us good and the good is true: this is the optimism that shapes the Christian faith, because this faith has been granted the vision of the *Logos,* of creative Reason that, in God's incarnation, revealed itself as the Good, as Goodness itself.

In medieval theology there was a detailed disputation on the relationship between theory and practice, on the proper relationship between knowledge and action—a disputation that we need not explore here. *De facto,* the medieval university with its four faculties expresses this correlation. Let us begin with the faculty that was understood at the time to rank as the fourth—the faculty of medicine. Even if it was considered more as an "art" than a science, the inclusion of medicine within the ambit of the *universitas* clearly indicated that it was placed within the realm of rationality—that the art of healing was under the guidance of reason and had been removed from the realm of magic. Healing is a task that always requires more than plain reason, but this is precisely why it depends on the connection between knowledge and power: it needs to belong to the sphere of *ratio.* Inevitably the question of the relationship between praxis and theory, between knowledge and action, also arose in the faculty of jurisprudence. Here it was a matter of giving the correct form to human freedom, which is always a freedom shared with others. Law is the presupposition of freedom, not its opponent. At this point, however, the question immediately arises: How is it possible to identify criteria of justice that make shared freedom possible and help man to be good? Here a leap into the present is necessary. The point in question is: how can a juridical body of norms be established that serves as an ordering of freedom, of human dignity and human rights? This is the issue with which we are grappling today in the democratic processes that form opinion—the issue that also causes us to be anxious about the future of humanity. In my opinion, Jürgen Habermas articulates a vast consensus of contemporary thought when he says that the legitimacy of a constitutional charter, as a basis for what is legal, derives from two sources: from the equal participation of all citizens in the political process and from the reasonable manner in which political disputes are resolved. With regard to this "reasonable manner," he notes that it cannot simply be a fight for arithmetical majorities, but must have the character of a "process of argumentation sensitive to the truth" (*wahrheitssensibles Argumentationsverfahren*). The point is well made, but it is far from easy to put it into practice politically. The representatives of that public "process of argumentation" are—as we know—principally political parties, inasmuch as these are responsible for the formation of political will. *De facto,* they will always aim to achieve majorities and hence will almost inevitably attend to interests that they promise to satisfy, even though these interests are often particular and do not truly serve the whole. Sensibility to the truth is repeatedly subordinated to sensibility to interests. I find it significant that Habermas speaks of sensibility to the truth as a necessary element in the process of political argument, thereby reintroducing the concept of truth into philosophical and political debate.

At this point, though, Pilate's question becomes unavoidable: What is truth? And how can it be recognized? If in our search for an answer we have recourse to "public reason," as Rawls does, then further questions necessarily follow: What is reasonable? How is reason shown to be true? In any case, on this basis it becomes clear that in the search for a set of laws embodying freedom, in the search for the truth about a just polity, we must listen to claims other than those of parties and interest groups, without in any way wishing to deny the importance of the latter. Let us return now to the structure of the medieval university. Besides the faculty of jurisprudence, there were faculties of philosophy and theology that were entrusted with the task of studying the human being in his totality, thus safeguarding sensibility to the truth. One might even say that this was the permanent and true purpose of both faculties: to be custodians of sensibility to the truth, not to allow man to be distracted from his search for the truth. Yet how could the faculties measure up to this task? This is a question that must be constantly worked at, and is never asked and answered once and for all. So, at this point, I cannot offer a satisfactory answer, either, but only an invitation to continue exploring the question—exploring in company with the great minds throughout history that have grappled and re-searched, engaging with their answers and their passion for the truth that invariably points beyond each individual answer.

Theology and philosophy in this regard form a strange pair of twins, in which neither of the two can be totally separated from the other, and yet each must preserve its own task and its own identity. It is the historical merit of St. Thomas Aquinas—in the face of the rather different answer offered by the fathers, owing to their historical context—to have highlighted the autonomy of philosophy, and with it the laws and the responsibility proper to reason, which inquires on the basis of its own dynamic. Dis-tancing themselves from neo-Platonic philosophies, in which religion and philosophy were inseparably interconnected, the fathers had presented the Christian faith as the true philosophy and had emphasized that this faith fulfills the demands of reason in search of truth; that faith is the "yes" to the truth, in compar-ison with the mythical religions that had become mere custom. By the time the university came to birth, though, those religions no longer existed in the West—there was only Christianity, and thus it was necessary to give new emphasis to the specific re-sponsibility of reason, which is not absorbed by faith. Thomas was writing at a privileged moment: for the first time, the philo-sophical works of Aristotle were accessible in their entirety; the Jewish and Arab philosophies were available as specific appro-priations and continuations of Greek philosophy. Christianity, in a new dialogue with the reasoning of the interlocutors it was now encountering, was thus obliged to argue a case for its own reasonableness. The faculty of philosophy, which as a so-called "arts faculty" had until then been no more than a preparation for theology, now became a faculty in its own right, an autonomous partner of theology and the faith on which theology reflected. We cannot digress to consider the fascinating consequences of this development. I would say that St. Thomas' idea concerning the relationship between philosophy and theology could be expressed using the formula that the Council of Chalcedon adopted for Christology: philosophy and theology must be interrelated "without confusion and without separation." "Without confusion" means that each of the two must preserve its own identity. Philosophy must truly remain a quest conducted by reason with freedom and responsibility; it must recognize its limits and likewise its greatness and immensity.

Theology must continue to draw upon a treasury of knowledge that it did not invent, that always surpasses it, the depths of which can never be fully plumbed through reflection, and that for that reason constantly gives rise to new thinking. Balancing "without confusion," there is always "without separation": philosophy does not start again from zero with every thinking subject in total isolation, but takes its place within the great dialogue of historical wisdom, which it continually accepts and develops in a manner both critical and docile. It must not exclude what religions, and the Christian faith in particular, have received and have given to humanity as signposts for the journey. Various things said by theologians in the course of history, or even adopted in practice by ecclesiastical authorities, have been shown by history to be false, and today make us feel ashamed. Yet at the same time it has to be acknowledged that the history of the saints, the history of the humanism that has grown out of the Christian faith, demonstrates the truth of this faith in its essential nucleus, thereby giving it a claim upon public reason. Of course, much of the content of theology and faith can only be appropriated within the context of faith, and therefore cannot be demanded of those to whom this faith remains inaccessible. Yet at the same time it is true that the message of the Christian faith is never solely a "comprehensive religious doctrine" in Rawls' sense, but is a purifying force for reason, helping it to be more fully itself. On the basis of its origin, the Christian message should always be an encouragement toward truth, and thus a force against the pressure exerted by power and interests.

Up to this point I have spoken only of the medieval university, while seeking nonetheless to indicate the unchanging nature of the university and its task. In modern times, new dimensions of knowledge have opened up, which have been explored within the university under two broad headings: first, the natural sciences, which have developed on the basis of the connection between experimentation and the presumed rationality of matter; and second, the historical and human sciences, in which man, contemplating his history as in a mirror and clarifying the dimensions of his nature, seeks to understand himself better. In this process, not only has an immense quantity of knowledge and power been made available to humanity, but knowledge and recognition of human rights and dignity have also evolved, and for this we can only be grateful. Yet the human journey never simply comes to an end, and the danger of falling into inhumanity is never totally overcome, as is only too evident from the panorama of recent history! The danger for the Western world—to speak only of this—is that today, precisely because of the greatness of his knowledge and power, man will fail to face up to the question of the truth. This would mean at the same time that reason would ultimately bow to the pressure of interests and the attraction of utility, constrained to recognize this as the ultimate criterion. To put it from the point of view of the structure of the university: there is a danger that philosophy, no longer considering itself capable of its true task, will degenerate into positivism; and that theology, with its message addressed to reason, will be limited to the private sphere of a more or less numerous group.

Yet if reason, out of concern for its alleged purity, becomes deaf to the great message that comes to it from Christian faith and wisdom, then it withers like a tree whose roots can no longer reach the waters that give it life. It loses the courage for truth and thus becomes not greater, but smaller. Applied to our European culture, this means: if our culture seeks only to build itself on the basis of the circle of its own argumentation, on what convinces it at the time, and if—anxious to preserve its secularism—it detaches itself from its life-giving roots, then it will not become more reasonable or purer, but will fall apart and disintegrate.

This brings me back to my starting point. What should the pope do or say at the university? Certainly, he must not seek to impose the faith upon others in an authoritarian manner—as faith can only be given in freedom. Over and above his ministry as shepherd of the Church, and on the basis of the intrinsic nature of this pastoral ministry, it is the pope's task to safeguard sensibility to the truth; to invite reason to set out ever anew in search of what is true and good, in search of God; to urge reason, in the course of this search, to discern the illuminating lights that have emerged during the history of the Christian faith, and thus to recognize Jesus Christ as the Light that illumines history and helps us find the path toward the future.

Widen the Horizons of Rationality

From *Address to Participants at the Sixth European Symposium for University Professors,* June 7, 2008

In continuity with last year's European meeting of university lecturers, your symposium takes up a very important academic and cultural theme. I would like to express my gratitude to the organizing committee for this choice that permits us, among other things, to celebrate the tenth anniversary of the publication of the encyclical letter *Fides et Ratio* of my beloved predecessor, Pope John Paul II. Already on that occasion fifty civil and ecclesial philosophy professors of the public and pontifical universities of Rome manifested their gratitude to the pope with a declaration that confirmed the urgency of relaunching the study of philosophy in universities and schools. Sharing this concern and encouraging fruitful collaboration among the professors of various Roman and European athenaeums, I wish to address a particular invitation to philosophy professors to continue with confidence in philosophical research, investing intellectual energy and involving new generations in this task.

The events that have taken place in the last ten years since the encyclical's publication have further delineated the historical and cultural scene in which philosophical research is called to enter. Indeed, the crisis of modernity is not synonymous with the decline in philosophy; instead, philosophy must commit itself to a new path of research to comprehend the true nature of this crisis and to identify new prospectives toward which to be oriented.[16] Modernity, if well understood, reveals an "anthropological question" that presents itself in a much more complex and articulated way than what has taken place in the philosophical reflections of the last centuries, above all in Europe. Without diminishing the attempts made, much still remains to be probed and understood. Modernity is not simply a cultural phenomenon, historically dated; in reality it implies a new planning, a more exact understanding of human nature. It is not difficult to gather from the writings of authoritative thinkers an honest reflection on the difficulties that arise in the resolution of this prolonged crisis. Giving credit to some authors' proposals in regard to religions, and in particular to Christianity, is an evident sign of the sincere desire to exist from the self-sufficiency of philosophical reflection.

From the beginning of my pontificate I have listened attentively to the requests that reach me from the men and women of our time and, in view of their expectations, I have wished to

16. Cf. Benedict XVI, *Address to European Meeting of University Lecturers,* June 23, 2007.

offer a pointer for research that seems to me capable of raising interest in relaunching philosophy and its irreplaceable role in the academic and cultural world. You have made it the object of reflection of your symposium: it is the proposal to "widen the horizons of rationality." This allows me to reflect on it with you as among friends who desire to pursue a common journey. I would like to begin with a deep conviction that I have expressed many times: "Christian faith has made its clear choice: against the gods of religion for the God of philosophers, in other words against the myth of mere custom for the truth of being."[17] This affirmation, which reflects the Christian journey from its dawning, shows itself completely actual in the cultural historical context that we are living. In fact, only beginning from this premise, which is historic and theological at the same time, is it possible to meet the new expectations of philosophical reflection. The risk that religion, even Christianity, be instrumentalized as a surreptitious phenomenon is very concrete, even today.

But Christianity, as I recalled in the encyclical *Spe Salvi,* is not only "informative," but "performative."[18] This means that from the beginning Christian faith cannot be enclosed within an abstract world of theories, but must descend into the concrete historic experience that reaches humanity in the most profound truth of his existence. This experience, conditioned by new cultural and ideological situations, is the place in which theological research must evaluate and upon which it is urgent to initiate a fruitful dialogue with philosophy—the understanding of Christianity as a real transformation of human existence: if on the one hand it impels theological reflection to a new approach in regard to religion, on the other, it encourages it not to lose confidence in being able to know reality. The proposal to "widen the horizons of rationality," therefore, must not simply be counted among the new lines of theological and philosophical thought, but it must

17. Cf. Joseph Ratzinger, *Introduction to Christianity,* chap. 3.
18. Cf. Benedict XVI, Encyclical Letter *Spe Salvi* (November 30, 2007), n. 2.

be understood as the requisite for a *new opening* onto the reality that the human person in his uni-totality is, rising above ancient prejudices and reductionisms, to open himself also to the way toward a true understanding of modernity. Humanity's desire for fullness cannot be disregarded. The Christian faith is called to take on this historical emergency by involving the men and women of good will in a simple task. The new dialogue between faith and reason required today cannot happen in the terms and in the ways in which it happened in the past. If it does not want to be reduced to a sterile intellectual exercise, it must begin from the present concrete situation of humanity, and upon this develop a reflection that draws from the ontological-metaphysical truth.

Dear friends, you have before you a very exacting journey. First of all, it is necessary to promote high-level academic centers in which philosophy can dialogue with other disciplines, in particular with theology, favoring new, suitable cultural syntheses to orient society's journey. The European dimension of your meeting in Rome—indeed, you come from twenty-six countries—can favor a truly fruitful comparison and exchange. I trust that the Catholic academic institutions are ready to open true cultural laboratories. I would also like to invite you to encourage youth to engage in philosophical studies, opportunely favoring initiatives with a university orientation. I am certain that the new generations, with their enthusiasm, will know how to respond generously to the expectations of the Church and society.

The Achievement of Reason

From *Address to Participants in a Congress Held on the Occasion of the 10th Anniversary of the Publication of Pope John Paul II's Encyclical Fides Et Ratio,* October 16, 2008

Ten years after its publication, an attentive look at the encyclical *Fides et Ratio* enables one to perceive admiringly its lasting topicality; it reveals the farsighted depth of my unforgettable predecessor. In fact, the encyclical is characterized by its great openness to reason, especially in a period in which its weakness was theorized. John Paul II, on the other hand, underlines the importance of combining faith and reason in their reciprocal relationship, while also respecting the sphere of autonomy of each. With this magisterium the Church has voiced an emerging need within the contemporary cultural context. She has chosen to defend the power of reason and its ability to attain the truth, presenting faith once again as a special form of knowledge, thanks to which we are opened to the truth of revelation.[19] We read in the encyclical that we must trust in the abilities of human reason and not set ourselves goals that are too modest: "It is faith which stirs reason to move beyond all isolation and willingly to run risks so that it may attain whatever is beautiful, good and true."[20] Moreover, it is in the passing of time that the achievement of reason's goals, motivated by the passion for truth, is manifest. Who could deny the contribution that the great philosophical systems have made to the development of human self-awareness and the progress of various cultures? What is more, these cultures become fruitful when they are opened to the truth, enabling all those who participate in them to reach goals that make social life ever more human. The quest for the truth bears most fruit when it is sustained by love for the truth. Augustine wrote, "What one holds with the mind is held by knowing it, but no good may be known perfectly unless one loves perfectly."[21]

Yet we cannot deny that a shift has occurred from predominantly speculative thought to that which is primarily experimental. Research has above all involved the observation of nature in the attempt to discover its secrets. The desire to know nature then became the desire to reproduce it. This transformation was far from painless; the evolution of concepts damaged the rela-

19. Cf. John Paul II, *Fides et Ratio*, n. 13.
20. John Paul II, *Fides et Ratio*, n. 56.
21. Augustine, *De diversis quaestionibus* 35.2.

tionship between *fides* and *ratio,* resulting in each taking its own separate path. Scientific and technological breakthroughs, which *fides* is increasingly challenged to face, have modified the age-old concept of *ratio;* in a certain way they have marginalized the reason that was seeking the ultimate truth of things in order to make room for a reason content with discovering the contingent truths of the laws of nature. Scientific research undoubtedly has its positive value. The discovery of and increase in the mathematical, physical, chemical, and applied sciences are the product of reason and express the intelligence with which man succeeds in penetrating the depth of creation. Faith, for its part, does not fear scientific progress and the developments to which scientific achievements lead when they are aimed toward the human being, his well-being, and the progress of humanity as a whole. As the anonymous author of the *Letter to Diognetus* recalled, "The tree of knowledge does not kill, but disobedience kills. For there cannot be life without knowledge any more than there can be sound knowledge without genuine life, and so the two trees were planted close together."[22]

Nonetheless, it happens that scientists do not always direct their research to these aims. Easy earnings or, even worse, the arrogance of replacing the Creator, at times play a decisive role. This is a form of the *hubris* of reason, which can acquire characteristics that are dangerous to humanity itself. Science, moreover, is unable to work out ethical principles; it can only accept them and recognize them as necessary to eradicate its potential pathologies. In this context, philosophy and theology become indispensable aids that must be placed alongside science in order to prevent it from proceeding on its own down a twisting path, full of unexpected accidents and not without risks. This does not mean restricting scientific research or preventing technology from producing the means for development; rather, it consists in maintaining vigilance about the sense of responsibility that rea-

---

22. Anonymous, *Letter to Diognetus* XII.2.4.

son possesses in regard to science, so that it stays on track in its service to the human being.

Augustine's lesson is still meaningful, even in today's context: "What does someone who can use reason well attain other than the truth?" the holy bishop of Hippo asks. "The truth is not obtained by itself with reasoning but it is what those who use reason seek.... It confesses that what the truth is, is not you, for it does not seek itself; you, on the other hand, have not attained it by passing from one place to another, but by seeking it with the disposition of your mind."[23] In other words, wherever the search for the truth comes from, it remains as a given that is both offered and recognizable as already present in nature. The intelligibility of creation, in fact, is not the result of the scientist's effort, but a condition offered to him to enable him to discover the truth that is present within it. "*These things are not made by the process of reasoning, but discovered,*" Augustine continues in his reflection. "*Therefore they abide in themselves even before they are discovered, and once they are discovered they renew us.*"[24] In brief, reason must fully run its course, strong in its autonomy and its rich intellectual tradition.

Reason also understands and discovers that, in addition to what it has already attained and achieved, there exists a truth that it will never be able to discover based solely on itself, but only receive as a gift freely given. The truth of revelation does not superimpose the truth achieved by reason; rather, it purifies and exalts reason, thereby enabling it to broaden its horizons to enter into a field of research as unfathomably expansive as mystery itself. The truth revealed, when "the time had fully come" (Gal 4:4), assumed the Face of a person, Jesus of Nazareth, who brought the ultimate and definitive answer to the question of human meaning. The truth of Christ, since it affects every person in search of joy, happiness, and meaning, far exceeds any

23. Augustine, *De Vera Religione* XXXIX.72.
24. Augustine, *De Vera Religione* XXXIX.73.

other truth that reason can discover. It surrounds mystery so that *fides* and *ratio* might find the real possibility of a common path.

The Synod of Bishops on the theme "The Word of God in the life and mission of the Church" is taking place in these days. How can we fail to see the providential coincidence of this event with your congress? Passion for the truth impels us to reenter into our interior selves to grasp the profound meaning of our lives. True philosophy must take every person by the hand and bring him to discover how fundamental it is to his dignity to know the truth of revelation. Before this demand for meaning, which gives no respite until it flows into Jesus Christ, the Word of God reveals his character as a definitive response: one Word of revelation that becomes life and that asks to be welcomed as an inexhaustible source of truth.

As I hope that each one of you will increasingly feel within you this passion for the truth and will do everything in your power to satisfy its demands, I would like to assure you that I am following your commitment with appreciation and pleasure, accompanying your research with my prayers.

The University: The "House" Where One Seeks the Truth Proper to the Human Person

From *Address to Young University Professors,*
Apostolic Journey to Madrid (Spain) on the Occasion
of the 26th World Youth Day, August 19, 2011

I have looked forward to this meeting with you, young professors in the universities of Spain. You provide a splendid service in the spread of truth, in circumstances that are not always easy. I greet you warmly and I thank you for your kind words of welcome and for the music that has marvelously resounded in this magnificent monastery, for centuries an eloquent witness to the life of prayer and study. In this highly symbolic place, reason and faith have harmoniously blended in the austere stone to shape one of Spain's most renowned monuments.

I also greet with particular affection those of you who took part in the recent World Congress of Catholic Universities held in Avila on the theme "The Identity and Mission of the Catholic University."

Being here with you, I am reminded of my own first steps as a professor at the University of Bonn. At the time, the wounds of war were still deeply felt, and we had many material needs; these were compensated by our passion for an exciting activity, our interaction with colleagues of different disciplines, and our desire to respond to the deepest and most basic concerns of our students. This experience of a "Universitas" of professors and students who together seek the truth in all fields of knowledge, or, as Alfonso X the Wise put it, this "counsel of masters and students with the will and understanding needed to master the various disciplines,"[25] helps us to see more clearly the importance, and even the definition, of the university.

The theme of the present World Youth Day—"Rooted and Built Up in Christ, and Firm in the Faith" (cf. Col 2:7) can also shed light on your efforts to understand more clearly your own identity and what you are called to do. As I wrote in my Message to Young People in preparation for these days, the terms "rooted, built up and firm" all point to solid foundations on which we can construct our lives.[26]

But where will young people encounter those reference points in a society that is increasingly confused and unstable? At times one has the idea that the mission of a university professor nowadays is exclusively that of forming competent and efficient professionals capable of satisfying the demand for labor at any given time. One also hears it said that the only thing that matters at the present moment is pure technical ability. This sort of utilitarian approach to education is in fact becoming more widespread, even at the university level, promoted especially by sectors outside the

25. Alfonso X, *Siete Partidas* II.31.
26. Cf. Benedict XVI, *Message for the Twenty-Sixth World Youth Day*, n. 2, August 6, 2010.

university. All the same, you who, like myself, have had an experience of the university and now are members of the teaching staff, surely are looking for something more lofty and capable of embracing the full measure of what it is to be human. We know that when mere utility and pure pragmatism become the principal criteria, much is lost, and the results can be tragic, from the abuses associated with a science that acknowledges no limits beyond itself to the political totalitarianism that easily arises when one eliminates any higher reference than the mere calculus of power. The authentic idea of the university, on the other hand, is precisely what saves us from this reductionist and curtailed vision of humanity.

In truth, the university has always been, and is always called to be, the "house" where one seeks the truth proper to the human person. Consequently it was not by accident that the Church promoted the universities, for Christian faith speaks to us of Christ as the Word through whom all things were made (cf. Jn 1:3) and of men and women as made in the image and likeness of God. The gospel message perceives a rationality inherent in creation and considers man as a creature participating in, and capable of attaining to, an understanding of this rationality. The university thus embodies an ideal that must not be attenuated or compromised, whether by ideologies closed to reasoned dialogue or by truckling to a purely utilitarian and economic conception that would view man solely as a consumer.

Here we see the vital importance of your own mission. You yourselves have the honor and responsibility of transmitting the ideal of the university: an ideal that you have received from your predecessors, many of whom were humble followers of the gospel and, as such, became spiritual giants. We should feel ourselves their successors, in a time quite different from their own, yet one in which the essential human questions continue to challenge and stimulate us. With them we realize that we are a link in that chain of men and women committed to teaching the faith and making it credible to human reason. And we do this not simply by our teaching, but by the way we live our faith and embody it, just as the Word took flesh and dwelt among us. Young people need authentic teachers: persons open to the fullness of truth in the various branches of knowledge; persons who listen to and experience in their own hearts that interdisciplinary dialogue; persons who, above all, are convinced of our human capacity to advance along the path of truth. Youth is a privileged time for seeking and encountering truth. As Plato said, "Seek truth while you are young, for if you do not, it will later escape your grasp."[27] This lofty aspiration is the most precious gift that you can give to your students, personally and by example. It is more important than mere technical know-how or cold and purely functional data.

I urge you, then, never to lose that sense of enthusiasm and concern for truth. Always remember that teaching is not just about communicating content, but about forming young people. You need to understand and love them, to awaken their innate thirst for truth and their yearning for transcendence. Be for them a source of encouragement and strength.

For this to happen, we need to realize in the first place that the path to the fullness of truth calls for complete commitment: it is a path of understanding and love, of reason and faith. We cannot come to know something unless we are moved by love; or, for that matter, love something that does not strike us as reasonable. "Understanding and love are not in separate compartments: love is rich in understanding and understanding is full of love."[28] If truth and goodness go together, so too do knowledge and love. This unity leads to consistency in life and thought, that ability to inspire demanded of every good educator.

In the second place, we need to recognize that truth itself will always lie beyond our grasp. We can seek it and draw near

27. Plato, *Parmenides* 135d.
28. Benedict XVI, Encyclical Letter *Caritas in Veritate* (June 29, 2009), n. 30.

to it, but we cannot completely possess it; or put better, truth possesses us and inspires us. In intellectual and educational activity the virtue of humility is also indispensable, since it protects us from the pride that bars the way to truth. We must not draw students to ourselves, but set them on the path toward the truth that we seek together. The Lord will help you in this, for he asks you to be plain and effective like salt, or like the lamp that quietly lights the room (cf. Mt 5:13).

All these things, finally, remind us to keep our gaze fixed on Christ, whose face radiates the Truth that enlightens us. Christ is also the Way that leads to lasting fulfillment; he walks constantly at our side and sustains us with his love. Rooted in him, you will prove good guides to our young people.

Faith and Knowledge: The Daily Work of a Catholic University

From *Address at the Inauguration of the Academic Year at the Catholic University of the Sacred Heart,* November 25, 2005

Today the Catholic University of the Sacred Heart has about 40,000 students enrolled in its five branches and fourteen faculties. The thought "what a responsibility!" springs spontaneously to mind. Thousands and thousands of young people pass through the halls of the "Catholic University." How do they leave it? What culture did they encounter, assimilate, or work out?

This is the great challenge, which concerns in the first place the group that directs the athenaeum, the teaching staff, and hence, the students themselves: to give life to an authentic Catholic university that excels in the quality of its research and teaching and, at the same time, its fidelity to the gospel and the Church's magisterium.

In this regard it is providential that the Catholic University of the Sacred Heart is structurally linked to the Holy See through the Toniolo Institute for Advanced Studies, whose task it was and is to guarantee the attainment of the institutional goals of this athenaeum for Italian Catholics. This original definition, always confirmed by my predecessors, collegially guarantees that the university is firmly anchored to the Chair of Peter and to the patrimony of values bequeathed as a legacy by the founders. To all members of this praiseworthy institution, I offer my heartfelt thanks.

So, let us return to the question: what culture? I am delighted that the rector in his presentation placed the emphasis on the original and ever up-to-date "mission" of the Catholic university —that is, to undertake scientific research and teaching activities in accordance with a consistent cultural and formative project at the service of the young generations and the human and Christian development of society.

In this regard the patrimony of teaching that Pope John Paul II bequeathed to us, which culminated in his Apostolic Constitution *Ex Corde Ecclesiae* of 1990, is of great value. He always showed that the "Catholic" identity is in no way reductive, but rather exalts the university.

Indeed, if the fundamental mission of every university is "a continuous quest for the truth through its research, and the preservation and communication of knowledge for the good of society,"[29] a Catholic academic community is distinguished by the Christian inspiration of individuals and of the university community itself in the light of the faith that illuminates thought, for the fidelity to the Christian message as it is presented by the Church and for the institutional commitment to the service of the people of God.[30]

The Catholic university is therefore a vast laboratory where, in accordance with the different disciplines, ever new areas of research are developed in a stimulating confrontation between faith and reason that aims to recover the harmonious synthesis

29. John Paul II, *Ex Corde Ecclesiae*, n. 30.
30. Cf. John Paul II, *Ex Corde Ecclesiae*, n. 13.

achieved by Thomas Aquinas and other great Christian thinkers, a synthesis that is unfortunately challenged by important currents of modern philosophy.

The consequence of this contestation has been that, as a criterion of rationality, empirical proof by experimentation has become ever more exclusive. The fundamental human questions—how to live and how to die—thus appear to be excluded from the context of rationality and are left to the sphere of subjectivity.

Consequently, the issue that brought universities into being—the question of the true and the good—in the end disappears, to be replaced by the question of feasibility.

This then is the great challenge to Catholic universities: to impart knowledge in the perspective of true rationality, different from that of today that largely prevails, in accordance with a reason open to the question of the truth and to the great values inscribed in being itself, hence open to the transcendent, to God.

We now know that this is possible precisely in the light of the revelation of Christ, who united in himself God and man, eternity and time, spirit and matter. "In the beginning was the Word," the Logos, creative reason ... and "the Word became flesh" (Jn 1:1, 14).

The divine *Logos,* eternal reason, is the origin of the universe and was united once and for all with humanity, the world and history, in Christ. In the light of this capital truth of faith and of reason at the same time, it was once again possible, in 2000, to combine faith and knowledge.

The daily work of a Catholic university, I should say, takes place on this basis. Is this not an exciting adventure? Yes, it is, because one discovers, moving within this horizon of meaning, the intrinsic unity that links the different branches of knowledge: theology, philosophy, medicine, economics, every discipline, even the most specialized technologies, since everything is connected.

Choosing a Catholic university means choosing this approach that, despite the inevitable historical limitations, characterizes the European culture, for whose formation the universities were, not for nothing, born historically "*ex corde Ecclesiae*" [from the heart of the Church] and have made a fundamental contribution.

Therefore, dear friends, with renewed passion for the truth and for human beings, cast your nets into the deep, into the open seas of knowledge, trusting in Christ's words, even when it happens that you experience the exhaustion and disappointment of having "caught" nothing.

In the vast ocean of culture Christ always needs "fishers of men"—that is, knowledgeable and well-qualified people who put their professional skills at the service of good, ultimately at the service of the kingdom of God.

If research work in a university is carried out in a faith perspective, it is also part of this service to the kingdom and to humankind! I am thinking of all the research work being carried out in the many institutes of the Catholic university: it is destined to the glory of God and to the spiritual and material promotion of humanity.

At this moment I am thinking in particular of the scientific institute that your athenaeum wished to offer to Pope John Paul II on November 9, 2000, on the occasion of his visit here to solemnly inaugurate the academic year.

I should like to state that I also have very much at heart the "Paul VI International Scientific Institute for Research on Human Fertility and Infertility" for responsible procreation.[31] Indeed, because of its institutional goals, it is presented as an eloquent example of that synthesis of truth and love that constitutes the vital center of Catholic culture.

The Institute, which came into being in response to the appeal launched by Pope Paul VI in the encyclical *Humanae Vitae,*

31. Cf. *L'Osservatore Romano,* English edition, November 22, 2000.

suggested giving a stable scientific basis both to the natural regulation of human fertility and to the commitment to overcome
possible infertility using natural methods.

As I make my own my venerable predecessor's grateful appreciation for this scientific initiative, I hope that it will be able
to find the support it needs to carry out its important research
activities.

2. THE SYMPHONY OF FREEDOM
AND TRUTH

Catholic Institutions: Helping to Overcome
the Crisis of Universities

From *Address to the Bishops of the United States of America*
(Regions X–XIII) on Their "Ad Limina" Visit, Rome, May 5, 2012

I greet all of you with affection in the Lord, and I offer you my prayerful good wishes for a grace-filled pilgrimage *ad limina Apostolorum.* In the course of our meetings I have been reflecting with you and your brother bishops on the intellectual and cultural challenges of the new evangelization in the context of contemporary American society. In the present talk I wish to address the question of religious education and the faith formation of the next generation of Catholics in your country.

Before all else, I would acknowledge the great progress that has been made in recent years in improving catechesis, reviewing texts and bringing them into conformity with the *Catechism of the Catholic Church.* Important efforts are also being made to preserve the great patrimony of America's Catholic elementary and high schools, which have been deeply affected by changing demographics and increased costs, while at the same time ensuring that the education they provide remains within the reach of all families, whatever their financial status. As has often been mentioned in our meetings, these schools remain an essential resource for the new evangelization, and the significant contribution that they make to American society as a whole ought to be better appreciated and more generously supported.

On the level of higher education, many of you have pointed to a growing recognition on the part of Catholic colleges and universities of the need to reaffirm their distinctive identity in fidelity to their founding ideals and the Church's mission in service of the gospel. Yet much remains to be done, especially in such basic areas as compliance with the mandate laid down in Canon 812 for those who teach theological disciplines. The importance of this canonical norm as a tangible expression of ecclesial communion and solidarity in the Church's educational apostolate becomes all the more evident when we consider the confusion created by instances of apparent dissidence between some representatives of Catholic institutions and the Church's pastoral leadership: such discord harms the Church's witness and, as experience has shown, can easily be exploited to compromise her authority and her freedom.

It is no exaggeration to say that providing young people with a sound education in the faith represents the most urgent internal challenge facing the Catholic community in your country. The deposit of faith is a priceless treasure, which each generation must pass on to the next by winning hearts to Jesus Christ and shaping minds in the knowledge, understanding, and love of his Church. It is gratifying to realize that, in our day too, the Christian vision, presented in its breadth and integrity, proves immensely appealing to the imagination, idealism, and aspirations of the young, who have a right to encounter the faith in all its beauty, its intellectual richness, and its radical demands.

Here I would simply propose several points, which I trust will prove helpful for your discernment in meeting this challenge.

First, as we know, the essential task of authentic education at every level is not simply that of passing on knowledge, essential as this is, but also of shaping hearts. There is a constant need to balance intellectual rigor in communicating effectively, attractively, and integrally, the richness of the Church's faith with forming the young in the love of God, the praxis of the Christian moral and sacramental life, and, not least, the cultivation of personal and liturgical prayer.

It follows that the question of Catholic identity, not least at the university level, entails much more than the teaching of religion or the mere presence of a chaplaincy on campus. All too often, it seems, Catholic schools and colleges have failed to challenge students to reappropriate their faith as part of the exciting intellectual discoveries that mark the experience of higher education. The fact that so many new students find themselves dissociated from the family, school, and community support systems that previously facilitated the transmission of the faith should continually spur Catholic institutions of learning to create new and effective networks of support. In every aspect of their education, students need to be encouraged to articulate a vision of the harmony of faith and reason capable of guiding a lifelong pursuit of knowledge and virtue. As ever, an essential role in this process is played by teachers who inspire others by their evident love of Christ, their witness of sound devotion and their commitment to that *sapientia Christiana* that integrates faith and life, intellectual passion and reverence for the splendor of truth, both human and divine.

In effect, faith by its very nature demands a constant and all-embracing conversion to the fullness of truth revealed in Christ. He is the creative Logos, in whom all things were made and in whom all reality "holds together" (Col 1:17); he is the new Adam who reveals the ultimate truth about man and the world in which we live. In a period of great cultural change and societal displacement not unlike our own, Augustine pointed to this intrinsic connection between faith and the human intellectual enterprise by appealing to Plato, who held, he says, that "to love wisdom is to love God."[1] The Christian commitment to learn-

---

1. Cf. Augustine, *De Civitate Dei,* Bk. viii, 8.

ing, which gave birth to the medieval universities, was based upon this conviction that the one God, as the source of all truth and goodness, is likewise the source of the intellect's passionate desire to know and the will's yearning for fulfillment in love.

Only in this light can we appreciate the distinctive contribution of Catholic education, which engages in a "diakonia of truth" inspired by an intellectual charity that knows that leading others to the truth is ultimately an act of love.[2] Faith's recognition of the essential unity of all knowledge provides a bulwark against the alienation and fragmentation that occurs when the use of reason is detached from the pursuit of truth and virtue; in this sense, Catholic institutions have a specific role to play in helping to overcome the crisis of universities today. Firmly grounded in this vision of the intrinsic interplay of faith, reason, and the pursuit of human excellence, every Christian intellectual and all the Church's educational institutions must be convinced, and desirous of convincing others, that no aspect of reality remains alien to or untouched by the mystery of the redemption and the Risen Lord's dominion over all creation.

During my pastoral visit to the United States I spoke of the need for the Church in America to cultivate "a mindset, an intellectual culture which is genuinely Catholic."[3] Taking up this task certainly involves a renewal of apologetics and an emphasis on Catholic distinctiveness; ultimately, however, it must be aimed at proclaiming the liberating truth of Christ and stimulating greater dialogue and cooperation in building a society ever more solidly grounded in an authentic humanism inspired by the gospel and faithful to the highest values of America's civic and cultural heritage. At the present moment of your nation's history, this is the challenge and opportunity awaiting the entire

2. Cf. Benedict XVI, *Address to Catholic Educators at The Catholic University of America,* Apostolic Journey to the United States, Washington, April 17, 2008.

3. Cf. Benedict XVI, *Homily at National Stadium,* Apostolic Journey to the United States, Washington, April 17, 2008.

Catholic community, and it is one that the Church's educational institutions should be the first to acknowledge and embrace.

In concluding these brief reflections, I wish to express once more my gratitude, and that of the whole Church, for the generous commitment, often accompanied by personal sacrifice, shown by so many teachers and administrators who work in the vast network of Catholic schools in your country.

There Is No Freedom Without Truth

From *Address to the Pontifical Lateran University,*
Rome, October 21, 2006

EXTEMPORANEOUS GREETING ON HIS ARRIVAL

I am happy to be here in "my" university, because this is the University of the Bishop of Rome. I know that here the truth is sought, and so ultimately, Christ is sought, because he is the Truth in person. This journey toward the truth—trying to know the truth better in all of its expressions—is in reality a fundamental ecclesial service.

A great Belgian theologian wrote a book, "Love of the Arts and the Desire of God," and has shown that in the monastic tradition the two things go together, because God is Word and speaks to us through scripture. Therefore, suppose that we begin to read, study, and deepen the knowledge of the arts, and thus deepen our knowledge of the Word.

In this sense the opening of the library is both an academic university event and a spiritual, theological event, precisely because through reading, on the path toward the truth, studying the words to find the Word, we are at the service of the Lord—a service of the gospel for the world, because the world needs the truth. There is no freedom without truth; [without it] we are not in total harmony with the original idea of the Creator.

❖ ❖ ❖

I recall my last visit to the Lateran with pleasure and, as if time had not elapsed, I would like to take up again the theme then under discussion, almost as though we had been interrupted only for a few seconds.

A context such as the academic one invites us in its peculiar way to enter anew the theme of the crisis of culture and identity, which in these decades dramatically places itself before our eyes.

The university is one of the best qualified places to attempt to find opportune ways to exit from this situation. In the University, in fact, the wealth of tradition that remains alive through the centuries is preserved—and especially the library is an essential means to safeguard the richness of tradition—in it and can be illustrated in the fecundity of the truth when it is welcomed in its authenticity with a simple and open soul.

In the university the young generations are formed who await a serious, demanding proposal, capable of responding in new contexts to the perennial question on the meaning of our existence. This expectation must not be disappointed.

The contemporary context seems to give primacy to an artificial intelligence that becomes ever more dominated by experimental techniques, and in this way forgets that all science must always safeguard man and promote his aspiration for the authentic good.

To overrate "doing," obscuring "being" does not help to recompose the fundamental balance that everyone needs in order to give his own existence a solid foundation and valid goal.

Every man, in fact, is called to give meaning to his own actions, above all when this is put in the perspective of a scientific discovery that weakens the very essence of personal life.

To let oneself be taken up by the taste for discovery without safeguarding the criteria that come from a more profound vision would be to fall easily into the drama of which an ancient myth speaks: Young Icarus, exhilarated by the flight toward absolute freedom and heedless of the warning of his old father, Daedalus, flew ever nearer to the sun, forgetting that the wings with which he flew in the sky were made of wax. His violent fall and death were the price of his illusion.

The ancient fable has a perennially valid lesson. In life there are other illusions that one cannot trust without risking disastrous consequences for the existence of one's self and others.

The university professor has the duty not only to investigate the truth and to arouse perennial wonder from it, but also to foster its knowledge in every facet and to defend it from reductive and distorted interpretations.

To make the theme of truth central is not merely a speculative act, restricted to a small circle of thinkers; on the contrary, it is a vital question in order to give a more profound identity to personal life and to heighten responsibility in social relations (cf. Eph 4:25).

In fact, if the question of the truth and the concrete possibility for every person to be able to reach it are neglected, life ends up being reduced to a plethora of hypotheses, deprived of assurances and points of reference.

As the famous humanist Erasmus once said, "Opinions are the source of happiness at a cheap price! To understand the true essence of things, even if it treats of things of minimal importance, costs great endeavor."[4]

It is this endeavor that the university must commit itself to accomplish; it passes through study and research in a spirit of patient perseverance. This endeavor, however, enables one to enter progressively into the heart of questions and to open oneself to passion for the truth and to the joy of finding it.

The words of the holy Bishop Anselm of Aosta remain totally current: "That I may seek you desiring you, that I may desire you seeking you, that I may find you loving you, and that loving you I may find you again."[5]

May the space of silence and contemplation, which are the

4. Cf. *Desiderius* Erasmus, *The Praise of Folly.*
5. Cf. Bishop Anselm of Aosta, *Proslogion* 1.

indispensable background upon which to gather the questions the mind raises, find within these walls attentive persons who know how to value the importance, the efficacy, and the consequences for personal and social living.

God is the ultimate truth to whom all reason naturally tends, solicited by the desire to totally fulfill the journey assigned to it. God is not an empty word or an abstract hypothesis; on the contrary, he is the foundation upon which to build one's life.

To live in the world *"veluti si Deus daretur"* brings with it the assumption of a responsibility that knows how to be concerned with investigating every feasible route in order to come as near as possible to him who is the goal toward which everything tends (cf. 1 Cor 15:24).

The believer knows that this God has a Face and that once for all, with Jesus Christ, he has drawn near to each man.

The Second Vatican Council acutely recalled this: "For, by his Incarnation, he, the Son of God, has in a certain way united himself with each man. He worked with human hands, he thought with a human mind. He acted with a human will, and with a human heart he loved. Born of the Virgin Mary, he has truly been made one of us, like to us in all things except sin."[6] To know him is to know the full truth, thanks to which one can find freedom: "You will know the truth, and the truth will make you free" (Jn 8:32).

Diakonia of Truth

From *Address to Catholic Educators at the Catholic University of America,* Apostolic Journey to the United States, Washington, D.C., April 17, 2008

"How beautiful are the footsteps of those who bring good news" (Rom 10:15–17). With these words of Isaiah quoted by St. Paul, I warmly greet each of you—bearers of wisdom—and through

---

6. Second Vatican Council, Pastoral Constitution *Gaudium et Spes* (December 7, 1965), n. 22.

you the staff, students, and families of the many and varied institutions of learning that you represent. It is my great pleasure to meet you and to share with you some thoughts regarding the nature and identity of Catholic education today.

Education is integral to the mission of the Church to proclaim the Good News. First and foremost every Catholic educational institution is a place to encounter the living God who in Jesus Christ reveals his transforming love and truth.[7] This relationship elicits a desire to grow in the knowledge and understanding of Christ and his teaching. In this way those who meet him are drawn by the very power of the gospel to lead a new life characterized by all that is beautiful, good, and true; a life of Christian witness nurtured and strengthened within the community of our Lord's disciples, the Church.

The dynamic between personal encounter, knowledge, and Christian witness is integral to the *diakonia* of truth that the Church exercises in the midst of humanity. God's revelation offers every generation the opportunity to discover the ultimate truth about its own life and the goal of history. This task is never easy; it involves the entire Christian community and motivates each generation of Christian educators to ensure that the power of God's truth permeates every dimension of the institutions they serve. In this way Christ's Good News is set to work, guiding both teacher and student toward the objective truth that, in transcending the particular and the subjective, points to the universal and absolute that enables us to proclaim with confidence the hope that does not disappoint (cf. Rom 5:5). Set against personal struggles, moral confusion, and fragmentation of knowledge, the noble goals of scholarship and education, founded on the unity of truth and in service of the person and the community, become an especially powerful instrument of hope.

Dear friends, the history of this nation includes many examples of the Church's commitment in this regard. The Catholic

---

7. Cf. Benedict XVI, *Spe Salvi*, n. 4.

community here has in fact made education one of its highest priorities. This undertaking has not come without great sacrifice. Towering figures like St. Elizabeth Ann Seton and other founders and foundresses, with great tenacity and foresight, laid the foundations of what is today a remarkable network of parochial schools contributing to the spiritual well-being of the Church and the nation. Some, like St. Katharine Drexel, devoted their lives to educating those whom others had neglected—in her case, African Americans and Native Americans. Countless dedicated religious sisters, brothers, and priests, together with selfless parents, have, through Catholic schools, helped generations of immigrants to rise from poverty and take their place in mainstream society.

This sacrifice continues today. It is an outstanding apostolate of hope, seeking to address the material, intellectual, and spiritual needs of over three million children and students. It also provides a highly commendable opportunity for the entire Catholic community to contribute generously to the financial needs of our institutions. Their long-term sustainability must be assured. Indeed, everything possible must be done, in cooperation with the wider community, to ensure that they are accessible to people of all social and economic strata. No child should be denied his or her right to an education in faith, which in turn nurtures the soul of a nation.

Some today question the Church's involvement in education, wondering whether her resources might be better placed elsewhere. Certainly in a nation such as this, the state provides ample opportunities for education and attracts committed and generous men and women to this honorable profession. It is timely, then, to reflect on what is particular to our Catholic institutions. How do they contribute to the good of society through the Church's primary mission of evangelization?

All the Church's activities stem from her awareness that she is the bearer of a message that has its origin in God himself: in his goodness and wisdom, God chose to reveal himself and to make known the hidden purpose of his will.[8] God's desire to make himself known, and the innate desire of all human beings to know the truth, provide the context for human inquiry into the meaning of life. This unique encounter is sustained within our Christian community: the one who seeks the truth becomes the one who lives by faith.[9] It can be described as a move from "I" to "we," leading the individual to be numbered among God's people.

This same dynamic of communal identity—to whom do I belong?—vivifies the ethos of our Catholic institutions. A university or school's Catholic identity is not simply a question of the number of Catholic students. It is a question of conviction— do we really believe that only in the mystery of the Word made flesh does the mystery of man truly become clear?[10] Are we ready to commit our entire self—intellect and will, mind and heart— to God? Do we accept the truth Christ reveals? Is the faith tangible in our universities and schools? Is it given fervent expression liturgically, sacramentally, through prayer, acts of charity, a concern for justice, and respect for God's creation? Only in this way do we really bear witness to the meaning of who we are and what we uphold.

From this perspective one can recognize that the contemporary "crisis of truth" is rooted in a "crisis of faith." Only through faith can we freely give our assent to God's testimony and acknowledge him as the transcendent guarantor of the truth he reveals. Again, we see why fostering personal intimacy with Jesus Christ and communal witness to his loving truth is indispensable in Catholic institutions of learning. Yet we all know, and observe with concern, the difficulty or reluctance many people

8. Cf. Eph 1:9; Second Vatican Council, Dogmatic Constitution *Dei Verbum* (November 18, 1965), n. 2.

9. Cf. John Paul II, *Fides et Ratio,* n. 31.

10. Cf. Second Vatican Council, *Gaudium et Spes,* n. 22.

have today in entrusting themselves to God. It is a complex phenomenon, and one that I ponder continually. While we have sought diligently to engage the intellect of our young, perhaps we have neglected the will. Subsequently we observe, with distress, the notion of freedom being distorted. Freedom is not an opting out. It is an opting in—a participation in Being itself. Hence authentic freedom can never be attained by turning away from God. Such a choice would ultimately disregard the very truth we need in order to understand ourselves. A particular responsibility therefore for each of you, and your colleagues, is to evoke among the young the desire for the act of faith, encouraging them to commit themselves to the ecclesial life that follows from this belief. It is here that freedom reaches the certainty of truth. In choosing to live by that truth, we embrace the fullness of the life of faith that is given to us in the Church.

Clearly, then, Catholic identity is not dependent upon statistics. Neither can it be equated simply with orthodoxy of course content. It demands and inspires much more: namely, that each and every aspect of your learning communities reverberates within the ecclesial life of faith. Only in faith can truth become incarnate and reason truly human, capable of directing the will along the path of freedom.[11] In this way our institutions make a vital contribution to the mission of the Church and truly serve society. They become places in which God's active presence in human affairs is recognized and in which every young person discovers the joy of entering into Christ's "being for others."[12]

The Church's primary mission of evangelization, in which educational institutions play a crucial role, is consonant with a nation's fundamental aspiration to develop a society truly worthy of the human person's dignity. At times, however, the value of the Church's contribution to the public forum is questioned. It is important therefore to recall that the truths of faith and of

11. Cf. Benedict XVI, *Spe Salvi*, n. 23.
12. Cf. Benedict XVI, *Spe Salvi*, n. 28.

reason never contradict one another.[13] The Church's mission, in fact, involves her in humanity's struggle to arrive at truth. In articulating revealed truth she serves all members of society by purifying reason, ensuring that it remains open to the consideration of ultimate truths. Drawing upon divine wisdom, she sheds light on the foundation of human morality and ethics and reminds all groups in society that it is not praxis that creates truth, but truth that should serve as the basis of praxis. Far from undermining the tolerance of legitimate diversity, such a contribution illuminates the very truth that makes consensus attainable, and helps to keep public debate rational, honest, and accountable. Similarly the Church never tires of upholding the essential moral categories of right and wrong, without which hope could only wither, giving way to cold, pragmatic calculations of utility that render the person little more than a pawn on some ideological chessboard.

With regard to the educational forum, the *diakonia* of truth takes on a heightened significance in societies where secularist ideology drives a wedge between truth and faith. This division has led to a tendency to equate truth with knowledge and to adopt a positivistic mentality that, in rejecting metaphysics, denies the foundations of faith and rejects the need for a moral vision. Truth means more than knowledge: knowing the truth leads us to discover the good. Truth speaks to the individual in his or her entirety, inviting us to respond with our whole being. This optimistic vision is found in our Christian faith because such faith has been granted the vision of the *Logos,* God's creative Reason, which in the incarnation is revealed as Goodness itself. Far from being just a communication of factual data—"informative"—the loving truth of the gospel is creative and

13. Cf. First Vatican Council, Dogmatic Constitution *Dei Filius* IV, no. 3017 (April 24, 1870), in *Enchiridion Symbolorum Definitionum et Declarationum de Rebus Fidei et Morum,* edited by Heinrich Denzinger and Adolf Schönmetzer, no. 3017, 35th ed. (Rome: Herder, 1973); Augustine, *Contra Academicos,* III.20.43.

life-changing—"performative."[14] With confidence Christian educators can liberate the young from the limits of positivism and awaken receptivity to the truth, to God and his goodness. In this way you will also help to form their conscience, which, enriched by faith, opens a sure path to inner peace and to respect for others.

It comes as no surprise, then, that not just our own ecclesial communities, but society in general has high expectations of Catholic educators. This places upon you a responsibility and offers an opportunity. More and more people—parents in particular—recognize the need for excellence in the human formation of their children. As *mater et magistra* the Church shares their concern. When nothing beyond the individual is recognized as definitive, the ultimate criterion of judgment becomes the self and the satisfaction of the individual's immediate wishes. The objectivity and perspective, which can only come through a recognition of the essential transcendent dimension of the human person, can be lost. Within such a relativistic horizon the goals of education are inevitably curtailed. Slowly, a lowering of standards occurs. We observe today a timidity in the face of the category of the good and an aimless pursuit of novelty parading as the realization of freedom. We witness an assumption that every experience is of equal worth as well as a reluctance to admit imperfection and mistakes. And particularly disturbing is the reduction of the precious and delicate area of education in sexuality to management of "risk," bereft of any reference to the beauty of conjugal love.

How might Christian educators respond? These harmful developments point to the particular urgency of what we might call "intellectual charity." This aspect of charity calls the educator to recognize that the profound responsibility to lead the young to truth is nothing less than an act of love. Indeed, the dignity of education lies in fostering the true perfection and happiness

14. Cf. Benedict XVI, *Spe Salvi,* n. 2.

of those to be educated. In practice "intellectual charity" upholds the essential unity of knowledge against the fragmentation that ensues when reason is detached from the pursuit of truth. It guides the young toward the deep satisfaction of exercising freedom in relation to truth, and it strives to articulate the relationship between faith and all aspects of family and civic life. Once their passion for the fullness and unity of truth has been awakened, young people will surely relish the discovery that the question of what they can know opens up the vast adventure of what they ought to do. Here they will experience "in what" and "in whom" it is possible to hope and be inspired to contribute to society in a way that engenders hope in others.

Dear friends, I wish to conclude by focusing our attention specifically on the paramount importance of your own professionalism and witness within our Catholic universities and schools. First, let me thank you for your dedication and generosity. I know from my own days as a professor, and I have heard from your bishops and officials of the Congregation for Catholic Education, that the reputation of Catholic institutes of learning in this country is largely due to yourselves and your predecessors. Your selfless contributions—from outstanding research to the dedication of those working in inner-city schools—serve both your country and the Church. For this I express my profound gratitude.

In regard to faculty members at Catholic colleges and universities, I wish to reaffirm the great value of academic freedom. In virtue of this freedom you are called to search for the truth wherever careful analysis of evidence leads you. Yet it is also the case that any appeal to the principle of academic freedom in order to justify positions that contradict the faith and the teaching of the Church would obstruct or even betray the university's identity and mission: a mission at the heart of the Church's *munus docendi,* and not somehow autonomous or independent of it.

Teachers and administrators, whether in universities or schools, have the duty and privilege to ensure that students receive instruction in Catholic doctrine and practice. This requires that public witness to the way of Christ, as found in the gospel and upheld by the Church's magisterium, shapes all aspects of an institution's life, both inside and outside the classroom. Divergence from this vision weakens Catholic identity and, far from advancing freedom, inevitably leads to confusion, whether moral, intellectual, or spiritual.

I wish also to express a particular word of encouragement to both lay and religious teachers of catechesis who strive to ensure that young people become daily more appreciative of the gift of faith. Religious education is a challenging apostolate, yet there are many signs of a desire among young people to learn about the faith and practice it with vigor. If this awakening is to grow, teachers require a clear and precise understanding of the specific nature and role of Catholic education. They must also be ready to lead the commitment made by the entire school community to assist our young people, and their families, to experience the harmony between faith, life and culture.

Here I wish to make a special appeal to religious brothers, sisters, and priests: do not abandon the school apostolate; indeed, renew your commitment to schools, especially those in poorer areas. In places where there are many hollow promises that lure young people away from the path of truth and genuine freedom, the consecrated person's witness to the evangelical counsels is an irreplaceable gift. I encourage the religious present to bring renewed enthusiasm to the promotion of vocations. Know that your witness to the ideal of consecration and mission among the young is a source of great inspiration in faith for them and their families.

To all of you I say: bear witness to hope. Nourish your witness with prayer. Account for the hope that characterizes your lives (cf. 1 Pet 3:15) by living the truth that you propose to your students. Help them to know and love the One you have encountered, whose truth and goodness you have experienced with joy.

With St. Augustine, let us say, "We who speak and you who listen acknowledge ourselves as fellow disciples of a single teacher."[15]

Fidelity to Man Requires Fidelity to the Truth, Which Alone Is the Guarantee of Freedom

From *Address to Members of the Academic Community*,
Apostolic Journey to the Czech Republic, Prague,
September 27, 2009

The service of academia, upholding and contributing to the cultural and spiritual values of society, enriches the nation's intellectual patrimony and strengthens the foundations of its future development. The great changes that swept Czech society twenty years ago were precipitated not least by movements of reform that originated in university and student circles. That quest for freedom has continued to guide the work of scholars whose *diakonia* of truth is indispensable to any nation's well-being.

I address you as one who has been a professor, solicitous of the right to academic freedom and the responsibility for the authentic use of reason, and is now the pope who, in his role as shepherd, is recognized as a voice for the ethical reasoning of humanity. While some argue that the questions raised by religion, faith, and ethics have no place within the purview of collective reason, that view is by no means axiomatic. The freedom that underlies the exercise of reason—be it in a university or in the Church—has a purpose: it is directed to the pursuit of truth, and as such gives expression to a tenet of Christianity that in fact gave rise to the university. Indeed, man's thirst for knowledge prompts every generation to broaden the concept of reason and to drink at the wellsprings of faith. It was precisely the rich heritage of classical wisdom, assimilated and placed at the service of the gospel, which the first Christian missionaries brought to

15. Augustine, *Sermons*, 23:2.

these lands and established as the basis of a spiritual and cultural unity that endures to this day. The same spirit led my predecessor Pope Clement VI to establish the famed Charles University in 1347, which continues to make an important contribution to wider European academic, religious, and cultural circles.

The proper autonomy of a university, or indeed any educational institution, finds meaning in its accountability to the authority of truth. Nevertheless, that autonomy can be thwarted in a variety of ways. The great formative tradition, open to the transcendent, which stands at the base of universities across Europe, was in this land and others systematically subverted by the reductive ideology of materialism, the repression of religion, and the suppression of the human spirit. In 1989, however, the world witnessed in dramatic ways the overthrow of a failed totalitarian ideology and the triumph of the human spirit. The yearning for freedom and truth is inalienably part of our common humanity. It can never be eliminated and, as history has shown, it is denied at humanity's own peril. It is to this yearning that religious faith, the various arts, philosophy, theology, and other scientific disciplines, each with its own method, seek to respond, both on the level of disciplined reflection and on the level of a sound praxis.

Distinguished rectors and professors, together with your research there is a further essential aspect of the mission of the university in which you are engaged—namely, the responsibility for enlightening the minds and hearts of the young men and women of today. This grave duty is of course not new. From the time of Plato, education has been not merely the accumulation of knowledge or skills, but *paideia,* human formation in the treasures of an intellectual tradition directed to a virtuous life. While the great universities springing up throughout Europe during the Middle Ages aimed with confidence at the ideal of a synthesis of all knowledge, it was always in the service of an authentic *humanitas,* the perfection of the individual within the unity of a well-ordered society. And likewise today: once young people's understanding of the fullness and unity of truth has been awakened, they relish the discovery that the question of what they can know opens up the vast adventure of how they ought to be and what they ought to do.

The idea of an integrated education, based on the unity of knowledge grounded in truth, must be regained. It serves to counteract the tendency, so evident in contemporary society, toward a fragmentation of knowledge. With the massive growth in information and technology there comes the temptation to detach reason from the pursuit of truth. Sundered from the fundamental human orientation toward truth, however, reason begins to lose direction: it withers, either under the guise of modesty, resting content with the merely partial or provisional, or under the guise of certainty, insisting on capitulation to the demands of those who indiscriminately give equal value to practically everything. The relativism that ensues provides a dense camouflage behind which new threats to the autonomy of academic institutions can lurk. While the period of interference from political totalitarianism has passed, is it not the case that frequently, across the globe, the exercise of reason and academic research are—subtly and not so subtly—constrained to bow to the pressures of ideological interest groups and the lure of short-term utilitarian or pragmatic goals? What will happen if our culture builds itself only on fashionable arguments, with little reference to a genuine historical intellectual tradition, or on the viewpoints that are most vociferously promoted and most heavily funded? What will happen if, in its anxiety to preserve a radical secularism, it detaches itself from its life-giving roots? Our societies will not become more reasonable or tolerant or adaptable, but rather more brittle and less inclusive, and they will increasingly struggle to recognize what is true, noble, and good.

Dear friends, I wish to encourage you in all that you do to meet the idealism and generosity of young people today, not only with programs of study that assist them to excel, but also by an experience of shared ideals and mutual support in the great enterprise of learning. The skills of analysis and those required to generate a hypothesis, combined with the prudent art of discernment, offer an effective antidote to the attitudes of self-absorption, disengagement, and even alienation that are sometimes found in our prosperous societies, and that can particularly affect the young. In this context of an eminently humanistic vision of the mission of the university, I would like briefly to mention the mending of the breach between science and religion that was a central concern of my predecessor, Pope John Paul II. He, as you know, promoted a fuller understanding of the relationship between faith and reason as the two wings by which the human spirit is lifted to the contemplation of truth.[16] Each supports the other, and each has its own scope of action,[17] yet still there are those who would detach one from the other. Not only do the proponents of this positivistic exclusion of the divine from the universality of reason negate what is one of the most profound convictions of religious believers, they also thwart the very dialogue of cultures that they themselves propose. An understanding of reason that is deaf to the divine and that relegates religions into the realm of subcultures is incapable of entering into the dialogue of cultures that our world so urgently needs. In the end, "fidelity to man requires fidelity to the truth, which alone is the guarantee of freedom."[18] This confidence in the human ability to seek truth, to find truth, and to live by the truth led to the foundation of the great European universities. Surely we must reaffirm this today in order to bring courage to the intellectual forces necessary for the development of a future of authentic human flourishing, a future truly worthy of man.

With these reflections, dear friends, I offer you my prayerful

16. Cf. John Paul II, *Fides et Ratio,* Proemium.
17. Cf. John Paul II, *Fides et Ratio,* n. 17.
18. Benedict XVI, *Caritas in Veritate,* n. 9.

good wishes for your demanding work. I pray that it will always be inspired and directed by a human wisdom that genuinely seeks the truth that sets us free (cf. Jn 8:28).

Keep Alive the Search for Truth

From *Address During the Meeting with the World of Culture at the Cultural Center of Belém,* Apostolic Journey to Portugal, Lisbon, May 12, 2010

Today's culture is in fact permeated by a "tension" that at times takes the form of a "conflict" between the present and tradition. The dynamic movement of society gives absolute value to the present, isolating it from the cultural legacy of the past, without attempting to trace a path for the future. This emphasis on the "present" as a source of inspiration for the meaning of life, both individual and social, nonetheless clashes with the powerful cultural tradition of the Portuguese people, deeply marked by the millenary influence of Christianity and by a sense of global responsibility. This came to the fore in the adventure of the discoveries and in the missionary zeal that shared the gift of faith with other peoples. The Christian ideal of universality and fraternity inspired this common adventure, even though influences from the Enlightenment and laicism also made themselves felt. This tradition gave rise to what could be called a "wisdom"—that is to say, an understanding of life and history that included a corpus of ethical values and an "ideal" to be realized by Portugal, which has always sought to establish relations with the rest of the world.

The Church appears as the champion of a healthy and lofty tradition, whose rich contribution she sets at the service of society. Society continues to respect and appreciate her service to the common good, but distances itself from that "wisdom" that is part of her legacy. This "conflict" between tradition and the present finds expression in the crisis of truth, yet only truth can provide direction and trace the path of a fulfilled existence, both for individuals and for a people. Indeed, a people no longer conscious of its own truth ends up being lost in the maze of time and history, deprived of clearly defined values and lacking great and clearly formulated goals. Dear friends, much still needs to be learned about the form in which the Church takes her place in the world, helping society to understand that the proclamation of truth is a service that she offers to society, and opening new horizons for the future, horizons of grandeur and dignity. The Church in effect has "a mission of truth to accomplish, in every time and circumstance, for a society that is attuned to man, to his dignity, to his vocation.... Fidelity to man requires fidelity to the truth, which alone is the guarantee of freedom (cf. Jn 8:28), and of the possibility of integral human development. For this reason the Church searches for truth, proclaims it tirelessly and recognizes it wherever it is manifested. This mission of truth is something that the Church can never renounce."[19] For a society made up mainly of Catholics, and whose culture has been profoundly marked by Christianity, the search for truth apart from Christ proves dramatic. For Christians, Truth is divine; it is the eternal "Logos" that found human expression in Jesus Christ, who could objectively state: "I am the truth" (Jn 14:6). The Church, in her adherence to the eternal character of truth, is in the process of learning how to live with respect for other "truths" and for the truth of others. Through this respect, open to dialogue, new doors can be opened to the transmission of truth.

"The Church"—wrote Pope Paul VI—"must enter into dialogue with the world in which she lives. The Church becomes word, she becomes message, she becomes dialogue."[20] Dialogue, without ambiguity and marked by respect for those taking part, is a priority in today's world, and the Church does not intend to withdraw from it. A testimony to this is the Holy See's presence

19. Benedict XVI, *Caritas in Veritate*, n. 9.
20. Paul VI, Encyclical Letter *Ecclesiam Suam* (August 6, 1964), n. 67.

in several international organizations, as for example her presence at the Council of Europe's North-South Center, established twenty years ago here in Lisbon, which is focused on intercultural dialogue with a view to promoting cooperation between Europe, the southern Mediterranean, and Africa, and building a global citizenship based on human rights and civic responsibility, independent of ethnic origin or political allegiance, and respectful of religious beliefs. Given the reality of cultural diversity, people need not only accept the existence of the culture of others, but also to aspire to be enriched by it and offer to it whatever they possess that is good, true, and beautiful.

Ours is a time that calls for the best of our efforts, prophetic courage, and a renewed capacity to "point out new worlds to the world," to use the words of your national poet.[21] You who are representatives of culture in all its forms, forgers of thought and opinion, "thanks to your talent, have the opportunity to speak to the heart of humanity, to touch individual and collective sensibilities, to call forth dreams and hopes, to broaden the horizons of knowledge and of human engagement.... Do not be afraid to approach the first and last source of beauty, to enter into dialogue with believers, with those who, like yourselves, consider that they are pilgrims in this world and in history towards infinite Beauty!"[22]

Precisely so as "to place the modern world in contact with the life-giving and perennial energies of the Gospel,"[23] the Second Vatican Council was convened. There the Church, on the basis of a renewed awareness of the Catholic tradition, took seriously and discerned, transformed, and overcame the fundamental critiques that gave rise to the modern world, the Reformation, and the Enlightenment. In this way the Church herself accepted and refashioned the best of the requirements of modernity by tran-

21. Luís de Camões, *Os Lusíades* II.45.
22. Benedict XVI, *Address to Artists in the Sistine Chapel,* November 21, 2009.
23. John XXIII, Apostolic Constitution *Humanae Salutis* (December 25, 1961), n. 3.

scending them on the one hand and by avoiding their errors and dead ends on the other. The Council laid the foundation for an authentic Catholic renewal and for a new civilization—"the civilization of love"—as an evangelical service to man and society.

Dear friends, the Church considers that her most important mission in today's culture is to keep alive the search for truth and consequently for God; to bring people to look beyond penultimate realities and to seek those that are ultimate. I invite you to deepen your knowledge of God as he has revealed himself in Jesus Christ for our complete fulfillment. Produce beautiful things, but above all make your lives places of beauty.

3. EDUCATION AND LOVE

On Human Love

From *Address to Members of the Pontifical John Paul II Institute for Studies on Marriage and Family on the 25th Anniversary of Its Foundation,* May 11, 2006

As a young priest Karol Wojtyla already had the idea of "teaching how to love." It was later to fill him with enthusiasm when, as a young bishop, he confronted the difficult times that followed the publication of my predecessor Paul VI's prophetic and ever timely encyclical *Humanae Vitae.*

It was then that he realized the need for a systematic study of this topic. It was the basis of this teaching that he later offered to the entire Church in his unforgettable *Catechesis on human love.* Thus, *two* fundamental *elements* were highlighted that in recent years you have sought to examine more deeply and that give novelty to your institute as an academic reality with a specific mission in the Church.

The *first element* concerns the fact that marriage and the family are rooted in the inmost nucleus of the truth about man and his destiny. Sacred scripture reveals that the vocation to love is part of the authentic image of God that the Creator has desired to impress upon his creatures, calling them to resemble him precisely to the extent in which they are open to love.

Consequently the sexual difference that distinguishes the male from the female body is not a mere biological factor, but has a far deeper significance. It expresses that form of love with which man and woman, by becoming one flesh, as sacred scripture says, can achieve an authentic communion of people open to the transmission of life and who thus cooperate with God in the procreation of new human beings.

A *second element* marks the newness of John Paul II's teaching on human love: his original way of interpreting God's plan precisely in the convergence of divine revelation with the human experience. Indeed, in Christ, fullness of the revelation of the Father's love is also expressed in the full truth of the human vocation to love that can only be found completely in the sincere gift of self.

In my recent encyclical, *Deus Caritas Est,* I wanted to emphasize that it is precisely through love that "the Christian image of God and the resulting image of mankind and its destiny" shine forth.[1]

In other words, God used the way of love to reveal the intimate mystery of his Trinitarian life. Furthermore, the close relationship that exists between the image of God-Love and human love enables us to understand that "Corresponding to the image of a monotheistic God is monogamous marriage. Marriage based on exclusive and definitive love becomes the icon of the relationship between God and his people and vice versa. God's way of loving becomes the measure of human love."[2]

It is here that the duty incumbent on the Institute for Studies on Marriage and Family in academic structures overall stands out: to illumine the truth of love as a path to fullness in every form of human life. The great challenge of the new evangelization that John Paul II proposed with such enthusiasm needs to be sustained with a truly profound reflection on human love, since precisely this love is the privileged path that God chose to

---

1. Benedict XVI, Encyclical Letter *Deus Caritas Est* (December 25, 2005), n. 1.
2. Benedict XVI, *Deus Caritas Est,* n. 11.

reveal himself to man and in this love he calls human beings to communion in the Trinitarian life.

This approach enables us also to overcome a private conception of love that is so widespread today. Authentic love is transformed into a light that guides the whole of life toward its fullness, generating a society in which human beings can live. The communion of life and love, which is marriage, thus emerges as an authentic good for society.

Today the need to avoid confusing marriage with other types of unions based on weak love is especially urgent. It is only the rock of total, irrevocable love between a man and a woman that can serve as the foundation on which to build a society that will become a home for all mankind.

The importance of the institute's work in the Church's mission explains its structure: in fact, John Paul II approved a single institute, but with different headquarters located on the five continents, for the purpose of offering a reflection that would display the riches of the one truth in the plurality of cultures.

This unity of vision in research and teaching, embracing the diversity of places and sensibilities, constitutes a value that you must safeguard, developing the riches embedded in each culture. This feature of the institute has proven to be particularly suited to the study of a reality such as that of marriage and the family. Your work can express how the gift of creation lived in the different cultures was raised to a redeeming grace by Christ's redemption.

To be successful in your mission as the faithful heirs of the institute's founder, beloved John Paul II, I ask you to look to Mary Most Holy, mother of fair love. The redeeming love of the incarnate Word must be transformed into "fountains of living water in the midst of a thirsting world," for every marriage and in every family.[3]

---

3. Benedict XVI, *Deus Caritas Est,* n. 42.

Vocation to Love

From *Address to the Pontifical John Paul II Institute for
Studies on Marriage and Family,* May 13, 2011

With joy I welcome you today, a few days after the beatification of Pope John Paul II, who, thirty years ago, as we heard, chose to found at the same time the Pontifical Council for the Family and your Pontifical Institute, two entities that show how firmly convinced he was of the family's importance for the Church and for society....

The new blessed John Paul II, who, as was mentioned, was the victim of that terrible attack in St. Peter's Square thirty years ago, entrusted to you, in particular, the study, research, and dissemination of his "Catecheses on human love" that contain a profound reflection on the human body. Joining the theology of the body with that of love in order to find unity in the human journey: this is the theme I would like to point out to you as a horizon for your work.

Shortly after the death of Michelangelo, Paolo Veronese was summoned by the Inquisition, accused of having depicted inappropriate figures in his "Last Supper." The artist replied that even in the Sistine Chapel bodies were depicted nude, with little reverence. It was the Inquisitor himself who took Michelangelo's defense, with a reply that has become famous: "But in these figures what is there that is not inspired by the Holy Spirit?" As people of the modern age, we struggle to understand these words, because the body appears to us as inert matter, heavy, opposed to knowledge and to the freedom proper to the spirit. However, the bodies Michelangelo depicted are robed in love, life, splendor. He wanted in this way to show that our bodies hide a mystery. In them the spirit is manifest and active. They are called to be spiritual bodies, as St. Paul says (cf. 1 Cor 15:44).

Consequently we can ask ourselves: can this destiny of the body enlighten the stages of its journey? If our body is called to be spiritual, should not its history be that of the covenant between body and spirit? Indeed, far from being opposed to the spirit, the body is the place where the spirit can dwell. In this light it is possible to understand that our bodies are not inert, heavy matter, but, if we know how to listen, they speak the language of true love.

The first word of this language is found in the creation of the human person. The body speaks to us of an origin that we have not conferred upon ourselves. "You knit me in my mother's womb," the Psalmist says to the Lord (Ps 139:13). We can affirm that the body, in revealing our origin to us, bears within itself a filial significance because it reminds us that we are generated and leads us back, through our parents who passed on life to us, to God the Creator. Only when he recognizes the originating love that has given this life can the human person accept himself, be reconciled with nature and with the world.

The creation of Adam is followed by the creation of Eve. The flesh received from God is required to make possible the union of love between man and woman and transmit life. Before the fall the bodies of Adam and Eve appear in perfect harmony. There is a language in them that they did not create, an *eros* rooted in their nature that invites them to receive one another reciprocally from the Creator so as to be able to give themselves.

Thus we understand that in love the human person is "re-created." *Incipit vita nuova* [a new life begins], as Dante said,[4] the life of the new unity of the two in one flesh. The true appeal of sexuality is born of the vastness of this horizon that opens up: integral beauty, the universe of the other person and of the "we" that is born of the union, the promise of communion that is hidden therein, the new fruitfulness, the path toward God, the source of love, which love opens up.

The union in one flesh then becomes a union for the whole of life, until the man and woman become one spirit, as well. Thus

---

4. Dante Alighieri, *Vita Nuova* I.1.

a journey begins in which the body teaches us the value of time, of that slow maturation in love. In this light the virtue of chastity takes on new meaning. It is not a "no" to the pleasures and joys of life, but a great "yes" to love as a profound communication between persons, a communication that requires time and respect as they journey together toward fullness, and as a love that becomes capable of generating life and of generously welcoming the new life that is born.

It is true that the body also has a negative language: one hears talk of oppression of the other, of the desire to possess and exploit. However, we know that this language is not part of God's original plan, but rather is the result of sin. When it is separated from its filial meaning, from its connection with the Creator, the body rebels against the person, loses its capacity to let communion shine through, and becomes a place for the appropriation of the other. Is this not perhaps the drama of that sexuality that today remains enclosed in the narrow circle of one's own body and emotions, but that in reality can only find fulfillment in that call to something greater?

In this regard John Paul II spoke of the humility of the body. One of Claudel's characters says to his beloved, "I am not able to keep the promise that my body made to you," which prompts the reply, "You can break the body, but not the promise."[5]

The power of this promise explains how the fall is not the last word about the body in salvation history. God also offers the human person a process of the redemption of the body, the language of which is preserved in the family. If after the fall Eve is given the name "Mother of the Living," this testifies to the fact that the power of sin is not capable of obliterating the original language of the body, the blessing of life that God continues to offer when a man and woman are joined in one flesh. The family: this is the place where the theology of the body and the theology of love are interwoven. Here we learn the goodness of the body,

5. Paul Claudel, *Le soulier de satin* [The Satin Slipper], day 3, scene XIII.

its witness to a good origin, in the experience of the love we receive from our parents. Here lives the self-giving in a single flesh, in the conjugal charity that unites the spouses. Here we experience that the fruitfulness of love and life is interwoven with that of other generations. It is in the family that the human person discovers that he or she is not in a relationship as an autonomous person, but as a child, spouse, or parent, whose identity is founded in being called to love, to receive from others and to give him- or herself to others.

This journey of creation finds its fullness in the incarnation, in the coming of Christ. God took a body, revealed himself in it. The upward movement of the body is hence integrated in another, more original movement, the humble movement of God who lowers himself toward the body in order to raise it to him. As Son, he received a filial body in gratitude and in listening to the Father, and he gave this body for us, by so doing to generate the new body of the Church. The liturgy of the feast of the Ascension sings the story of the flesh, sinner in Adam, assumed and redeemed by Christ. It is a flesh that becomes increasingly filled with light and the Spirit, filled with God.

Thus we see the depth of the theology of the body. When it is interpreted in the whole of tradition, it does not run the risk of superficiality, and allows us to understand the greatness of the vocation to love, which is a call to a communion of persons in the twofold form of life of virginity and marriage.

Dear friends, your institute has been placed under the protection of Our Lady. Concerning Mary, Dante said some words that are enlightening for a theology of the body: "For in thy womb rekindling shone the love."[6] The Love that generates the Church was incarnate in her female body. May the Mother of the Lord continue to protect you on your journey and make fruitful your studies and your teaching in service to the Church's mission for the family and society.

6. Dante Alighieri, *Paradiso,* Canto XXXIII.7.

Every Scientific Approach Must Be
a Loving Approach

From *Address to Participants in an Interacademic Conference
on "The Changing Identity of the Individual," Organized by the
"Académie Des Sciences" of Paris and by the Pontifical
Academy of Sciences,* January 28, 2008

Whereas the exact, natural, and human sciences have progressed prodigiously in the knowledge of man and his universe, there is a strong temptation to seek to isolate the identity of the human being and to enclose this identity in the knowledge that can derive from it. In order to avoid moving in this direction it is important to support anthropological, philosophical, and theological research that allows the appearance and preservation in man of his own mystery, for no science can say who man is, where he comes from, or where he is going. Anthropology thus becomes the most vital science of all. This is what John Paul II said in his encyclical *Fides et Ratio:* "We face a great challenge ... to move from *phenomenon* to *foundation,* a step as necessary as it is urgent. We cannot stop short at experience alone; even if experience does reveal the human being's interiority and spirituality, speculative thinking must penetrate to the spiritual core and the ground from which it rises."[7] Man is always more than what is seen or perceived of him through experience. Failing to ask questions about man's being would lead inevitably to refusing to seek the objective truth about being as a whole, and hence, to no longer being able to recognize the basis on which human dignity, the dignity of every person, rests from the embryonic stage to natural death.

During your colloquium you have recognized that the sciences, philosophy, and theology can be mutually helpful for perceiving the human identity that is constantly developing. Starting with questions on the new being derived from cellular fusion and on who bears a new and specific genetic patrimony, you have

7. John Paul II, *Fides et Ratio,* n. 83.

brought to the fore some essential elements of the mystery of man, marked by otherness: a being created by God, a being in the image of God, a being who is loved and is made to love. As a human person, man is never closed in on himself; he is always a bearer of otherness and from the very first moment of his existence interacts with other human beings, as the human sciences increasingly bring to light. How is it possible not to recall here the marvelous meditation of the Psalmist on the human being, knit together in the secret of his mother's womb and at the same time known in his identity and mystery to God alone, who loves and protects him? (cf. Ps 139:1–16)

Man is neither the result of chance, nor of a bundle of convergences, nor of forms of determinism, nor physiochemical interaction; he is a being who enjoys freedom, which, while taking his nature into account, transcends it and symbolizes this mystery of otherness that dwells within him. It is in this perspective that the great thinker Pascal said, "Man is infinitely more than man." This freedom that is a distinctive feature of the being called man enables him to orient his life toward an end that he can direct with his actions toward the happiness to which he is called for eternity. This freedom reveals that human existence has meaning. In the exercise of his authentic freedom, the person fulfills his vocation; it is completed and gives shape to his profound identity. It is also by putting his freedom into practice that the person exercises his own responsibility for his actions. In this sense the special dignity of the human being is both a gift of God and the promise of a future.

Man bears within himself a specific capacity for discerning what is good and right. Affixed in him as a seal by the Creator, synderesis urges him to do good. Impelled by it, the human being is required to develop his conscience by forming and using it in order to direct his life freely based on the essential laws that are natural law and moral law. In our day, when the development of the sciences attracts and seduces with the possibilities they offer, it is more important than ever to educate the consciences of our contemporaries in order to prevent science from becoming the criterion of good and to ensure that man is respected as the center of creation and not made the object of ideological manipulation, arbitrary decisions, or the abuse of the weaker by the stronger. These are some of the dangers we have experienced in human history, especially during the twentieth century.

Every scientific approach must also be a loving approach, called to be at the service of the human being and of humanity and to make its contribution to forming the identity of individuals. Indeed, as I emphasized in the encyclical *Deus Caritas Est,* "Love embraces the whole of existence in each of its dimensions, including the dimension of time.... Love is indeed 'ecstasy,' that is, a journey, an ongoing exodus out of the closed inward-looking self towards its liberation through self-giving, and thus towards authentic self-discovery."[8] Love brings one out of oneself in order to discover and recognize the other; in opening himself to otherness it also affirms the identity of the subject, for the other reveals me to myself. This is the experience made by numerous believers throughout the Bible, beginning with Abraham. The model of love par excellence is Christ. It is in the act of giving his life for his brethren, in giving himself totally, that his profound identity is expressed and we have the key to interpreting the unfathomable mystery of his being and his mission.

Heart Speaks Unto Heart

From *Homily of Mass with the Beatification of Venerable Cardinal John Henry Newman,* Apostolic Journey to the United Kingdom, Birmingham, September 19, 2010

This day that has brought us together here in Birmingham is a most auspicious one. In the first place, it is the Lord's day, Sunday, the day when our Lord Jesus Christ rose from the dead and

8. Benedict XVI, *Deus Caritas Est,* n. 6.

changed the course of human history forever, offering new life and hope to all who live in darkness and in the shadow of death. That is why Christians all over the world come together on this day to give praise and thanks to God for the great marvels he has worked for us. This particular Sunday also marks a significant moment in the life of the British nation, as it is the day chosen to commemorate the seventieth anniversary of the Battle of Britain. For me as one who lived and suffered through the dark days of the Nazi regime in Germany, it is deeply moving to be here with you on this occasion, and to recall how many of your fellow citizens sacrificed their lives, courageously resisting the forces of that evil ideology. My thoughts go in particular to nearby Coventry, which suffered such heavy bombardment and massive loss of life in November 1940. Seventy years later, we recall with shame and horror the dreadful toll of death and destruction that war brings in its wake, and we renew our resolve to work for peace and reconciliation wherever the threat of conflict looms. Yet there is another, more joyful reason that this is an auspicious day for Great Britain, for the Midlands, for Birmingham. It is the day that sees Cardinal John Henry Newman formally raised to the altars and declared blessed.

I thank Archbishop Bernard Longley for his gracious welcome at the start of Mass this morning. I pay tribute to all who have worked so hard over many years to promote the cause of Cardinal Newman, including the fathers of the Birmingham Oratory and the members of the Spiritual Family *Das Werk*. And I greet everyone here from Great Britain, Ireland, and further afield; I thank you for your presence at this celebration, in which we give glory and praise to God for the heroic virtue of a saintly Englishman.

England has a long tradition of martyr saints, whose courageous witness has sustained and inspired the Catholic community here for centuries. Yet it is right and fitting that we should recognize today the holiness of a confessor, a son of this nation, who, while not called to shed his blood for the Lord, nevertheless bore eloquent witness to him in the course of a long life devoted to the priestly ministry and especially to preaching, teaching, and writing. He is worthy to take his place in a long line of saints and scholars from these islands, St. Bede, St. Hilda, St. Aelred, blessed Duns Scotus, to name but a few. In blessed John Henry, that tradition of gentle scholarship, deep human wisdom, and profound love for the Lord has borne rich fruit as a sign of the abiding presence of the Holy Spirit deep within the heart of God's people, bringing forth abundant gifts of holiness.

Cardinal Newman's motto, *Cor ad cor loquitur,* or "Heart speaks unto heart," gives us an insight into his understanding of the Christian life as a call to holiness, experienced as the profound desire of the human heart to enter into intimate communion with the heart of God. He reminds us that faithfulness to prayer gradually transforms us into the divine likeness. As he wrote in one of his many fine sermons, "a habit of prayer, the practice of turning to God and the unseen world in every season, in every place, in every emergency—prayer, I say, has what may be called a natural effect in spiritualizing and elevating the soul. A man is no longer what he was before; gradually ... he has imbibed a new set of ideas, and become imbued with fresh principles."[9] Today's gospel tells us that no one can be the servant of two masters (cf. Lk 16:13), and blessed John Henry's teaching on prayer explains how the faithful Christian is definitively taken into the service of the one true Master, who alone has a claim to our unconditional devotion (cf. Mt 23:10). Newman helps us to understand what this means for our daily lives: he tells us that our divine Master has assigned a specific task to each one of us, a "definite service," committed uniquely to every single person: "I have my mission," he wrote, "I am a link in a chain, a bond of connection between persons. He has not created me for naught.

9. Bl. John Henry Newman, *Parochial and Plain Sermons* (New York: Longmans, Green, 1909), 4:230–31.

I shall do good, I shall do his work; I shall be an angel of peace, a preacher of truth in my own place ... if I do but keep his commandments and serve him in my calling."[10]

The definite service to which blessed John Henry was called involved applying his keen intellect and his prolific pen to many of the most pressing "subjects of the day." His insights into the relationship between faith and reason, into the vital place of revealed religion in civilized society, and into the need for a broadly based and wide-ranging approach to education were not only of profound importance for Victorian England, but continue today to inspire and enlighten many all over the world. I would like to pay particular tribute to his vision for education, which has done so much to shape the ethos that is the driving force behind Catholic schools and colleges today. Firmly opposed to any reductive or utilitarian approach, he sought to achieve an educational environment in which intellectual training, moral discipline, and religious commitment would come together. The project to found a Catholic university in Ireland provided him with an opportunity to develop his ideas on the subject, and the collection of discourses that he published as *The Idea of a University* holds up an ideal from which all those engaged in academic formation can continue to learn. And indeed, what better goal could teachers of religion set themselves than Blessed John Henry's famous appeal for an intelligent, well-instructed laity: "I want a laity, not arrogant, not rash in speech, not disputatious, but men who know their religion, who enter into it, who know just where they stand, who know what they hold and what they do not, who know their creed so well that they can give an account of it, who know so much of history that they can defend it."[11] On this day when the author of those words is raised to the altars, I pray that, through his intercession and example, all

10. Newman, *Meditations and Devotions* (New York: Longmans, Green, 1907), 301–2.

11. Newman, *Lectures on the Present Position of Catholics in England* (New York: Longmans, Green, 1908), lecture 9, 390.

who are engaged in the task of teaching and catechesis will be inspired to greater effort by the vision he so clearly sets before us.

While it is John Henry Newman's intellectual legacy that has understandably received most attention in the vast literature devoted to his life and work, I prefer on this occasion to conclude with a brief reflection on his life as a priest, a pastor of souls. The warmth and humanity underlying his appreciation of the pastoral ministry is beautifully expressed in another of his famous sermons: "Had Angels been your priests, my brethren, they could not have condoled with you, sympathized with you, have had compassion on you, felt tenderly for you, and made allowances for you, as we can; they could not have been your patterns and guides, and have led you on from your old selves into a new life, as they can who come from the midst of you."[12] He lived out that profoundly human vision of priestly ministry in his devoted care for the people of Birmingham during the years that he spent at the Oratory he founded, visiting the sick and the poor, comforting the bereaved, caring for those in prison. No wonder that on his death so many thousands of people lined the local streets as his body was taken to its place of burial not half a mile from here. One hundred and twenty years later, great crowds have assembled once again to rejoice in the Church's solemn recognition of the outstanding holiness of this much-loved father of souls. What better way to express the joy of this moment than by turning to our heavenly Father in heartfelt thanksgiving, praying in the words that Blessed John Henry Newman placed on the lips of the choirs of angels in heaven:

> Praise to the Holiest in the height
> And in the depth be praise;
> In all his words most wonderful,
> Most sure in all his ways![13]

---

12. Newman, "Men, Not Angels: The Priests of the Gospel," *Discourses to Mixed Congregations* (New York: Longmans, Green, 1906), 47–48, 3.

13. Newman, "The Dream of Gerontius" [1865], in *Versus on Various Occasions* (New York: Longmans, Green, 1903), 353.

To Educate Is an Act of Love

From *Address to Participants in the Plenary Assembly of the
Congregation for Catholic Education,* February 7, 2011

The topics you are addressing in these days have education and
formation as a common denominator, which today constitute one
of the most urgent challenges that the Church and her institutions
are called to address. The educational endeavor seems to have become ever more arduous because, in a culture that too often makes
relativism its creed, the light of truth is lacking; more than that, it
is considered dangerous to speak of truth, thus instilling doubt on
the basic values of personal and community life. Important, because of this, is the service carried out in the world by the numerous formative institutions that are inspired in the Christian vision
of man and of reality: to educate is an act of love, the exercise of
"intellectual charity," which requires responsibility, dedication,
consistency of life. The work of your congregation and the choices
you will make in these days of reflection and study will certainly
contribute to respond to the present "educational emergency."

Your congregation, created in 1915 by Benedict XV, has carried out its work for almost one hundred years at the service of
the various Catholic institutions of formation. Among these,
undoubtedly, the seminary is one of the most important for the
life of the Church; hence it exacts a formative plan that takes
into account the context referred to above. Several times I have
stressed how the seminary is a precious stage of life, in which the
candidate to the priesthood experiences being "a disciple of Jesus." Required for this time destined to formation is a certain de-
tachment, a certain "desert," because the Lord speaks to the heart
with a voice that is heard if there is silence (cf. 1 Kings 19:12); but
required also is willingness to live together, to love "family life"
and the community dimension that anticipate that "sacramental
fraternity" that must characterize every diocesan presbyter[14] and

---

14. Cf. Second Vatican Council, Decree *Presbyterorum Ordinis* (December 7, 1965),
n. 8.

that I also wished to recall in my recent Letter to Seminarians: "one does not become a priest on one's own. There is the 'community of disciples,' the totality of those who wish to serve the common Church."

In these days you also studied the draft of the document on the Internet and formation in the seminaries. Because of its capacity to surmount distances and put people in mutual contact, the Internet presents great possibilities for the Church and her mission. With the necessary discernment for its intelligent and prudent use, it is an instrument that can serve not only for studies, but also for the pastoral action of future presbyters in different ecclesial fields, such as evangelization, missionary action, catechesis, educational projects, the management of institutes. Also of extreme importance in this field is to be able to count on adequately prepared formators who will be faithful guides and always up to date in order to support the candidates to the priesthood in the correct and positive use of the media.

This year, then, is the seventieth anniversary of the Pontifical Work for Priestly Vocations, instituted by the venerable Pius XII to foster collaboration between the Holy See and the local churches in the precious work of promotion of vocations to the ordained ministry. This anniversary could be the occasion to know and evaluate the most significant vocational initiatives promoted in the local churches. In addition to stressing the value of the universal call to follow Jesus, the vocational pastoral must insist more clearly on the profile of the ministerial priesthood, characterized by its specific configuration to Christ, which distinguishes it essentially from the other faithful and puts itself at their service.

Moreover, you also undertook a revision of what the apostolic constitution "Sapientia Christiana" prescribes on ecclesiastical studies regarding canon law, the higher institutes of religious studies, and, recently, philosophy. A sector on which to reflect particularly is that of theology. It is important to render ever more solid the bond between theology and the study of sacred scripture so that the latter is really its soul and heart.[15]

However, the theologian must not forget that he is also the one who speaks to God. Hence, it is indispensable to have theology closely united with personal and community prayer, especially liturgical prayer. Theology is *sciencia fidei,* and prayer nourishes faith. In the union with God, mystery is, in some way, savored, it comes close, and this proximity is light for the intelligence. I would also like to stress the connection between theology and the other disciplines, considering that theology is taught in Catholic universities and, in many cases, in civil ones. Blessed John Henry Newman spoke of the "circle of knowledge" to indicate that an interdependence exists between the different branches of knowledge; but God is he who has a relationship only with the totality of the real; consequently, to eliminate God means to break the circle of knowledge.

In this perspective the Catholic universities, with their very precise identity and their openness to the "totality" of the human being, can carry out a valuable work of promoting the unity of knowledge, orienting students and teachers to the Light of the world, "the true light that enlightens every man" (Jn 1:9). These are considerations that are valid also for Catholic schools. First of all there must be the courage to proclaim the "great" value of education, to form solid persons able to collaborate with others, and to give meaning to their life. Today there is talk of intercultural education, an object of study also in your plenary assembly.

Required in this realm is a courageous and innovative fidelity, which is able to combine the clear awareness of one's identity with openness to others because of the exigencies of living together in multicultural societies. Emerging also for this end is the educational role of the teaching of the Catholic religion as a scholastic discipline in interdisciplinary dialogue with oth- .

15. Cf. Benedict XVI, Apostolic Exhortation *Verbum Domini* (September 30, 2010), n. 31.

ers. In fact, this contributes widely not only to the integral development of the student, but also to knowledge of the other, to mutual understanding and respect. To attain such objectives particular attention must be given to the care of the formation of leaders and formators, not only from a professional point of view, but also from a religious and spiritual view, so that, with the consistency of one's life and with personal involvement, the presence of the Christian educator will be an expression of the love and witness of the truth.

Education in Life

From *Address to Participants in the International Congress Organized by the Pontifical Lateran University on the 40th Anniversary of the Encyclical "Humanae Vitae,"* May 10, 2008

In the Pastoral Constitution on the Church in the Modern World, *Gaudium et Spes,* the Second Vatican Council was already addressing scientists, urging them to join forces to achieve unity in knowledge and a consolidated certainty on the conditions that can favor "the proper regulation of births."[16] My predecessor of venerable memory, the servant of God Paul VI, published his encyclical letter *Humanae Vitae* on July 25, 1968. The document very soon became a sign of contradiction. Drafted to treat a difficult situation, it constitutes a significant show of courage in reasserting the continuity of the Church's doctrine and tradition. This text, all too often misunderstood and misinterpreted, also sparked much discussion because it was published at the beginning of profound contestations that marked the lives of entire generations. Forty years after its publication this teaching not only expresses its unchanged truth, but also reveals the farsightedness with which the problem is treated. In fact, conjugal love is described within a global process that does not stop at the division between soul and body and is not subjected to mere

16. Second Vatican Council, *Gaudium et Spes,* n. 52.

sentiment, often transient and precarious, but rather takes charge of the person's unity and the total sharing of the spouses who, in their reciprocal acceptance, offer themselves in a promise of faithful and exclusive love that flows from a genuine choice of freedom. How can such love remain closed to the gift of life? Life is always a precious gift; every time we witness its beginnings we see the power of the creative action of God who trusts man and thus calls him to build the future with the strength of hope.

The magisterium of the Church cannot be exonerated from reflecting in an ever new and deeper way on the fundamental principles that concern marriage and procreation. What was true yesterday is true also today. The truth expressed in *Humanae Vitae* does not change; on the contrary, precisely in the light of the new scientific discoveries, its teaching becomes more timely and elicits reflection on the intrinsic value it possesses. The key word to enter coherently into its content remains "love." As I wrote in my first encyclical, *Deus Caritas Est,* "Man is truly himself when his body and soul are intimately united.... Yet it is neither the spirit alone nor the body alone that loves: it is man, the person, a unified creature composed of body and soul, who loves."[17] If this unity is removed, the value of the person is lost, and there is a serious risk of considering the body a commodity that can be bought or sold.[18] In a culture subjected to the prevalence of "having" over "being," human life risks losing its value. If the practice of sexuality becomes a drug that seeks to enslave one's partner to one's own desires and interests, without respecting the cycle of the beloved, then what must be defended is no longer solely the true concept of love, but, in the first place, the dignity of the person. As believers we could never let the domination of technology invalidate the quality of love and the sacredness of life.

It was not by chance that Jesus, in speaking of human love, alluded to what God created at the beginning of the creation

17. Benedict XVI, *Deus Caritas Est,* n. 5.
18. Benedict XVI, *Deus Caritas Est,* n. 5.

(cf. Mt 19:4–6). His teaching refers to a free act with which the Creator not only meant to express the riches of his love that is open, giving itself to all, but he also wanted to impress upon it a paradigm in accordance with which humanity's action must be declined. In the fruitfulness of conjugal love, the man and the woman share in the Father's creative act and make it clear that at the origin of their spousal life they pronounce a genuine "yes" that is truly lived in reciprocity, remaining ever open to life. This word of the Lord with its profound truth endures unchanged and cannot be abolished by the different theories that have succeeded one another in the course of the years, and at times have even been contradictory. Natural law, which is at the root of the recognition of true equality between persons and peoples, deserves to be recognized as the source that inspires the relationship between the spouses in their responsibility for begetting new children. The transmission of life is inscribed in nature, and its laws stand as an unwritten norm to which all must refer. Any attempt to turn one's gaze away from this principle is in itself barren and does not produce a future.

We urgently need to rediscover a new covenant that has always been fruitful when it has been respected: it puts reason and love first. A perceptive teacher like William of Saint-Thierry could write words that we feel are profoundly valid even for our time: "If reason instructs love and love illumines reason, if reason is converted into love and love consents to be held within the bounds of reason, they can do something great."[19] What is this "something great" that we can witness? It is the promotion of responsibility for life, which brings to fruition the gift that each one makes of him- or herself to the other. It is the fruit of a love that can think and choose in complete freedom, without letting itself be conditioned unduly by the possible sacrifice requested. From this comes the miracle of life that parents experience in

19. William of Saint-Thierry, *De Natura et Dignitate Amoris* 21.8.

themselves as they sense the extraordinary nature of what takes place in them and through them. No mechanical technique can substitute the act of love that husband and wife exchange as the sign of a greater mystery that (as protagonists and sharers in creation) sees them playing the lead and sharing in creation.

Unfortunately, more and more often we see sorrowful events that involve adolescents, whose reactions show their incorrect knowledge of the mystery of life and of the risky implications of their actions. The urgent need for education to which I often refer primarily concerns the theme of life. I sincerely hope that young people in particular will be given very special attention so that they may learn the true meaning of love and prepare for it with an appropriate education in sexuality without letting themselves be distracted by ephemeral messages that prevent them from reaching the essence of the truth at stake. To circulate false illusions in the context of love or to deceive people concerning the genuine responsibilities that they are called to assume with the exercise of their own sexuality does not do honor to a society based on the principles of freedom and democracy. Freedom must be conjugated with truth and responsibility with the force of dedication to the other, even with sacrifice; without these components the human community does not grow, and the risk of enclosing itself in an asphyxiating cycle of selfishness is always present.

The teaching expressed by the encyclical *Humanae Vitae* is not easy. Yet it conforms to the fundamental structure through which life has always been transmitted since the world's creation, with respect for nature and in conformity with its needs. Concern for human life and safeguarding the person's dignity require us not to leave anything untried, so that all may be involved in the genuine truth of responsible conjugal love in full adherence to the law engraved on the heart of every person.

A Heart That "Sees"

*From Address to Participants in an International Congress
Organized by the John Paul II Institute for Studies on
Marriage and Family, April 5, 2008*

I meet you with great joy on the occasion of the International Congress on "'Oil on the Wounds': A Response to the Ills of Abortion and Divorce," promoted by the John Paul II Pontifical Institute for Studies on Marriage and Family in collaboration with the *Knights of Columbus.* I congratulate you on the topical and complex theme that has been the subject of your reflections in these days, and in particular for the reference to the Good Samaritan (Lk 10:25–37), which you chose as a key to approach the evils of abortion and divorce that bring so much suffering to the lives of individuals, families, and society. Yes, the men and women of our day sometimes truly find themselves stripped and wounded on the wayside of the routes we take, often without anyone listening to their cry for help or attending to them to alleviate and heal their suffering. In the often purely ideological debate a sort of conspiracy of silence is created in their regard. Only by assuming an attitude of merciful love is it possible to approach in order to bring help and enable victims to pick themselves up and resume their journey through life.

In a cultural context marked by increasing individualism and hedonism, and all too often by a lack of solidarity and adequate social support, human freedom, as it faces life's difficulties, is prompted in its weakness to make decisions that conflict with the indissolubility of the matrimonial bond or with the respect due to human life from the moment of conception, while it is still protected in its mother's womb. Of course, divorce and abortion are decisions of a different kind, which are sometimes made in difficult and dramatic circumstances that are often traumatic and a source of deep suffering for those who make them. They also affect innocent victims: the infant just conceived and not yet born, children involved in the break-up of family ties. These decisions indelibly mark the lives of all those involved. The Church's ethical opinion with regard to divorce and procured abortion is unambivalent and known to all: these are grave sins that, to a different extent and taking into account the evaluation of subjective responsibility, harm the dignity of the human person, involve a profound injustice in human and social relations, and offend God himself, Guarantor of the conjugal covenant and the Author of life. Yet the Church, after the example of her Divine Teacher, always has the people themselves before her, especially the weakest and most innocent who are victims of injustice and sin, and also those other men and women who, having perpetrated these acts, stained by sin and wounded within, are seeking peace and the chance to begin anew.

The Church's first duty is to approach these people with love and consideration, with caring and motherly attention, to proclaim the merciful closeness of God in Jesus Christ. Indeed, as the fathers teach, it is he who is the true Good Samaritan, who has made himself close to us, who pours oil and wine on our wounds and takes us into the inn, the Church, where he has us treated, entrusting us to her ministers and personally paying in advance for our recovery. Yes, the gospel of love and life is also always the *gospel of mercy,* which is addressed to the actual person and sinner that we are, to help us up after any fall and to recover from any injury. My beloved predecessor, the servant of God John Paul II, the third anniversary of whose death we celebrated recently, said in inaugurating the new Shrine of Divine Mercy in Krakow, "Apart from the mercy of God there is no other source of hope for mankind."[20] On the basis of this mercy the Church cultivates an indomitable trust in human beings and in their capacity for recovery. She knows that with the help of grace human freedom is capable of the definitive and faithful gift

20. John Paul II, *Address at the Dedication of the Shrine of Divine Mercy*, Apostolic Journey to Poland, Krakow-Lagiewniki, August 17, 2002.

of self that makes possible the marriage of a man and woman as an indissoluble bond; she knows that even in the most difficult circumstances human freedom is capable of extraordinary acts of sacrifice and solidarity to welcome the life of a new human being. Thus, one can see that the "no" that the Church pronounces in her moral directives on which public opinion sometimes unilaterally focuses, is in fact a great "yes" to the dignity of the human person, to human life, and to the person's capacity to love. It is an expression of the constant trust with which, despite their frailty, people are able to respond to the loftiest vocation for which they are created: the vocation to love.

On that same occasion, John Paul II continued, "This fire of mercy needs to be passed on to the world. In the mercy of God the world will find peace."[21] The great task of disciples of the Lord Jesus who find themselves the traveling companions of so many brothers, men and women of good will, is hinged on this. Their program, the program of the Good Samaritan, is a "'heart which sees.' This heart sees where love is needed and acts accordingly."[22] In these days of reflection and dialogue you have stooped down to victims suffering from the wounds of divorce and abortion. You have noted first of all the sometimes traumatic suffering that afflicts the so-called "children of divorce," marking their lives to the point of making their way far more difficult. It is in fact inevitable that when the conjugal covenant is broken, those who suffer most are the children who are the living sign of its indissolubility. Supportive pastoral attention must therefore aim to ensure that the children are not the innocent victims of conflicts between parents who divorce. It must also endeavor to ensure that the continuity of the link with their parents is guaranteed as far as possible, as well as the links with their own family and social origins, which are indispensable for balanced psychological and human growth.

21. John Paul II, *Address at the Dedication of the Shrine of Divine Mercy.*
22. Benedict XVI, *Deus Caritas Est,* n. 31.

You also focused on the tragedy of procured abortion that leaves profound and sometimes indelible marks in the women who undergo it and in the people around them, as well as devastating consequences on the family and society, partly because of the materialistic mentality of contempt for life that it encourages. What selfish complicity often lies at the root of an agonizing decision that so many women have had to face on their own, who still carry in their heart an open wound! Although what has been done remains a grave injustice and is not in itself remediable, I make my own the exhortation in *Evangelium Vitae* addressed to women who have had an abortion: "Do not give in to discouragement and do not lose hope. Try rather to understand what happened and face it honestly. If you have not already done so, give yourselves over with humility and trust to repentance. The Father of mercies is ready to give you his forgiveness and his peace in the Sacrament of Reconciliation. To the same Father and his mercy you can with sure hope entrust your child."[23]

I express deep appreciation for all those social and pastoral initiatives being taken for the reconciliation and treatment of people injured by the drama of abortion and divorce. Together with numerous other forms of commitment, they constitute essential elements for building that civilization of love that humanity needs today more than ever.

How Can We Remain Indifferent to Such Love?

From *Address to the Community of the Pontifical Theological Faculty "Teresianum" of Rome*, May 19, 2011

Three quarters of a century have passed since that July 16, 1935, liturgical memorial of the Blessed Virgin of Mount Carmel in which the then International College of the Order of Discalced Carmelites in the city was promoted to the status of theological faculty. From the beginning it was oriented to deepening spiri-

23. John Paul II, Encyclical Letter *Evangelium Vitae* (March 25, 1995), n. 99.

tual theology in the framework of the anthropological question. Over the course of the years, an institute of spirituality was established, which together with the theological faculty, makes up the academic group that has the name of Teresianum.

Taking a retrospective glance over the history of this institution, we want to praise the Lord for the wonders he has accomplished in and through it, in the many students who have attended it—first of all, because to be part of such an academic community constitutes a unique ecclesial experience, strengthened by all the richness of a great spiritual family such as the Order of Discalced Carmelites. We think of the vast renewal movement begun in the Church by the testimony of Sts. Teresa of Jesus and John of the Cross. It aroused a rekindling of the ideals and fervor of contemplative life, which in the sixteenth century set afire, so to speak, Europe and the whole world.

Dear students, placed in the wake of this charism is your work of anthropological and theological reflection, as well—the task of penetrating the mystery of Christ with that intelligence of heart that is at the same time a knowing and a loving; this calls for Jesus to be placed at the center of everything—your affections and thoughts, your time of prayer, study, and action, the whole of your life. He is the Word, the living book, as he was for St. Teresa of Avila, who affirmed, "To learn the truth, there is no other book than God."[24] I wish for each one of you that you will be able to say with St. Paul: I count everything as loss because of the surpassing worth of knowing Christ Jesus my Lord (Phil 3:8).

To this end I would like to recall St. Teresa's description of the interior experience of conversion, just as she herself lived it one day before the crucifix. She writes, "As soon as I looked at him ... the sorrow I felt was so great, the sorrow of ingratitude with which I responded to his love, that it seemed to me my heart would break. I threw myself at his feet all in tears and begged him to give me the grace not to offend him anymore."[25]

24. Teresa of Avila, *Vita* 26.5.   25. Teresa of Avila, *Autobiography* 9.1.

With the same force, the saint seems to ask us, too: How can we remain indifferent to such love? How can we ignore him who has loved us with such great mercy? The love of the Redeemer merits all the heart's and mind's attention, and can activate also in us that wonderful circle in which love and knowledge reciprocally nourish one another.

During your theological studies, always have your sight turned to the ultimate reason for which you undertook them—that is, to Jesus who has loved us and given his life for us (cf. 1 Jn 3:16). Be conscious that these years of study are a precious gift of Divine Providence, a gift that must be received with faith and lived diligently, as an unrepeatable opportunity to grow in knowledge of the mystery of Christ.

In the present context an in-depth study of Christian spirituality from its anthropological foundations is of great importance. The specific preparedness that this furnishes is certainly important because it gives a person the proper profile and qualifies him for teaching this discipline, but it constitutes an even greater grace because of the sapiential weight it carries with it, geared to the delicate task of spiritual direction.

As she has never failed to do, again today the Church continues to recommend the practice of spiritual direction, not only to all those who wish to follow the Lord up close, but to every Christian who wishes to live responsibly his baptism—that is, the new life in Christ. Everyone, in fact, and in a particular way all those who have received the divine call to a closer following, needs to be supported personally by a sure guide in doctrine and expert in the things of God. A guide can help defend oneself from facile subjectivist interpretations, making available his own supply of knowledge and experiences in following Jesus. [Spiritual direction] is a matter of establishing that same personal relationship that the Lord had with his disciples, that special bond with which he led them, following him, to embrace the will of the Father (cf. Lk 22:42)—that is, to embrace the cross.

You also, dear friends, in the measure in which you are called to this invaluable task, make a treasure of all that you will have learned in these years of study, to support all those whom Divine Providence will entrust to you, helping them in the discernment of spirits and in the capacity to second the motions of the Holy Spirit, with the objective of leading them to the fullness of grace, until we all attain, as St. Paul says, "to the measure of the fullness of Christ" (Eph 4:13).

4. PEDAGOGY AND LEARNING

Educating Young People in Justice and Peace

From *Message for the Celebration of the 45th World Day
of Peace,* January 1, 2012

The beginning of a new year, God's gift to humanity, prompts me
to extend to all, with great confidence and affection, my heartfelt good wishes that this time now before us may be marked
concretely by justice and peace.

With what attitude should we look to the new year? We find
a very beautiful image in Psalm 130. The Psalmist says that people
of faith wait for the Lord "more than those who watch for the
morning" (Ps 130:6); they wait for him with firm hope because
they know that he will bring light, mercy, salvation. This waiting
was born of the experience of the Chosen People, who realized
that God taught them to look at the world in its truth and not
to be overwhelmed by tribulation. I invite you to look to 2012
with this attitude of confident trust. It is true that the year now
ending has been marked by a rising sense of frustration at the crisis looming over society, the world of labor, and the economy, a
crisis whose roots are primarily cultural and anthropological. It
seems as if a shadow has fallen over our time, preventing us from
clearly seeing the light of day.

In this shadow, however, human hearts continue to wait for

the dawn of which the Psalmist speaks. Because this expectation is particularly powerful and evident in young people, my thoughts turn to them and to the contribution, which they can and must make to society. I would like therefore to devote this message for the forty-fifth World Day of Peace to the theme of education: "Educating Young People in Justice and Peace," in the conviction that the young, with their enthusiasm and idealism, can offer new hope to the world.

My message is also addressed to parents, families, and all those involved in the area of education and formation, as well as to leaders in the various spheres of religious, social, political, economic, and cultural life and in the media. Attentiveness to young people and their concerns, the ability to listen to them and appreciate them, is not merely something expedient; it represents a primary duty for society as a whole, for the sake of building a future of justice and peace.

It is a matter of communicating to young people an appreciation for the positive value of life and of awakening in them a desire to spend their lives in the service of the Good. This is a task that engages each of us personally.

The concerns expressed in recent times by many young people around the world demonstrate that they desire to look to the future with solid hope. At the present time they are experiencing apprehension about many things: they want to receive an education that prepares them more fully to deal with the real world; they see how difficult it is to form a family and to find stable employment; they wonder if they can really contribute to political, cultural, and economic life in order to build a society with a more human and fraternal face.

It is important that this unease and its underlying idealism receive due attention at every level of society. The Church looks to young people with hope and confidence; she encourages them to seek truth, to defend the common good, to be open to the world around them and be willing to see "new things" (Is 42:9; 48:6).

EDUCATORS

Education is the most interesting and difficult adventure in life. Educating—from the Latin *educere*—means leading young people to move beyond themselves and introducing them to reality, toward a fullness that leads to growth. This process is fostered by the encounter of two freedoms, that of adults and that of the young. It calls for responsibility on the part of the learners, who must be open to being led to the knowledge of reality, and on the part of educators, who must be ready to give of themselves. For this reason, today more than ever, we need authentic witnesses, and not simply people who parcel out rules and facts: we need witnesses capable of seeing farther than others because their life is so much broader. A witness is someone who first lives the life that he proposes to others.

Where does true education in peace and justice take place? First of all, in the family, since parents are the first educators. The family is the primary cell of society; "it is in the family that children learn the human and Christian values which enable them to have a constructive and peaceful coexistence. It is in the family that they learn solidarity between the generations, respect for rules, forgiveness and how to welcome others."[1] The family is the first school in which we are trained in justice and peace.

We are living in a world where families, and life itself, are constantly threatened and not infrequently fragmented. Working conditions that are often incompatible with family responsibilities, worries about the future, the frenetic pace of life, the need to move frequently to ensure an adequate livelihood, to say nothing of mere survival—all this makes it hard to ensure that children receive one of the most precious of treasures: the presence of their parents. This presence makes it possible to share more deeply in the journey of life and thus to pass on experiences

1. Benedict XVI, *Address to Administrators of the Lazio Region and of the Municipality and Province of Rome,* January 14, 2011.

and convictions gained with the passing of the years, experiences, and convictions that can only be communicated by spending time together. I would urge parents not to grow disheartened! May they encourage children by the example of their lives to put their hope before all else in God, the one source of authentic justice and peace.

I would also like to address a word to those in charge of educational institutions: with a great sense of responsibility may they ensure that the dignity of each person is always respected and appreciated. Let them be concerned that every young person be able to discover his or her own vocation and be helped to develop his or her God-given gifts. May they reassure families that their children can receive an education that does not conflict with their consciences and their religious principles.

Every educational setting can be a place of openness to the transcendent and to others—a place of dialogue, cohesiveness, and attentive listening, where young people feel appreciated for their personal abilities and inner riches and can learn to esteem their brothers and sisters. May young people be taught to savor the joy that comes from the daily exercise of charity and compassion toward others and from taking an active part in the building of a more humane and fraternal society.

I ask political leaders to offer concrete assistance to families and educational institutions in the exercise of their right and duty to educate. Adequate support should never be lacking to parents in their task. Let them ensure that no one is ever denied access to education and that families are able freely to choose the educational structures they consider most suitable for their children. Let them be committed to reuniting families separated by the need to earn a living. Let them give young people a transparent image of politics as a genuine service to the good of all.

I cannot fail also to appeal to the world of the media to offer its own contribution to education. In today's society the mass media have a particular role: they not only inform, but also form the minds of their audiences, and so they can make a significant contribution to the education of young people. It is important never to forget that the connection between education and communication is extremely close: education takes place through communication, which influences, for better or worse, the formation of the person.

Young people too need to have the courage to live by the same high standards that they set for others. Theirs is a great responsibility: may they find the strength to make good and wise use of their freedom. They too are responsible for their education, including their education in justice and peace!

EDUCATING IN TRUTH AND FREEDOM

Saint Augustine once asked, *"Quid enim fortius desiderat anima quam veritatem?*—What does man desire more deeply than truth?"[2] The human face of a society depends very much on the contribution of education to keep this irrepressible question alive. Education, indeed, is concerned with the integral formation of the person, including the moral and spiritual dimension, focused upon man's final end and the good of the society to which he belongs. Therefore, in order to educate in truth, it is necessary first and foremost to know who the human person is, to know human nature. Contemplating the world around him, the Psalmist reflects, "When I see the heavens, the work of your hands, the moon and the stars which you arranged, what is man that you should keep him in mind, mortal man that you care for him?" (Ps 8:4–5). This is the fundamental question that must be asked: *who is man?* Man is a being who bears within his heart a thirst for the infinite, a thirst for truth—a truth that is not partial, but capable of explaining life's meaning—since he was created in the image and likeness of God. The grateful recognition that life is an inestimable gift, then, leads to the discovery of one's own profound dignity and the inviolability of every single person. Hence the first step in ed-

---

2. Augustine, *Commentary on the Gospel of John* 26.5.

ucation is learning to recognize the Creator's image in man, and consequently learning to have a profound respect for every human being and helping others to live a life consonant with this supreme dignity. We must never forget that "authentic human development concerns the whole of the person in every single dimension,"[3] including the transcendent dimension, and that the person cannot be sacrificed for the sake of attaining a particular good, whether this be economic or social, individual or collective.

Only in relation to God does man come to understand also the meaning of human freedom. It is the task of education to form people in authentic freedom. This is not the absence of constraint or the supremacy of free will; it is not the absolutism of the self. When man believes himself to be absolute, to depend on nothing and no one, to be able to do anything he wants, he ends up contradicting the truth of his own being and forfeiting his freedom. On the contrary, man is a relational being, who lives in relationship with others and especially with God. Authentic freedom can never be attained independently of God.

Freedom is a precious value, but a fragile one; it can be misunderstood and misused. "Today, a particularly insidious obstacle to the task of educating is the massive presence in our society and culture of that relativism which, recognizing nothing as definitive, leaves as the ultimate criterion only the self with its desires. And under the semblance of freedom it becomes a prison for each one, for it separates people from one another, locking each person into his or her own self. With such a relativistic horizon, therefore, real education is not possible without the light of the truth; sooner or later, every person is in fact condemned to doubting the goodness of his or her own life and the relationships of which it consists, the validity of his or her commitment to build with others something in common."[4]

3. Benedict XVI, *Caritas in Veritate,* n. 11; cf. Paul VI, Encyclical Letter *Populorum Progressio* (March 26, 1967), n. 14.

4. Benedict XVI, *Address for the Opening of the Diocesan Ecclesial Convention of Rome,* June 6, 2005.

In order to exercise his freedom, then, man must move beyond the relativistic horizon and come to know the truth about himself and the truth about good and evil. Deep within his conscience, man discovers a law that he did not lay upon himself, but that he must obey. Its voice calls him to love and to do what is good, to avoid evil, and to take responsibility for the good he does and the evil he commits.[5] Thus the exercise of freedom is intimately linked to the natural moral law, which is universal in character, expresses the dignity of every person, and forms the basis of fundamental human rights and duties; consequently, in the final analysis, it forms the basis for just and peaceful co-existence.

The right use of freedom, then, is central to the promotion of justice and peace, which require respect for oneself and others, including those whose way of being and living differs greatly from one's own. This attitude engenders the elements without which peace and justice remain merely words without content: mutual trust, the capacity to hold constructive dialogue, the possibility of forgiveness, which one constantly wishes to receive but finds hard to bestow, mutual charity, compassion toward the weakest, as well as readiness to make sacrifices.

EDUCATING IN JUSTICE

In this world of ours, in which, despite the profession of good intentions, the value of the person, of human dignity and human rights, is seriously threatened by the widespread tendency to have recourse exclusively to the criteria of utility, profit, and material possessions, it is important not to detach the concept of justice from its transcendent roots. Justice, indeed, is not simply a human convention, since what is just is ultimately determined not by positive law, but by the profound identity of the human being. It is the integral vision of man that saves us from falling

5. Cf. Second Vatican Council, *Gaudium et Spes,* n. 16.

into a contractual conception of justice and enables us to locate justice within the horizon of solidarity and love.[6]

We cannot ignore the fact that some currents of modern culture, built upon rationalist and individualist economic principles, have cut off the concept of justice from its transcendent roots, detaching it from charity and solidarity: "The 'earthly city' is promoted not merely by relationships of rights and duties, but to an even greater and more fundamental extent by relationships of gratuitousness, mercy and communion. Charity always manifests God's love in human relationships as well, it gives theological and salvific value to all commitment for justice in the world."[7]

"Blessed are those who hunger and thirst for righteousness, for they shall be satisfied" (Mt 5:6). They shall be satisfied because they hunger and thirst for right relations with God, with themselves, with their brothers and sisters, and with the whole of creation.

EDUCATING IN PEACE

"Peace is not merely the absence of war, and it is not limited to maintaining a balance of powers between adversaries. Peace cannot be attained on earth without safeguarding the goods of persons, free communication among men, respect for the dignity of persons and peoples, and the assiduous practice of fraternity."[8] We Christians believe that Christ is our true peace: in him, by his cross, God has reconciled the world to himself and has broken down the walls of division that separated us from one another (cf. Eph 2:14–18); in him, there is but one family, reconciled in love.

Peace, however, is not merely a gift to be received; it is also a task to be undertaken. In order to be true peacemakers, we must educate ourselves in compassion, solidarity, working together,

---

6. Cf. Benedict XVI, *Address to the Bundestag*, Apostolic Journey to Germany, Berlin, September 22, 2011.

7. Benedict XVI, *Caritas in Veritate*, n. 6.

8. *Catechism of the Catholic Church* (1993), n. 2304.

fraternity, in being active within the community and concerned to raise awareness about national and international issues and the importance of seeking adequate mechanisms for the redistribution of wealth, the promotion of growth, cooperation for development, and conflict resolution. "Blessed are the peacemakers, for they shall be called sons of God," as Jesus says in the Sermon on the Mount (Mt 5:9).

Peace for all is the fruit of justice for all, and no one can shirk this essential task of promoting justice according to one's particular areas of competence and responsibility. To the young, who have such a strong attachment to ideals, I extend a particular invitation to be patient and persevering in seeking justice and peace, in cultivating the taste for what is just and true, even when it involves sacrifice and swimming against the tide.

RAISING ONE'S EYES TO GOD

Before the difficult challenge of walking the paths of justice and peace, we may be tempted to ask, in the words of the Psalmist: "I lift up my eyes to the mountains: from where shall come my help?" (Ps 121:1).

To all, and to young people in particular, I wish to say emphatically, "It is not ideologies that save the world, but only a return to the living God, our Creator, the guarantor of our freedom, the guarantor of what is really good and true ... an unconditional return to God who is the measure of what is right and who at the same time is everlasting love. And what could ever save us apart from love?"[9] Love takes delight in truth; it is the force that enables us to make a commitment to truth, to justice, to peace, because it bears all things, believes all things, hopes all things, endures all things (cf. 1 Cor 13:1–13).

Dear young people, you are a precious gift for society. Do not yield to discouragement in the face of difficulties, and do not

9. Benedict XVI, *Address at Youth Vigil,* Apostolic Journey to Cologne on the Occasion of the 20th World Youth Day, Cologne-Marienfeld, August 20, 2005.

abandon yourselves to false solutions, which often seem the easiest way to overcome problems. Do not be afraid to make a commitment, to face hard work and sacrifice, to choose the paths that demand fidelity and constancy, humility and dedication. Be confident in your youth and its profound desires for happiness, truth, beauty, and genuine love! Live fully this time in your life so rich and so full of enthusiasm.

Realize that you yourselves are an example and an inspiration to adults, even more so to the extent that you seek to overcome injustice and corruption and strive to build a better future. Be aware of your potential; never become self-centered, but work for a brighter future for all. You are never alone. The Church has confidence in you, follows you, encourages you, and wishes to offer you the most precious gift she has: the opportunity to raise your eyes to God, to encounter Jesus Christ, who is himself justice and peace.

All you men and women throughout the world, who take to heart the cause of peace: peace is not a blessing already attained, but rather a goal to which each and all of us must aspire. Let us look with greater hope to the future; let us encourage one another on our journey; let us work together to give our world a more humane and fraternal face; and let us feel a common responsibility toward present and future generations, especially in the task of training them to be people of peace and builders of peace.

Taught by God

From *Address to Catholic Religion Teachers,* April 25, 2009

The teaching of the Catholic religion is an integral part of the history of schools in Italy, and the religion teacher is a very important figure on the teaching staff. It is significant that so many children keep in touch with their teachers even after leaving school. Furthermore, the large number of those who choose to study this subject is a sign of its irreplaceable value in the educational process and proof of the high standard of quality it has attained. In a recent message the presidency of the Italian Bishops' Conference (CEI) said that, "the teaching of the Catholic religion encourages reflection on the deep meaning of life, helping people to rediscover, beyond individual forms of knowledge, a sense of unity and an overall intuition. This is possible because such teaching focuses on the human person and his or her inalienable dignity, letting itself be illuminated by the unique life of Jesus of Nazareth, whose identity it takes care to investigate. Thus for 2,000 years it has not ceased to call men and women into question."

Putting man created in the image of God at the center (cf. Gen 1:27) is in fact the distinctive mark of your daily work, in unity of intention with other educators and teachers. On the occasion of the Ecclesial Convention in Verona in October 2006, I myself had the opportunity to touch on the "fundamental and decisive question" of education, indicating the need "to enlarge the area of our rationality, to reopen it to the larger questions of the truth and the good, to link theology, philosophy and science between them in full respect for the methods proper to them and for their reciprocal autonomy, but also in the awareness of the intrinsic unity that holds them together."[10] The religious dimension is in fact intrinsic to culture. It contributes to the overall formation of the person and makes it possible to transform knowledge into the wisdom of life.

Your service, dear friends, fits precisely into this fundamental crossroads, in which without improper invasion or the confusion of roles the universal aspiration to truth and the two-thousand-year-old testimony offered by believers in the light of faith converge—the extraordinary peaks of knowledge and art acquired by the human spirit and the fruitfulness of the Christian message that so deeply nourishes the culture and life of the Italian people. With the full and recognized scholastic digni-

10. Benedict XVI, *Address to the Participants in the Fourth National Ecclesial Convention,* Pastoral Visit to Verona, October 19, 2006.

ty of your teaching, you contribute on the one hand to giving school a soul and, on the other, to assuring to the Christian faith full citizenship in the places of education and culture in general. Thanks to the teaching of the Catholic religion, school and society are enriched with true laboratories of culture and humanity in which, by deciphering the significant contribution of Christianity, the person is equipped to discover goodness and to grow in responsibility, to seek comparisons and to refine his or her critical sense, to draw from the gifts of the past to understand the present better and to be able to plan wisely for the future.

Today's meeting is also taking place in the context of the Pauline year. The apostle to the gentiles continues to exercise great fascination on all of us. In him we recognize the humble and faithful disciple, the courageous herald, the gifted mediator of revelation. These are characteristics to which I invite you to look to nourish your identity as educators and witnesses in the world of the school. It is Paul, in the First Letter to the Thessalonians (4:9) who defines believers with the beautiful expression *theodidaktoi*—that is, "taught by God"—who have God as teacher. In this word we find the secret of education itself, as St. Augustine also recalls, "We who speak and you who listen, recognize each other as faithful disciples of one Teacher."[11]

In addition, in the Pauline teaching religious formation is not separate from human formation. The last letters of his correspondence, the so-called "pastoral" letters, are full of significant references to the social and civil life that Christ's disciples must keep clearly in mind. St. Paul is a true teacher who has at heart both the salvation of the person in whom has been inculcated a mentality of faith and the person's human and civil formation, so that the disciple of Christ may express to the full a free personality, a human life that is "complete and well prepared," which is also shown by attention for culture, professionalism, and competence in the various fields of knowledge for the benefit of all.

11. Augustine, *De Serm.* 23.2.

Consequently the religious dimension is not a superstructure; it is an integral part of the person from the very earliest infancy; it is fundamental openness to otherness and to the mystery that presides over every relationship and every encounter with human beings. The religious dimension makes the person more human. May your teaching always be able, like Paul's, to open students to this dimension of freedom and the full appreciation of man redeemed by Christ as he is in God's plan, thereby expressing true intellectual charity to countless children and their families.

One of the main aspects of your teaching is of course the communication of the truth and beauty of the word of God, and knowledge of the Bible is an essential element of the curriculum for teaching the Catholic religion. There is a connection between the scholastic teaching of religion and the existential deepening of faith, as happens in parishes and in the various ecclesial structures. The very person of the Catholic religion teacher constitutes this bond: to you, in fact, in addition to the duty of the human, cultural, and didactic competence proper to every teacher, belongs the vocation to make it clear that the God of whom you speak in the classrooms is the essential reference point of your life. Far from constituting interference or a curtailment of freedom, your presence on the contrary is an effective example of that positive spirit of secularism that makes it possible to promote a constructive civil coexistence, based on reciprocal respect and loyal dialogue, values that a country always needs.

In Order to Understand Man, One Must Be Open to Transcendence

From *Address to the Pontifical Gregorian University,*
Rome, November 3, 2006

[I]f the effort of study and teaching is to have any meaning in relation to God's kingdom, it must be sustained by the theological virtues. In fact, the immediate object of the different branches of theological knowledge is God himself, revealed in Jesus Christ, God with a human face.

Even when, as in canon law and in Church history, the immediate object is the people of God in their visible, historical dimension, the deeper analysis of the topic urges us once again to contemplation, in the faith, of the mystery of the risen Christ. It is he, present in his Church, who leads her among the events of the time toward eschatological fullness, a goal to which we have set out sustained by hope.

However, knowing God is not enough. For a true encounter with him one must also love him. Knowledge must become love.

The study of theology, canon law, and Church history is not only knowledge of the propositions of the faith in their historical formulation and practical application, but is also always knowledge of them in faith, hope, and charity.

The Spirit alone searches the depths of God (cf. 1 Cor 2:10); thus, only in listening to the Spirit can one search the depths of the riches, wisdom, and knowledge of God (cf. Rom 11:33).

We listen to the Spirit in prayer when the heart opens to contemplation of God's mystery that was revealed to us in Jesus Christ the Son, image of the invisible God (cf. Col 1:15), constituted head of the Church and Lord of all things (cf. Eph 1:10; Col 1:18).

Since its origins as the *Collegium Romanum,* the Gregorian University has been distinguished for the study of philosophy and theology. It would take too long to list the names of the outstanding philosophers and theologians who have followed one another in the chairs of this academic center; we should also add to them those of the famous canon lawyers and Church historians who expended their energies within these prestigious walls.

They all made a substantial contribution to the progress of the branches of knowledge they studied, hence they offered a precious service to the apostolic see in the exercise of its doctrinal, disciplinary, and pastoral role. With the development of the times, outlooks necessarily change.

Today one must take into account the confrontation with secular culture in many parts of the world, which not only tends to deny every sign of God's presence in the life of society and of the individual, but, with various means that bewilder and cloud the upright human conscience, is seeking to corrode the human being's capacity and readiness to listen to God.

Moreover, it is impossible to ignore relations with other religions, which will only prove constructive if we avoid all forms of ambiguity, which in a certain way undermine the essential content of Christian faith in Christ, the one Savior of all mankind (cf. Acts 4:12), and in the Church, the necessary sacrament of salvation for all humanity.[12]

Here I cannot forget the other human sciences that are encouraged at this famous university in the wake of the glorious academic tradition of the Roman College. The great prestige the Roman College acquired in the fields of mathematics, physics, and astronomy is well-known to all.

It suffices to remember that the "Gregorian" calendar, so-called because it was desired by my predecessor, Gregory XIII, and currently in use throughout the world, was compiled in 1582 by Fr. Christopher Clavius, a lecturer at the Roman College.

It suffices also to mention Fr. Matteo Ricci, who took to as far as distant China the knowledge he had acquired as a disciple of Fr. Clavius, in addition to his witness to the faith.

Today the above-mentioned disciplines are no longer taught at the Gregorian University, but have been replaced by other human sciences such as psychology, the social sciences, and social communications.

Thus man desires to be more deeply understood, both in his profound personal dimension and his external dimension as a builder of society in justice and peace, and as a communicator of the truth.

---

12. Cf. Congregation for the Doctrine of the Faith, Declaration *Dominus Iesus* (August 6, 2000), nn. 13–15; nn. 20–22.

For the very reason that these sciences concern the human being, they cannot set aside reference to God. In fact man, both in his interiority and in his exteriority, cannot be fully understood unless he recognizes that he is open to transcendence.

Deprived of his reference to God, man cannot respond to the fundamental questions that trouble and will always trouble his heart concerning the end of his life, hence the meaning of his existence. As a result it is no longer possible to introduce into society those ethical values that alone can guarantee a coexistence worthy of man.

Human destiny without reference to God cannot but be the desolation of anguish, which leads to desperation.

Only in reference to God's love, which is revealed in Jesus Christ, can man find the meaning of his existence and live in hope, even if he must face evils that injure his personal existence and the society in which he lives.

Hope ensures that man does not withdraw into a paralyzing and sterile nihilism, but opens himself instead to generous commitment within the society where he lives in order to improve it. This is the task that God entrusted to man when he created him in his own image and likeness, a task that fills every human being with the greatest possible dignity, but also with an immense responsibility.

It is in this perspective that you, professors and lecturers at the Gregorian, are called to train the students whom the Church entrusts to you. The integral formation of young people has been one of the traditional apostolates of the Society of Jesus since its origins; this is why the Roman College took on this mission at the outset.

The entrustment to the Society of Jesus in Rome, close to the Apostolic See, of the [Pontifical] German College, the Roman Seminary, the German-Hungarian College, the English College, the Greek College, the Scots College, and the Irish College, was intended to ensure the formation of the clergy of those nations where the unity of the faith and communion with the Apostolic See had been broken.

These colleges still send almost all their students, or large numbers of them, to the Gregorian University in continuity with that original mission.

Down through history many other colleges have joined those mentioned above, so the task that weighs heavily upon your shoulders, dear professors and lecturers, is more demanding than ever!

Appropriately, therefore, after deep reflection, you have drafted a "Declaration of Intentions" that is essential for an institution like yours, since it sums up its nature and its mission.

On this basis you are nearing the conclusion of your revision of the statutes and the general rules of the university, as well as the statutes and rules of the various faculties, institutes, and centers.

This will help to define the identity of the Gregorian University more clearly and allow for the drafting of academic programs better suited to the fulfillment of your mission, which is at the same time both easy and difficult.

It is easy because the identity and mission of the Gregorian University have been clear since its earliest days on the basis of the indications reaffirmed by so many Roman pontiffs, of whom at least sixteen were students at this university.

At the same time, it is a difficult mission because it implies constant fidelity to its own history and tradition so as not to lose its historical roots and openness to contemporary reality to respond creatively, after attentive discernment, to the needs of the Church and the world today.

As a pontifical ecclesiastical university this academic center is committed to *sentire in Ecclesia et cum Ecclesia*. It is a commitment born from love for the Church, our mother and the bride of Christ. We must love her as Christ himself loved her, assuming the suffering of the world to complete what is lacking in Christ's afflictions in our own flesh (cf. Col 1:24).

In this way it will be possible to form new generations of

priests, religious, and committed lay people. Indeed, it is only right to ask ourselves what type of formation we wish to impart to our students, whether priest, religious, or lay person.

Dear professors and lecturers, it is of course your intention to form priests who are learned, but at the same time prepared to spend their lives serving all those whom the Lord entrusts to their ministry with an undivided heart, in humility and in austerity of life.

Thus you intend to offer a solid intellectual training to men and women religious, so that they will be able to joyfully live the consecration God has given to them and to offer themselves as an eschatological sign of that future life to which we are all called.

Likewise, you wish to prepare competent lay men and women who will be able to carry out services and offices in the Church and, first and foremost, to be leaven of the kingdom of God in the temporal sphere.

In this perspective, this very year, the university has initiated an interdisciplinary program to train lay people to live their specifically ecclesial vocation of ethical commitment in the public arena.

However, formation is also your responsibility, dear students.

There is no doubt that studying demands constant ascesis and self-denial, but it is precisely on this path that the person is trained in self-denial and the sense of duty.

In fact, what you learn today is what you will communicate tomorrow, when the sacred ministry or other services and offices for the benefit of the community will have been entrusted to you by the Church. What in all circumstances will give joy to your hearts will be the knowledge that you have always fostered upright intentions, thanks to which one may be certain of having sought and done the will of God alone. Obviously all these things require a purification of the heart and discernment.

Dear sons of St. Ignatius, once again the pope entrusts to you

this university, such an important institution for the universal
Church and for so many particular Churches. It has always been
a priority among the priorities of the apostolates of the Society
of Jesus. It was in the university environment of Paris that St. Ignatius of Loyola and his first companions developed the ardent
desire to help souls by loving and serving God in all things, for
his greater glory.

Impelled by the inner promptings of the Spirit, St. Ignatius
came to Rome, center of Christianity, the see of the successor of
Peter, to found the *Collegium Romanum* here, the first university
of the Society of Jesus.

Today the Gregorian University is the university environment
in which, even after 456 years, the desire of St. Ignatius and his
first companions to help souls to love and serve God in all things
for his greater glory is being fulfilled.

I would say that here, within these walls, is achieved what
Pope Julius III said on July 21, 1550, established in the *"formula
Istituti,"* establishing that every member of the Society of Jesus
was bound to *"sub crucis vexillo Deo militare, et soli Domino ac
Ecclesiae Ipsius sponsae, sub Romano Pontifice, Christi in terris
Vicario, servire,"* committing himself *"potissimum … ad fidei
defensionem et propagationem, et profectum animarum in vita et
doctrina christiana, per publicas praedicationes, lectiones et aliud
quodcumque verbi Dei ministerium."*[13]

This charismatic specificity of the Society of Jesus, expressed
institutionally in the fourth vow of total availability to the Roman pontiff in anything he may see fit to command *"ad profectum animarum et fidei propagationem,"*[14] is also evident in the
fact that the superior general of the Company of Jesus summons
from across the world the Jesuits best suited to carrying out the
task of teaching at this university.

Knowing that this might involve the sacrifice of other works

13. Pope Julius III, Bull *Exposcit Debitum* (July 21, 1550), n. 1.
14. Julius III, Bull *Exposcit Debitum*, n. 3.

and services to further the aims the Society proposes to achieve, the Church is deeply grateful to it and desires the Gregorian to preserve the Ignatian spirit that enlivens it, expressed in its pedagogical method and curriculum.

God Wants Us for Himself: A Complete and Unified Vision

From *Address to Priests, Seminarians, and Students of the Pontifical Theological Faculty of Sardinia,* Pastoral Visit to Cagliari (Sardinia), September 7, 2008

Meeting with you, dear priests here present, I think with affection and gratitude of your brethren who work on the island, on a terrain plowed and cultivated with apostolic ardor by those who have preceded you. Yes! Sardinia has known priests who, as authentic teachers of the faith, have left wonderful examples of loyalty to Christ and to the Church. The same inestimable treasure of faith, of spirituality, and of culture is entrusted to you today. It is placed in your hands so that you may be attentive and wise administrators of it. Take care of it and guard it with gospel joy and passion!

Now I affectionately address the community of seminarians and of the theological faculty, where many of you have been able to carry out doctrinal and pastoral formation, and where currently many young people go to prepare for their future ministerial priesthood. I am anxious to thank the teachers and professors who dedicate themselves daily to such an important apostolic work. To accompany candidates for the priestly mission on their formative journey means above all to help them conform themselves to Christ. In this duty, you, dear educators and professors, are called to play an irreplaceable role, since it is truly during these years that one lays the foundations of their future priestly ministry. This is why, as on different occasions I have been able to emphasize, it is necessary to guide seminarians to a personal experience of God through personal and communal daily prayer, and above all through the Eucharist, celebrated and experienced as the center of their very existence. In the post-synodal exhortation *Pastores Dabo Vobis* John Paul II wrote, "Intellectual formation in theology and formation in the spiritual life, in particular the life of prayer, meet and strengthen each other, without detracting in any way from the soundness of research or from the spiritual tenor of prayer."[15]

Dear seminarians and students of the theological faculty, you know that theological formation—as my venerable predecessor recalled further in the cited apostolic exhortation—is very complex and demanding work. It must lead you to possess a "complete and unified" vision of revealed truths and of their acceptance into the faith experience of the Church. From this pours forth the double demand of knowing the entirety of Christian truth and knowing those truths not as truths separated one from the other, but in an organic way, as a union, as the one truth of faith in God, building "a synthesis which will be the result of the contributions of the different theological disciplines, the specific nature of which acquires genuine value only in their profound coordination."[16] This [synthesis] demonstrates to us the unity of truth, the unity of our faith. Besides, in these years, each activity and initiative must dispose you to administer the charity of Christ the Good Shepherd. To him you are called to be tomorrow's ministers and witnesses: ministers of his grace and witnesses of his love. Next to study and pastoral and apostolic experience from which you can draw, do not forget, however, to put the constant quest for intimate communion with Christ in the first place. Here, only here, rests the secret of your true apostolic success.

Dear priests, dear aspirants to the priesthood and to consecrated life, God wants you for himself and calls you to be workers

15. John Paul II, Apostolic Exhortation *Pastores Dabo Vobis* (March 25, 1992), n. 53.
16. John Paul II, *Pastores Dabo Vobis*, n. 54.

in his vineyard, just as he did many men and women throughout the Christian history of your beautiful island. They knew to respond with a generous "yes" to his call. I am thinking of, for example, the evangelizing work carried out by the religious: from the Franciscans to the Mercenaries, from the Dominicans to the Jesuits, from the Benedictines to the Vincentians, from the Salesians to the Scolipians, from the Christian School Brothers to the Josephine Fathers, to the Orioni Fathers and so many others still. And how could the great flowering of female religious vocations, for which Sardinia has been a true and proper garden, be forgotten? In many orders and congregations Sardinian women are present, especially in cloistered monasteries. Without this great "cloud of witnesses" (cf. Heb 12:1), it certainly would have been much more difficult to spread the love of Christ in the towns, families, schools, hospitals, prisons, and workplaces. What a heritage of good has come, accumulating grace by their dedication! Without the seed of Christianity Sardinia would be more fragile and poor. Together with you I thank God who never lets the witnesses of saints fail to guide his people!

Dear brothers and sisters, it is now up to you to carry on the work of good accomplished by those who have gone before you. To you, in particular, dear priests—and I address with affection all the priests of Sardinia—I assure my spiritual nearness, so that you may respond to the Lord's call with total loyalty as, even recently, some of your brothers have done. I recall Fr. Graziano Muntoni, a priest of the diocese of Nuoro, killed on Christmas Eve of 1998 while he was going to celebrate Mass, and Fr. Battore Carzedda of the P.I.M.E., who gave his life so that believers of all religions would open to sincere dialogue sustained by love. Do not be frightened, do not be discouraged by difficulties: the grain and the weeds, as we know, will grow together until the end of the world (cf. Mt 13:30). It is important to be seeds of good grain that, fallen to earth, bear fruit. Deepen the awareness of your identity: the priest, for the Church and in the Church, is a humble but real sign of the one, eternal Priest who is Jesus. He must proclaim his word authoritatively, renew his acts of pardon and offering, and exercise loving concern in the service of his flock, in communion with the pastors and faithfully docile to the teaching of the magisterium. Therefore, rekindle the charism you have received with the imposition of hands (cf. 2 Tm 1:6) each day, identifying with Jesus Christ in his triple function of sanctifying, teaching, and shepherding the flock.

"A New Humanistic Synthesis"

From *Address to the Communities of the Pontifical Universities and Athenaeums of Rome for the Solemn Inauguration of the Academic Year,* November 19, 2009

I am pleased to commemorate with you these important anniversaries, which give me the opportunity to highlight once again the irreplaceable role of ecclesiastical faculties and Catholic universities in the Church and in society. The Second Vatican Council clearly stressed this in the declaration *Gravissimum Educationis* when it urged ecclesiastical faculties to promote research in the various sectors of the sacred sciences for an ever deeper understanding of revelation in order to explore the inheritance of Christian wisdom, to foster ecumenical and inter-religious dialogue, and to find answers to the problems that are emerging in the cultural context.[17] The same conciliar document recommended the promotion of Catholic universities, opening them throughout the various regions of the world and, above all, ensuring that they maintain a high standard in order to educate people steeped in knowledge, ready to witness in the world to their faith and to undertake the responsible duties of society.[18] The Council's invitation has reverberated throughout the

17. Cf. Second Vatican Council, Declaration *Gravissimum Educationis* (October 28, 1965), n. 11.
18. Cf. Second Vatican Council, *Gravissimum Educationis,* n. 10.

Church. Today, in fact, there are more than 1,300 Catholic universities and about four hundred ecclesiastical faculties, spread throughout the continents, many of which have been founded in recent decades; they are proof of the increasing attention of particular Churches to the formation of clerics and lay people in culture and research.

From its very first words the apostolic constitution *Sapientia Christiana* points out the urgent, ever timely need to bridge the gap between faith and culture. It calls for a greater commitment to evangelization in the firm conviction that Christian revelation is a transforming force, destined to permeate mindsets, standards of judgment, and behavioral norms. It is able to illuminate, purify, and renew people's morals and culture,[19] and must constitute the focal point of teaching and research, as well as the horizon that illumines the nature and objective of every ecclesiastical faculty. In this perspective the duty of scholars of the sacred disciplines to achieve, through theological research, a more profound knowledge of the revealed truth is emphasized. At the same time, interactions with other fields of knowledge are encouraged for fruitful dialogue, especially in order to make a precious contribution to the mission the Church is called to carry out in the world. After thirty years the fundamental lines of the apostolic constitution *Sapientia Christiana* retain all their timeliness. Indeed, in contemporary society where knowledge is becoming ever more specialized and compartmentalized but is profoundly marked by relativism, it is more necessary than ever to be open to the wisdom that comes from the gospel. The human being, in fact, is incapable of fully understanding himself and the world without Jesus Christ. Christ alone illumines his true dignity, his vocation, and his ultimate destiny and opens the heart to firm and lasting hope.

Dear friends, your commitment to serving the truth that God has revealed to us is part of the evangelizing mission that

---

19. Cf. Second Vatican Council, *Gravissimum Educationis*, Foreword, i, n. i.

Christ has entrusted to the Church: it is therefore an ecclesial service. *Sapientia Christiana* cites in this regard the conclusion of the Gospel according to Matthew: "Go therefore and make disciples of all nations, baptizing them in the name of the Father and of the Son and of the Holy Spirit, teaching them to observe all that I have commanded you" (Mt 28:19–20). It is important for everyone, teachers and students alike, never to lose sight of the objective to be pursued—namely, that of being an instrument for proclaiming the gospel. The years of advanced ecclesiastical studies can be compared to the experience that the apostles lived with Jesus: in being with him they learned the truth in order to become its heralds everywhere. At the same time it is important to remember that the study of the sacred sciences must never be separated from prayer, from union with God, from contemplation, as I recalled in my recent catecheses on medieval monastic theology; otherwise, reflection on the mysteries risks becoming a vain intellectual exercise. Every sacred science, in the end, refers to the "knowledge of the saints," to their intuition of the mysteries of the living God, to wisdom, which is a gift of the Holy Spirit and the soul of the *"fides quaerens intellectum."*[20]

The FUCI [*Italian Catholic University Federation*] came into being in 1924 at the initiative of several rectors and was recognized twenty-five years later by the Holy See. Dear rectors of Catholic universities, the sixtieth anniversary of the canonical erection of your federation is an especially favorable opportunity to review its achievements and to plot the course of its future commitments.

Celebrating an anniversary means giving thanks to God who has guided our footsteps, but it is also drawing from our own history a further impetus to renew the will to serve the Church. In this regard your motto is also a program for the federation's future: *"Sciat ut serviat,"* to know in order to serve. In a culture that demonstrates "a lack of wisdom and reflection, a lack of think-

20. Cf. Benedict XVI, *General Audience Address,* October 21, 2009.

ing capable of formulating a guiding synthesis,"[21] faithful to their own identity that makes Christian inspiration a defining feature, Catholic universities are called to promote a "new humanistic synthesis,"[22] knowledge that is "wisdom capable of directing man in the light of his first beginnings and his final ends,"[23] knowledge illumined by faith.

The Correlation of Consecrated Life and Education

From *Address of the Holy Father to Pupils of St. Mary's University College,* Apostolic Journey to the United Kingdom, Twickenham, September 17, 2010

As you know, the task of a teacher is not simply to impart information or to provide training in skills intended to deliver some economic benefit to society; education is not and must never be considered as purely utilitarian. It is about forming the human person, equipping him or her to live life to the full—in short, it is about imparting wisdom. And true wisdom is inseparable from knowledge of the Creator, for "both we and our words are in his hand, as are all understanding and skill in crafts" (Ws 7:16).

This transcendent dimension of study and teaching was clearly grasped by the monks who contributed so much to the evangelization of these islands. I am thinking of the Benedictines who accompanied St. Augustine on his mission to England, of the disciples of St. Columba, who spread the faith across Scotland and Northern England, of St. David and his companions in Wales. Since the search for God, which lies at the heart of the monastic vocation, requires active engagement with the means by which he makes himself known—his creation and his revealed word—it was only natural that the monastery should have a library and a

21. Benedict XVI, *Caritas in Veritate,* n. 31.
22. Benedict XVI, *Caritas in Veritate,* n. 21.
23. *Benedict XVI, Caritas in Veritate,* n. 30.

school.[24] It was the monks' dedication to learning as the path on which to encounter the incarnate word of God that was to lay the foundations of our Western culture and civilization.

Looking around me today, I see many apostolic religious whose charism includes the education of the young. This gives me an opportunity to give thanks to God for the life and work of the venerable Mary Ward, a native of this land whose pioneering vision of apostolic religious life for women has borne so much fruit. I myself as a young boy was taught by the "English Ladies," and I owe them a deep debt of gratitude. Many of you belong to teaching orders that have carried the light of the gospel to far-off lands as part of the Church's great missionary work, and for this too I give thanks and praise to God. Often you laid the foundations of educational provision long before the state assumed a responsibility for this vital service to the individual and to society. As the relative roles of Church and state in the field of education continue to evolve, never forget that religious have a unique contribution to offer to this apostolate, above all through lives consecrated to God and through faithful, loving witness to Christ, the supreme Teacher.

Indeed, the presence of religious in Catholic schools is a powerful reminder of the much-discussed Catholic ethos that needs to inform every aspect of school life. This extends far beyond the self-evident requirement that the content of the teaching should always be in conformity with Church doctrine. It means that the life of faith needs to be the driving force behind every activity in the school, so that the Church's mission may be served effectively, and the young people may discover the joy of entering into Christ's "being for others."[25]

Before I conclude, I wish to add a particular word of appreciation for those whose task it is to ensure that our schools provide

---

24. Cf. Benedict XVI, *Address to Representatives from the World of Culture at the "Collège des Bernardins" in Paris,* Apostolic Journey to France, Paris, September 12, 2008.

25. Benedict XVI, *Spe Salvi,* n. 28.

a safe environment for children and young people. Our responsibility toward those entrusted to us for their Christian formation demands nothing less. Indeed, the life of faith can only be effectively nurtured when the prevailing atmosphere is one of respectful and affectionate trust. I pray that this may continue to be a hallmark of the Catholic schools in this country.

Study Can Open the Heart of Man

From *Address to Members of the Italian Catholic University Federation,* November 9, 2007

FUCI is celebrating its 110 years: a fitting occasion to review the ground covered and its future prospects. Safeguarding the historic memory is valuable because, by considering the validity and consistency of its own roots, it is more enthusiastic in continuing the itinerary begun. On this joyful occasion I willingly take up the words that approximately ten years ago my venerable and beloved predecessor John Paul II addressed to you on the occasion of your centenary: "The history of the past 100 years," he said, "actually confirms that the FUCI experience is a significant chapter of the Church's life in Italy, especially of that vast and multiform lay movement which found in Catholic Action its main support."[26]

How can one fail to recognize that FUCI has contributed to the formation of entire generations of exemplary Christians, who have been able to transform the gospel *into* life and *with* life, committing themselves on the cultural, civil, social, and ecclesial levels? I am thinking in the first place of the young blesseds Pier Giorgio Frassati and Alberto Marvelli. I recall illustrious personalities like Aldo Moro and Vittorio Bachelet, both barbarously assassinated. Nor can I forget my venerable predecessor Paul VI, who was an attentive and courageous general ecclesial chaplain

26. John Paul II, *Address to Participants in the National Congress of the Italian Catholic University Federation (FUCI),* April 29, 1996; *L'Osservatore Romano,* English edition, May 22, 1996.

of FUCI in the difficult years of Fascism, and also Bishop Emilio Guano and Bishop Franco Costa. Moreover, the recent ten years have been characterized by FUCI's decisive commitment to rediscover its true university dimension. After several debates and heated discussions, Italy began during the mid-1990s a radical reform of its academic system, which now presents a new profile, rich in promising perspectives, combined, however, with elements that raise legitimate concern. And you, both at the recent congresses and on the pages of the *Ricerca* journal, are constantly concerned with the new configuration of academic studies, the relative legislative modifications, the topic of student participation, and the ways in which the global dynamics of communication affect formation and the transmission of knowledge.

It is precisely in this environment that FUCI can fully express even today its original and ever-current charism: the convinced witness of the "possible friendship" between intelligence and faith, which implies the ceaseless effort to unite maturation in faith with growth in studies and the acquisition of scientific knowledge. In this context the expression so dear to you, "To believe in study," is meaningful. In effect, why should one who holds the faith renounce the freedom to seek the truth, and why should one who freely seeks the truth renounce the faith? Instead, it is possible, precisely during the university years and thanks to them, to realize an authentic human, scientific, and spiritual maturation. "To believe in study" means to recognize that study and research—especially during the university years—have an intrinsic power to widen the horizons of human intelligence, as long as academic study remains demanding, rigorous, serious, methodical, and progressive. Indeed, on these conditions it represents an advantage for the global formation of the human person, as Bl. Giuseppe Tovini used to say, observing that with study young people would never have been poor, while without study they would never have been rich.

At the same time study constitutes a providential opportunity to advance on the journey of faith, because a well-cultivated intelligence opens the heart of man to listen to the voice of God, emphasizing the importance of discernment and humility. I referred precisely to the value of humility at the recent *Agora* [meeting] at Loreto when I exhorted Italian youth not to follow the dictates of pride, but rather the realistic sense of life open to the transcendent dimension. Today, as in the past, whoever wants to be a disciple of Christ is called to go against the tide, not to be attracted by the interesting and persuasive appeals that come from various platforms that propagandize behavior marked by arrogance and violence, presumption, and gaining success by every means. Contemporary society is marked by such an unbridled race for appearances and possessions, unfortunately to the detriment of being, and the Church, expert in humanity, does not tire to exhort especially the young generations to which you belong to remain vigilant and not to be afraid to choose "alternative" ways that only Christ can indicate.

Yes, dear friends, Jesus summons all his friends to characterize their existence by a sober, solidary way of life, to weave sincere and free emotional relationships with others. He asks you, dear young students, to commit yourselves honestly to study, cultivating a mature sense of responsibility and a shared interest in the common good. The university years are therefore a training ground for convinced and courageous gospel witness. To accomplish your mission, seek to cultivate an intimate friendship with the divine Teacher, placing yourself at the school of Mary, seat of wisdom.

Jesus Has Risen: Educating for Hope in Prayer, Action, and Suffering

From *Address to the Ecclesial Convention of the Diocese of Rome,* June 9, 2008

After dedicating special attention to the family for three years, we have now focused for two years on the topic of the education of the new generations. It is a theme that involves the family first of all, but also very directly concerns the Church, schools, and society as a whole. Thus we seek to respond to that "educational emergency" that, for everyone, is a great and unavoidable challenge. The goal we have set ourselves for the coming pastoral year on which we shall be reflecting at this convention once again refers to education, in the perspective of theological hope nourished by faith and trust in God who revealed himself in Jesus Christ as man's true friend. "Jesus is risen: educating for hope in prayer, action and suffering" will therefore be our theme this evening. Jesus raised from the dead is truly the faultless foundation that supports our faith and hope. He has been from the outset, since the time of the apostles who were direct witnesses of his resurrection and proclaimed him to the world at the cost of their lives. He is today and always will be. As the Apostle Paul wrote in chapter 15 of his First Letter to the Corinthians, "If Christ has not been raised, then our preaching is in vain and your faith is in vain" (1 Cor 15:14), "if our hope in Christ has been for this life only, we are the most unfortunate of all people" (1 Cor 15:19). I repeat to you what I said on October 19, 2006, at the Ecclesial Convention in Verona: "The Resurrection of Christ is a fact that occurred in history, of which the Apostles were witnesses and certainly not its inventors. At the same time, it was not simply a return to our earthly life. Instead, it is the greatest 'mutation' that ever occurred, the decisive 'jump' towards a profoundly new dimension of life, the entry into a decidedly different order that regards above all Jesus of Nazareth, but with him also us, the whole human family, history and the entire universe."[27]

In the light of Jesus risen from the dead we can thus understand the true dimensions of the Christian faith as "a life-changing and life-sustaining hope,"[28] setting us free from those misinter-

27. Benedict XVI, *Address to the Fourth National Ecclesial Convention*, Pastoral Visit to Verona, October 19, 2006.
28. Benedict XVI, *Spe Salvi*, n. 10.

pretations and false alternatives that have restricted and weakened the breath of our hope down the centuries. In practice the hope of those who believe in the God who raised Jesus from the dead aspires with its whole being to that happiness and full and total joy that we call eternal life, but for this very reason it clothes, enlivens, and transforms our daily existence on earth, gives a direction and enduring significance to our small hopes and the efforts we make to change, and makes the world in which we live less unjust. Of course, Christian hope likewise concerns each one of us personally, the eternal salvation of our self and our life in this world. However, it is also a community hope, a hope for the Church and for the entire human family—that is, it is "always essentially also hope for others; only thus is it truly hope for me too."[29]

In contemporary society and culture, and thus also in our beloved city of Rome, it is not easy to live under the banner of Christian hope. On the one hand, distrust, disappointment, and resignation frequently prevail. Not only do they contradict the "great hope" of faith, but also the "little hopes" that generally comfort us in our efforts to attain the goals of daily life. In other words, we have the feeling that for Italy, as for Europe, the best years are now behind us and a precarious and uncertain future awaits the new generations. On the other hand, the expectations of great innovations and improvements are focused on science and technology, hence on human efforts and discoveries, as though solutions to our problems could come from them alone. It would be nonsensical to deny or to minimize the enormous contribution made by science and technology in transforming the world and our actual standard of living, but it would be equally short-sighted to ignore that their progress puts into the hands of men and women abysmal possibilities for evil and that, nonetheless, it is not science and technology that give our lives meaning and teach us to distinguish good from evil. Therefore,

29. Benedict XVI, *Spe Salvi*, n. 48.

as I wrote in *Spe Salvi,* it is not science, but love that redeems man, and this also means the earthly and worldly aspects.[30]

Thus we approach the deepest and most crucial cause of the weakness of hope in the world we live in. Ultimately this cause is no different from that which the Apostle Paul pointed out to the Christians of Ephesus when he reminded them that before encountering Christ they had "no hope and [were] without God in the world" (Eph 2:12). Our civilization and culture, which encountered Christ 2,000 years ago, would be unrecognizable without his presence, especially here in Rome. Yet it tends all too often to put God in parentheses, to organize personal and social life without him, even to claim that it is impossible to know anything about God and to go so far as to deny his existence. However, when God is left aside, none of the things that truly matter to us can find a permanent place; all our great and small hopes are founded on emptiness. Thus, to "educate for hope," as we propose to do at this convention and throughout the coming pastoral year, it is first necessary to open our hearts, our minds, and our entire lives to God, to be his credible witnesses among our brothers and sisters.

At our previous diocesan conventions we have already considered the causes of the current educational crisis and the proposals that can help to overcome it. Moreover, in recent months, also with my letter on the urgent task of education, we have sought to involve the whole city, especially families and schools, in this joint undertaking. It is not necessary here, therefore, to return to these aspects. Rather, let us see how we can really teach ourselves to hope, turning our attention to certain "places" where this can be learned practically and exercised effectively and which I identified in *Spe Salvi.* Among these places, prayer has priority. In prayer we open ourselves to the One who is the origin and foundation of our hope. The prayerful person is never totally alone, for God is the One who in every situation and in

30. Cf. Benedict XVI, *Spe Salvi,* n. 26.

any trial is always able to listen to and help him or her. Through perseverance in prayer the Lord broadens our desires and expands our mind, rendering us better able to receive him within ourselves. The correct way to pray is, therefore, a process of inner purification. We must open ourselves to God's gaze, to God himself so that, in the light of God's Face, lies and hypocrisy fall away. This manner of exposing oneself in prayer to God's Face is really a purification that renews us, sets us free, and opens us not only to God, but also to our brothers and sisters. Hence it is the opposite of escaping from our responsibilities toward our neighbor. On the contrary, it is through prayer that we learn to keep the world open to God and to become ministers of hope for others. It is in speaking with God that we see the whole community of the Church, a human community, as all our brethren, and thus we learn responsibility for others and the hope that God will help us on our way. Teaching prayer, learning "the art of prayer" from the lips of the divine Teacher, like the first disciples who asked him, "Lord, teach us to pray" (Lk 11:1), is thus an essential task. By learning to pray we learn to live, and on our journey we must pray ever better with the Church and with the Lord in order to live in a better way. As the beloved servant of God, John Paul II reminded us in his apostolic letter *Novo Millennio Ineunte,* "Our Christian communities must become *genuine 'schools' of prayer*, where the encounter with Christ is expressed not just in imploring help but also in thanksgiving, praise, adoration, contemplation, listening and ardent devotion, until the heart truly 'falls in love'";[31] thus Christian hope will grow within us. And love of God and neighbor will grow with hope.

I wrote in the encyclical *Spe Salvi,* "All serious and upright human conduct is hope in action."[32] As disciples of Jesus, let us therefore participate joyfully in the effort to make the face of this city of ours more beautiful, more human and fraternal in

31. John Paul II, Apostolic Letter *Novo Millennio Ineunte* (January 6, 2001), n. 33.
32. Benedict XVI, *Spe Salvi,* n. 35.

order to revive its hope and the joy of belonging to it together. Dear brothers and sisters, it is precisely the acute and widespread awareness of the evils and problems that exist in Rome
that is reawakening the will to make a concerted effort to rec-
tify them: it is our duty to make our own specific contribution,
starting with the crucial structure that consists of education and
the person's formation, but also constructively facing the many
other concrete problems that often make the lives of this city's
inhabitants stressful. We will seek in particular to promote a
more family-friendly culture and a social organization that is
ready to welcome life as well as to appreciate the elderly who are
so numerous in Rome's population. We will work to respond to
primary needs such as employment and housing, especially for
young people. We will share the commitment to make our city
safer and more "livable," but we will also strive to make it so for
everyone, in particular for the poorest people, so that immigrants who come among us, with the intention of finding a living
space and who respect our laws, may not be excluded.

I do not need to enter further into these problems with
which you are familiar, because you live them daily. Rather, I
wish to emphasize the attitude and approach with which those
who put their hope in God first work and commit themselves.
Their primary attitude is humility; they do not claim to be successful always or to be able to solve every problem by their own
efforts. Yet it is also, and for the same reason, an attitude of great
trust, tenacity, and courage: in fact, believers know that despite
all the difficulties and failures, their life, work, and history overall are protected through the indestructible power of God's love;
that consequently they are never fruitless or meaningless. In this
perspective we can understand more easily that Christian hope
also lives in suffering—indeed, that suffering itself educates and
fortifies our hope in a special way. Certainly we must "do whatever we can to reduce suffering: to avoid as far as possible the
suffering of the innocent; to soothe pain; to give assistance in

overcoming mental suffering."[33] Great progress has effectively been made, particularly in the struggle against physical pain. Yet we cannot entirely eliminate the world's suffering, because we are powerless to dry its sources: the finiteness of our being and the power of evil and sin. Indeed, the suffering of the innocent and mental imbalances are, unfortunately, tending to increase in the world. Actually, human experience, today and always, and especially the experience of the saints and martyrs, confirms the great Christian truth that it is not escape from suffering that cures the human being, but rather the ability to accept tribulation and mature through it, finding meaning therein through union with Christ. For each one of us and for the society in which we live the measure of our humanity is defined in our relationship with suffering and with people who are suffering. Christian faith deserves the historical merit of having inspired in men and women, in a new way and with new depth, the capacity for sharing also inwardly the suffering of others, hence one is not alone in suffering, and also to suffer for love of goodness, truth, and justice: all this is far beyond our own strength, but becomes possible on the basis of God's com-passion through his love of humanity in Christ's Passion.

Dear brothers and sisters, let us teach ourselves every day the hope that matures in suffering. We are called to do so in the first place when we are personally afflicted by a serious illness or some other harsh trial. We will grow equally in hope through concrete help and daily closeness to the suffering of our neighbors and of our relatives, and of every person who is our brother, because we draw near with a loving attitude. Furthermore, let us learn to offer to God, rich in mercy, the small efforts of our daily existence, inserting them humbly into the great "com-passion" of Jesus, in that treasure of compassion of which the human race stands in need. The hope of believers in Christ cannot, in any case, stop at this world, but is intrinsically oriented to full and eternal com-

33. Benedict XVI, *Spe Salvi*, n. 36.

munion with the Lord. Therefore, toward the end of my encyclical I reflected on God's judgment as a place in which to learn and exercise hope. I thus sought once again to make in some way familiar and comprehensible to humanity and to the culture of our time the salvation that is promised to us in the world beyond death, even if we cannot have a true and proper experience of that world here below. To restore its true dimensions and crucial motivation to education in hope, all of us, starting with priests and catechists, must put back at the center of the proposal of faith this great truth whose "first fruits" are in Jesus Christ raised from the dead (cf. 1 Cor 15:20–23).

Education Is a Crucial Theme
for Every Generation

From *Address to the Diplomatic Corps Accredited
to the Holy See,* January 9, 2012

Today's meeting traditionally takes place at the end of the Christmas season, during which the Church celebrates the coming of the Savior. He comes in the dark of night, and so his presence is immediately a source of light and joy (cf. Lk 2:9–10). Truly the world is gloomy wherever it is not brightened by God's light! Truly the world is dark wherever men and women no longer acknowledge their bond with the Creator and thereby endanger their relation to other creatures and to creation itself. The present moment is sadly marked by a profound disquiet and the various crises—economic, political, and social—are a dramatic expression of this.

Here I cannot fail to address before all else the grave and disturbing developments of the global economic and financial crisis. The crisis has not only affected families and businesses in the more economically advanced countries where it originated, creating a situation in which many people, especially the young, have felt disoriented and frustrated in their aspirations for a serene future, but it has also had a profound impact on the life of developing countries. We must not lose heart, but instead resolutely rediscover our way through new forms of commitment. The crisis can and must be an incentive to reflect on human existence and on the importance of its ethical dimension, even before we consider the mechanisms governing economic life: not only in an effort to stem private losses or to shore up national economies, but to give ourselves new rules that ensure that all can lead a dignified life and develop their abilities for the benefit of the community as a whole.

I would like next to point out that the effects of the present moment of uncertainty are felt particularly by the young. Their disquiet has given rise in recent months to agitation that has affected various regions, at times severely. I think first and foremost of North Africa and the Middle East, where young people, among others, who are suffering from poverty and unemployment and are fearful of an uncertain future, have launched what has developed into a vast movement calling for reforms and a more active share in political and social life. At present it is hard to make a definitive assessment of recent events and to understand fully their consequences for the stability of the region. Initial optimism has yielded to an acknowledgment of the difficulties of this moment of transition and change, and it seems evident to me that the best way to move forward is through the recognition of the inalienable dignity of each human person and of his or her fundamental rights. Respect for the person must be at the center of institutions and laws; it must lead to the end of all violence and forestall the risk that due concern for popular demands and the need for social solidarity turn into mere means for maintaining or seizing power. I invite the international community to dialogue with the actors in the current processes, in a way respectful of peoples and in the realization that the building of stable and reconciled societies, opposed to every form of unjust discrimination, particularly religious discrimination, represents a much vaster horizon than that of short-term electoral gains. I am deeply concerned for the people of those countries where hostilities and acts of violence continue, particularly Syria, where I pray for a rapid end to the bloodshed and the beginning of a fruitful dialogue between the political forces, encouraged by the presence of independent observers. In the Holy Land, where tensions between Palestinians and Israelis affect the stability of the entire Middle East, it is necessary that the leaders of these two peoples adopt courageous and farsighted decisions in favor of peace. I was pleased to learn that, following an initiative of the kingdom of Jordan, dialogue has been resumed; I express my hope that it will be maintained, and that it will lead to a lasting peace that guarantees the right of the two peoples to dwell in security in sovereign states and within secure and international- ly recognized borders. For its part, the international community must become more creative in developing initiatives that pro- mote this peace process and are respectful of the rights of both parties. I am also following closely the developments in Iraq, and I deplore the attacks that have recently caused so much loss of life; I encourage the nation's leaders to advance firmly on the path to full national reconciliation.

Blessed John Paul II stated that "the path of peace is at the same time the path of the young," inasmuch as young people embody "the youth of the nations and societies, the youth of every family and of all humanity."[34] Young people thus impel us to take seriously their demand for truth, justice, and peace. For this reason I chose them as the subject of my annual World Day of Peace Message entitled *Educating Young People in Justice and Peace.* Education is a crucial theme for every generation, for it determines the healthy development of each person and the future of all society. It thus represents a task of primary impor- tance in this difficult and demanding time. In addition to a clear

34. John Paul II, Apostolic Letter *Dilecti Amici* (March 31, 1985), n. 1.

goal, that of leading young people to a full knowledge of reality and thus of truth, education needs *settings*. Among these, pride of place goes to the *family*, based on the marriage of a man and a woman. This is not a simple social convention, but rather the fundamental cell of every society. Consequently, policies that undermine the family threaten human dignity and the future of humanity itself. The family unit is fundamental for the educational process and for the development both of individuals and states; hence there is a need for policies that promote the family and aid social cohesion and dialogue. It is in the family that we become open to the world and to life and, as I pointed out during my visit to Croatia, "openness to life is a sign of openness to the future."[35] In this context of openness to life, I note with satisfaction the recent sentence of the Court of Justice of the European Union forbidding patenting processes relative to human embryonic stem cells, as well as the resolution of the Parliamentary Assembly of the Council of Europe condemning prenatal selection on the basis of sex.

More generally, and with particular reference to the West, I am convinced that legislative measures that not only permit, but at times even promote abortion for reasons of convenience or for questionable medical motives, compromise the education of young people and, as a result, the future of humanity.

Continuing our reflection, a similarly essential role in the development of the person is played by *educational institutions:* these are the first instances that cooperate with the family, and they can hardly function properly unless they share the same goals as the family. There is a need to implement educational policies that ensure that schooling is available to everyone and that, in addition to promoting the cognitive development of the individual, show concern for a balanced personal growth, including openness to the transcendent. The Catholic Church

35. Benedict XVI, *Homily at the Mass for the National Day of Croatian Catholic Families,* Apostolic Journey to Croatia, Zagreb, June 5, 2011.

has always been particularly active in the field of education and schooling, making a valued contribution alongside that of state institutions. It is my hope that this contribution will be acknowledged and prized also by the legislation of the various nations.

From this perspective it is clear that an effective educational program also calls for respect for *religious freedom*. This freedom has individual, collective, and institutional dimensions. We are speaking of the first of human rights, for it expresses the most fundamental reality of the person. All too often, for various reasons, this right remains limited or is flouted. I cannot raise this subject without first paying tribute to the memory of the Pakistani minister Shahbaz Bhatti, whose untiring battle for the rights of minorities ended in his tragic death. Sadly, we are not speaking of an isolated case. In many countries Christians are deprived of fundamental rights and sidelined from public life; in other countries they endure violent attacks against their churches and their homes. At times they are forced to leave the countries they have helped to build because of persistent tensions and policies that frequently relegate them to being second-class spectators of national life. In other parts of the world we see policies aimed at marginalizing the role of religion in the life of society, as if it were a cause of intolerance rather than a valued contribution to education in respect for human dignity, justice, and peace. In the past year religiously motivated terrorism has also reaped numerous victims, especially in Asia and in Africa; for this reason, as I stated in Assisi, religious leaders need to repeat firmly and forcefully that "this is not the true nature of religion. It is the antithesis of religion and contributes to its destruction."[36] Religion cannot be employed as a pretext for setting aside the rules of justice and of law for the sake of the intended "good." In this context I am proud to recall, as I did in my native country, that the Christian vision of man was the true inspi-

---

36. Benedict XVI, *Address for the Day of Reflection, Dialogue and Prayer for Peace and Justice in the World*, Assisi, October 27, 2011.

ration for the framers of Germany's Basic Law, as indeed it was for the founders of a united Europe. I would also like to bring up several encouraging signs in the area of religious freedom. I am referring to the legislative amendment whereby the public juridical personality of religious minorities was recognized in Georgia; I think too of the sentence of the European Court of Human Rights upholding the presence of the crucifix in Italian schoolrooms. It is also appropriate for me to make particular mention of Italy at the conclusion of the 150th anniversary of her political unification. Relations between the Holy See and Italy experienced moments of difficulty following the unification. In the course of time, however, concord and the mutual desire for cooperation, each within its proper domain, prevailed for the promotion of the common good. I hope that Italy will continue to foster a stable relationship between Church and state and thus serve as an example to which other nations can look with respect and interest.

On the continent of Africa, to which I returned during my recent visit to Benin, it is essential that cooperation between Christian communities and governments favor progress along the path of justice, peace, and reconciliation, where respect is shown for members of all ethnic groups and all religions. It is painful to realize that in different countries of the continent this goal remains distant. I think in particular of the renewed outbreak of violence in Nigeria, as we saw from the attacks against several churches during the Christmas period, the aftermath of the civil war in Côte d'Ivoire, the continuing instability in the Great Lakes region, and the humanitarian emergency in the countries of the Horn of Africa. I once again appeal to the international community to make every effort to find a solution to the crisis that has gone on for years in Somalia.

Finally I would stress that education, correctly understood, cannot fail to foster *respect for creation*. We cannot disregard the grave natural calamities that in 2011 affected various regions of

Southeast Asia or ecological disasters like that of the Fukushima nuclear plant in Japan. Environmental protection and the connection between fighting poverty and fighting climate change are important areas for the promotion of integral human development. For this reason, I hope that, pursuant to the seventeenth session of the Conference of States Parties to the UN Convention on Climate Change recently concluded in Durban, the international community will prepare for the UN Conference on Sustainable Development ("Rio + 20") as an authentic "family of nations" with a great sense of solidarity and responsibility toward present and future generations....

The birth of the Prince of Peace teaches us that life does not end in a void; that its destiny is not decay, but eternal life. Christ came so that we might have life and have it in abundance (cf. Jn 10:10). "Only when the future is certain as a positive reality does it become possible to live the present as well."[37] Inspired by the certainty of faith, the Holy See continues to offer its proper contribution to the international community in accordance with the twofold desire clearly enunciated by the Second Vatican Council, whose fiftieth anniversary takes place this year: to proclaim the lofty grandeur of our human calling and the presence within us of a divine seed, and to offer humanity sincere cooperation in building a sense of universal fraternity corresponding to this calling.[38]

Prayer and Study

From *Address to Students and Teachers from the Ecclesiastical Universities of Rome*, October 25, 2007

Dear friends, the annual event here in the Vatican Basilica, which reunites in spirit the whole academic family of the Roman ecclesiastical universities, enables you to perceive more clearly

37. Benedict XVI, *Spe Salvi,* n. 2.
38. Cf. Second Vatican Council, *Gaudium et Spes,* n. 3.

the unique experience of communion and brotherhood that you can have in these years. If this experience is to be fruitful it needs the contribution of each and every one. Together you have taken part in the eucharistic celebration, and you will be spending this new year together. Try to create an atmosphere among yourselves in which the commitment to study and brotherly cooperation are a common enrichment for you, not only with regard to the cultural, scientific, and doctrinal aspects, but also the human and spiritual dimensions. May you learn to make the most of the opportunities in this regard that are offered to you in Rome, a truly unique city from this point of view.

Rome is rich in historical memorials, masterpieces of art and culture; it is above all full of eloquent Christian testimonies. In the course of time ecclesiastical universities and faculties, now more than a century old, came into being, where entire generations of priests and pastoral workers have been formed, among whom great saints and important men of the Church are not lacking.

You are following in their footsteps, dedicating important years of your life to acquire a deeper knowledge of various humanistic and theological disciplines. The purposes of these worthy institutions, as beloved John Paul II wrote in 1979 in his apostolic constitution *Sapientia Christiana,* are, among other things, "through scientific research to cultivate and promote their own disciplines, and especially to deepen knowledge of Christian revelation and of matters connected with it, to enunciate systematically the truths contained therein, to consider in the light of revelation the most recent progress of the sciences and to present them to the people of the present day in a manner adapted to various cultures."[39] This commitment is more urgently needed than ever in our postmodern age, in which we feel the need for a new evangelization that requires properly trained teachers of the faith and heralds and witnesses of the gospel.

39. John Paul II, Apostolic Constitution *Sapientia Christiana* (April 29, 1979), Section 1, Art. 3, n. 1.

In fact, your stay in Rome can and must serve to prepare you to carry out in the best possible way the task that awaits you in the various fields of apostolic action. The evangelizing mission proper to the Church in our time not only requires that the gospel message be disseminated everywhere, but also that it penetrate deeply peoples' ways of thinking and criteria of judgment and behavior. In a word, the entire culture of contemporary man must be permeated with the gospel. The multiplicity of the subjects taught at the athenaeums and study centers that you attend intends to respond to this vast and urgent cultural and spiritual challenge. May the possibility of studying in Rome, the see of the successor of Peter and hence of the Petrine ministry, help you to reinforce your sense of belonging to the Church and your commitment of fidelity to the pope's universal magisterium. In addition, the presence in the academic institutions and in the colleges and seminaries of teachers and students from every continent offers you a further opportunity to be acquainted with one another and to experience the beauty of belonging to the one large family of God: may you know how to make the very most of it!

Dear brothers and sisters, it is indispensable that the study of the humanistic and theological sciences always be accompanied by a gradual, intimate, and profound knowledge of Christ. This entails combining a sincere desire for holiness with your necessary concern for study and research. Therefore, in addition to being a serious and persevering intellectual commitment, may these years of formation in Rome be first and foremost a time of intense prayer, in constant harmony with the divine Teacher who has chosen you for his service. Likewise, may contact with the religious and social reality of the city be useful to you for a spiritual and pastoral enrichment. Let us invoke the intercession of Mary, the docile and wise Mother, so that she may help you to be ready in every circumstance to recognize the voice of the Lord, who safeguards you and accompanies you on your journey of formation and at every moment in your life.

Patience and Academic Life

*From Homily at the Celebration of Vespers with
University Students and Teachers of Rome in Preparation
for Christmas,* December 16, 2010

"Be patient, therefore, brethren, until the coming of the Lord" (Jas 5:7).

With these words the apostle James has ushered us into the process of immediate preparation for Holy Christmas, which, at this vespers liturgy, I have the joy of beginning with you, dear students and distinguished teachers of the athenaeums of Rome.

I address my cordial greeting to you all and in particular to the large group of those who are preparing to receive confirmation. I express my deep appreciation of your dedication to the Christian animation of our city's culture. I thank Professor Renato Lauro, rector magnificent of the University of Rome Tor Vergata, for his words of greeting to me on behalf of you all. I address a special and respectful greeting to the cardinal vicar and to the various academic and institutional authorities.

The invitation of the apostle points out to us the way that leads to Bethlehem, freeing our hearts from every ferment of intolerance and false expectation that can always lurk within us if we forget that God has already come. He is already at work in our personal and community story and asks to be received.

The God of Abraham, Isaac, and Jacob has revealed himself, he has shown his Face and has taken up residence in our flesh, in Jesus, Son of Mary—true God and true man—whom we shall meet once again in the grotto of Bethlehem. To return there, to that humble, narrow place, is not merely a journey in spirit: it is the path we are called to take, experiencing this day God's closeness and his action that renews and sustains our existence.

Christian patience and constancy, of which St. James speaks, are not synonymous with apathy or resignation; rather, they are virtues of those who know that they can and must not build on sand, but on the rock—virtues of those who can respect the times and ways of the human condition and therefore avoid clouding the deepest expectations of the mind with utopian or transient hopes that subsequently disappoint.

"Behold, the farmer waits for the precious fruit of the earth" (Jas 5:7). Dear friends, this invitation, which refers to the rural world and which marks time with nature's seasons, may sound surprising to us, immersed as we are in an ever more dynamic society.

Yet the comparison the apostle chose calls us to turn our gaze to the one true "farmer," the God of Jesus Christ, to his most profound mystery that was revealed in the incarnation of the Son. Indeed, the Creator of all things is not a despot who orders and intervenes peremptorily in history; rather, he is like a farmer who sows the seed and tends it while it grows so it may bear fruit.

With him, man, too, can be a good farmer who loves history and builds it in depth, recognizing and contributing to the growth of the seeds of good that the Lord has given to us. So let us too journey on to Bethlehem, our eyes fixed on God, patient and faithful, who knows how to wait, how to stop, and how to respect the seasons of our existence. The Child whom we shall meet is the full manifestation of the mystery of love of God, who loves by giving his life, who loves in a disinterested manner, who teaches us to love and asks only to be loved.

"Strengthen your hearts." The journey to the grotto of Bethlehem is a journey of inner liberation, an experience of profound freedom, because it impels us to come out of ourselves and to go toward God who has made himself close to us, who heartens us with his presence and with his freely given love, who precedes and accompanies us in our daily decisions, who speaks to us in the secrecy of our hearts and in the sacred scriptures.

He wants to imbue our lives with courage, especially in the moments when we feel tired and overworked and need to rediscover the serenity of the journey and feel joyfully that we are pilgrims bound for eternity.

"The Lord's coming is at hand." This is the announcement that fills this celebration with emotion, as well as hastening our steps on the way to the grotto. The Child we shall find between Mary and Joseph is the *Logos*-Love, the Word who can give our life its full consistence.

God has opened for us the treasures of his profound silence and, with his Word, has communicated himself to us. In Bethlehem the everlasting today of God brushes against our fleeting time that receives from it orientation and light for the journey through life.

Dear friends of the universities of Rome, who are walking on the fascinating and demanding path of research and cultural creativity, the incarnate Word asks you to share with him the patience of "building." Building your own lives and building society are not tasks that can be accomplished by distracted or superficial minds and hearts. They require profound educational action and continuous discernment that must involve the whole of the academic community, encouraging that synthesis between intellectual formation, moral discipline, and religious commitment that Bl. John Henry Newman proposed in his *The Idea of a University*.

People in our time feel the need for a new class of intellectuals who can interpret social and cultural dynamics by offering solutions that are practical and realistic, rather than abstract.

The university is called to play this indispensable role, and the Church gives it her convinced and effective support. The Church of Rome, in particular, has been for many years devoted to supporting the university's vocation and to serving it with the simple and discreet contribution of numerous priests who work in the chaplaincies and institutions of the Church.

I would like to express my appreciation to the cardinal vicar and to his collaborators for the pastoral program of university ministry, which, this year, in tune with the diocesan project, is summed up succinctly by the theme, "*Ite, missa est* ... in the courtyard of the Gentiles."

The greeting at the end of the eucharistic celebration, "*Ite, missa est,*" invites everyone to be witnesses of that love which transforms human life and thereby grafts in society the shoot of the civilization of love. Your program that offers the city of Rome a culture at the service of the integral development of the human person, as I pointed out in the encyclical *Caritas in Veritate,* is a concrete example of your commitment to promoting academic communities in which one develops and practices what Giovanni Battista Montini—when he was chaplain to FUCI—called "intellectual charity."

The community of the Roman universities, with its wealth of state, private, Catholic, and pontifical institutions, is called to perform an important historical task: to overcome the assumptions and prejudices that sometimes prevent the development of authentic culture.

By working in synergy, in particular with the theological faculties, the Roman universities can show that a new dialogue and new collaboration are possible between the Christian faith and the various branches of knowledge, without confusion and without separation, but sharing the same aspiration to serve the human being in his fullness.

Studying Is Essential: Only Thus Can We Stand Firm in These Times

From *Address to Seminarians,* Apostolic Journey to Germany, Freiburg in Breisgau, September 26, 2011

It is a great joy for me to be able to come together here with young people who are setting out to serve the Lord, young people who want to listen to his call and follow him....

It truly touched my heart to see how you had reflected on my letter, and developed your own questions and answers from it, and to see how seriously you are taking what I tried to say in my letter, on the basis of which you are now working out your own path.

Of course it would be wonderful if we could hold a conversation with one another, but my travel schedule, which I am bound to follow, sadly does not permit such things. So I can only try, in the light of what you have written and what I myself had written, to offer just one or two further ideas.

In considering the questions "What is the seminary for?" "What does this time mean?" I am always particularly struck by the account that St. Mark gives of the birth of the apostolic community in the third chapter of his gospel. Mark says, "And he appointed twelve." He makes something, he does something, it is a creative act; and he made them "to be with him, and to be sent out to preach" (Mk 12:14). That is a twofold purpose, which in many respects seems contradictory. "To be with him": they are to be with him, in order to come to know him, to hear what he says, to be formed by him; they are to go with him, to accompany him on his path, surrounding him and following him. But at the same time they are to be envoys who go out, who take with them what they have learned, who bring it to others who are also on a journey—into the margins, into the wide open spaces, even into places far removed from him. And yet this paradox holds together: if they are truly with him, then they are also always journeying toward others, they are searching for the lost sheep; they go out, they must pass on what they have found, they must make it known, they must become envoys. And conversely, if they want to be good envoys, then they must always be with him. As St. Bonaventure once said, the angels, wherever they go, however far away, always move within the inner being of God. This is also the case here: as priests we must go out onto the many different streets, where we find people whom we should invite to his wedding feast. But we can only do this if in the process we always remain with him. And learning this—this combination of, on the one hand, going out on mission, and on the other hand, being with him, remaining with him, is, I believe, precisely what we have to learn in the seminary. The right way of remaining with him, becoming deeply rooted in him—being more and more with him, knowing him more and more, being more and more inseparable from him—and at the same time going out more and more, bringing the message, passing it on, not keeping it to ourselves, but bringing the Word to those who are far away and who nevertheless, as God's creatures and as people loved by Christ, all have a longing for him in their hearts.

The seminary is therefore a time for training; also, of course, a time for discernment, for learning: does he want me for this? The mission must be tested, and this includes being in community with others and also of course speaking with your spiritual directors, in order to learn how to discern what his will is. And then learning to trust: if he truly wants this, then I may entrust myself to him. In today's world, which is changing in such an unprecedented way and in which everything is in a constant state of flux, in which human ties are breaking down because of new encounters, it is becoming more and more difficult to believe that I will hold firm for the whole of my life. Even for my own generation, it was not exactly easy to imagine how many decades God might assign to me, and how different the world might become. Will I be able to hold firm with him, as I have promised to do? ... It is a question that demands the testing of the vocation, but then also—the more I recognize that he does indeed want me—it demands trust: if he wants me, then he will also hold me, he will be there in the hour of temptation, in the hour of need, and he will send people to me, he will show me the path, he will hold me. And faithfulness is possible, because he is always there, because he is yesterday, today, and tomorrow, because he belongs not only to this time, but he is the future and he can support us at all times.

A time for discernment, a time for learning, a time for vocation … and then, naturally, a time for being with him, a time for praying, for listening to him. Listening, truly learning to listen to him—in the word of sacred scripture, in the faith of the Church, in the liturgy of the Church—and learning to understand the present time in his Word. In exegesis we learn much about the past: what happened, what sources there are, what communities there were, and so on. This is also important. But more important still is that from the past we should learn about the present, we should learn that he is speaking these words now, and that they all carry their present within them, and that over and above the historical circumstances in which they arose, they contain a fullness that speaks to all times. And it is important to learn this present-day aspect of his Word—to learn to listen out for it— and thus to be able to speak of it to others. Naturally, when one is preparing the homily for Sunday, it often seems … my goodness, so remote! But if I live with the Word, then I see that it is not at all remote, it is highly contemporary, it is right here, it concerns me and it concerns others. And then I also learn how to explain it. But for this, a constant inner journey with the word of God is needed.

Personally being with Christ, with the living God, is one thing; another is that we can only ever believe within the "we." I sometimes say that St. Paul wrote, "Faith comes from hearing"—not from reading. It needs reading as well, but it comes from hearing, that is to say from the living word, addressed to me by the other, whom I can hear, addressed to me by the Church throughout the ages, from her contemporary word, spoken to me the priests, bishops, and my fellow believers. Faith must include a "you" and it must include a "we." And it is very important to practice this mutual support, to learn how to accept the other as the other in his otherness, and to learn that he has to support me in my otherness, in order to become "we," so that we can also build community in the parish, calling people into the community of the Word, and journeying with one another toward the living God. This requires the very particular "we" that is the seminary, and also the parish, but it also requires us always to look beyond the particular, limited "we" toward the great "we" that is the Church of all times and places: it requires that we do not make ourselves the sole criterion. When we say, "We are Church"—well, it is true: that is what we are, we are not just anybody. But the "we" is more extensive than the group that asserts those words. The "we" is the whole community of believers, today and in all times and places. And so I always say: within the community of believers, yes, there is as it were the voice of the valid majority, but there can never be a majority against the apostles or against the saints: that would be a false majority. We are Church: let us be Church, let us be Church precisely by opening ourselves and stepping outside ourselves and being Church with others.

Well, now, according to the schedule, I daresay I ought really to draw to a close now. I would like to make just one more point to you. In preparing for the priesthood, study is very much a part of the journey. This is not an academic accident that has arisen in the Western Church; it is something essential. We all know that St. Peter said, "Always be prepared to make a defense to anyone who calls you to account for the hope that is in you" (1 Pet 3:15). Our world today is a rationalist and thoroughly scientific world, albeit often somewhat pseudoscientific. But this scientific spirit, this spirit of understanding, explaining, know-how, rejection of the irrational, is dominant in our time. There is a good side to this, even if it often conceals much arrogance and nonsense. The faith is not a parallel world of feelings that we can still afford to hold on to; rather it is the key that encompasses everything, gives it meaning, interprets it, and also provides its inner ethical orientation: making clear that it is to be understood and lived as tending toward God and proceeding from God. Therefore it is important to be informed and to understand, to have an open mind, to learn.

Naturally in twenty years' time, some quite different philosophical theories will be fashionable from those of today: when I think what counted as the highest, most modern philosophical fashion in our day, and how totally forgotten it is now ... still, learning these things is not in vain, for there will be some enduring insights among them. And most of all, this is how we learn to judge, to think through an idea—and to do so critically—and to ensure that in this thinking the light of God will serve to enlighten us and will not be extinguished. Studying is essential: only thus can we stand firm in these times and proclaim within them the reason for our faith. And it is essential that we study critically—because we know that tomorrow someone else will have something else to say—while being alert, open, and humble as we study, so that our studying is always with the Lord, before the Lord, and for him.

Yes, I could say much more, and perhaps I should ... but I thank you for your attention. In my prayers, all the seminarians of the world are present in my heart—and not only those known to me by name, like the individuals I had the pleasure of receiving here this evening; I pray, as they make their inner journey toward the Lord, that he may bless them all, give light to them all, and show them the right way, and that he may grant us to receive many good priests.

5. THE CHURCH—
EDUCATION IN FAITH AND
COMMUNITY

Educating in the Faith

From *Address to Participants in the Convention of
the Diocese of Rome,* June 11, 2007

For the third consecutive year our diocesan convention gives me the possibility of meeting and speaking to you all, addressing the theme on which the Church of Rome will be focusing in the coming pastoral year, in close continuity with the work carried out in the year now drawing to a close.

The theme of the convention is "Jesus is Lord: educating in the faith, in the 'sequela,' in witnessing": a theme that concerns us all because every disciple professes that Jesus is Lord and is called to grow in adherence to him, giving and receiving help from the great company of brothers and sisters in the faith.

Nevertheless, the verb "to educate," as part of the title of the convention, suggests special attention to children, boys and girls and young people, and highlights the duty proper first of all to the family; thus we are continuing the program that has been a feature of the pastoral work of our diocese in recent years.

It is important to start by reflecting on the first affirmation, which gives our convention its tone and meaning: "Jesus is Lord." We find it in the solemn declaration that concludes

Peter's discourse at Pentecost, in which the head of the apostles said, "Let all the house of Israel therefore know assuredly that God has made him both Lord and Christ, this Jesus whom you crucified" (Acts 2:36). The conclusion of the great hymn to Christ contained in Paul's Letter to the Philippians is similar: "every tongue [should] confess that Jesus Christ is Lord, to the glory of God the Father" (Phil 2:11).

Again, in the final salutation of his First Letter to the Corinthians, St. Paul exclaimed, "If anyone has no love for the Lord, let him be accursed. *Maranà tha:* Our Lord, come!" (1 Cor 16:22), thereby handing on to us the very ancient Aramaic invocation of Jesus as Lord.

Various other citations could be added; I am thinking of the twelfth chapter of the same Letter to the Corinthians, in which St. Paul says, "No one can say 'Jesus is Lord' except by the Holy Spirit" (1 Cor 12:3).

Thus the apostle declares that this is the fundamental confession of the Church, guided by the Holy Spirit. We might think also of the tenth chapter of the Letter to the Romans, where the apostle says, "if you confess with your lips that Jesus is Lord," (Rom 10:9) thus reminding the Christians of Rome that these words, "Jesus is Lord," form the common confession of the Church, the sure foundation of the Church's entire life.

The whole confession of the Apostolic Creed, of the Nicene Creed, developed from these words. St. Paul also says in another passage of his First Letter to the Corinthians, "Although there may be so-called gods in heaven or on earth …"—and we know that today too there are many so-called "gods" on earth—for us there is only "one God, the Father, from whom are all things and for whom we exist, and one Lord, Jesus Christ, through whom are all things and through whom we exist" (1 Cor 8:5–6).

Thus, from the outset the disciples recognized the risen Jesus as the One who is our brother in humanity, but is also one with God; the One who, with his coming into the world and throughout his life, in his death and in his resurrection, brought us God and in a new and unique way made God present in the world; the One, therefore, who gives meaning and hope to our life; in fact, it is in him that we encounter the true Face of God that we find what we really need in order to live.

Educating in the faith, in the *sequela,* and in witnessing means helping our brothers and sisters, or rather helping one another to enter into a living relationship with Christ and with the Father. This has been from the start the fundamental task of the Church as the community of believers, disciples, and friends of Jesus. The Church, the body of Christ and temple of the Holy Spirit, is that dependable company within which we have been brought forth and educated to become, in Christ, sons and heirs of God.

In the Church, we receive the Spirit through whom "we cry, '*Abba!* Father!'" (cf. Rom 8:14–17). We have just heard in St. Augustine's homily that God is not remote, that he has become the "Way," and the "Way" himself has come to us. He said, "Stand up, you idler, and start walking!" Starting to walk means moving along the path that is Christ himself, in the company of believers; it means while walking, helping one another to become truly friends of Jesus Christ and children of God.

Daily experience tells us—as we all know—that precisely in our day educating in the faith is no easy undertaking. Today, in fact, every educational task seems more and more arduous and precarious. Consequently, there is talk of a great "educational emergency," of the increasing difficulty encountered in transmitting the basic values of life and correct behavior to the new generations, a difficulty that involves both schools and families and, one might say, any other body with educational aims.

We may add that this is an inevitable emergency: in a society, in a culture, which all too often make relativism its creed—relativism has become a sort of dogma—in such a society the light of truth is missing; indeed, it is considered dangerous and "authoritarian" to speak of truth, and the end result is doubt about the goodness of life—is it good to be a person? Is it good to be alive?—and in the validity of the relationships and commitments in which it consists.

So how would it be possible to suggest to children and to pass on from generation to generation something sound and dependable, rules of life, an authentic meaning and convincing objectives for human existence, both as individuals and as a community?

For this reason education tends to be broadly reduced to the transmission of specific abilities or capacities for doing, while people endeavor to satisfy the desire for happiness of the new generations by showering them with consumer goods and transitory gratification. Thus both parents and teachers are easily tempted to abdicate their educational duties and even no longer to understand what their role, or rather, the mission entrusted to them, is.

Yet, in this way we are not offering to young people, to the young generations, what it is our duty to pass on to them. Moreover, we owe them the true values that give life a foundation.

However, this situation obviously fails to satisfy; it cannot satisfy because it ignores the essential aim of education that is the formation of a person to enable him or her to live to the full and to make his or her own contribution to the common good. However, on many sides the demand for authentic education and the rediscovery of the need for educators who are truly such are increasing.

Parents, concerned and often worried about their children's future, are asking for it; many teachers who are going through the sad experience of the deterioration of their schools are asking for it; society overall is asking for it, in Italy as in many other nations, because it sees the educational crisis cast doubt on the very foundations of coexistence.

In a similar context, the Church's commitment to providing education in the faith, in discipleship, and in witnessing to the Lord Jesus is more than ever acquiring the value of a contribution to extracting the society in which we live from the educational crisis that afflicts it, clamping down on distrust and on that strange "self-hatred" that seems to have become a hallmark of our civilization.

However, none of this diminishes the difficulties we encounter in leading children, adolescents, and young people to meet Jesus Christ and to establish a lasting and profound relationship with him. Yet precisely this is the crucial challenge for the future of the faith, of the Church, and of Christianity, and it is therefore an essential priority of our pastoral work: to bring close to Christ and to the Father the new generation that lives in a world largely distant from God.

Dear brothers and sisters, we must always be aware that we cannot carry out such a task with our own strength, but only with the power of the Spirit. We need enlightenment and grace, which come from God and which act within hearts and consciences. For education and Christian formation, therefore, it is above all prayer and our personal friendship with Jesus that are crucial: only those who know and love Jesus Christ can introduce their brothers and sisters into a living relationship with him. Indeed, moved by this need, I thought, it would be helpful to write a book on Jesus to make him known.

Let us never forget the words of Jesus: "I have called you friends, for all that I have heard from my Father I have made known to you. You did not choose me, but I chose you and appointed you that you should go and bear fruit and that your fruit should abide" (Jn 15:15–16).

Our communities will thus be able to work fruitfully and to teach the faith and discipleship of Christ while being in themselves authentic "schools" of prayer, where the primacy of God is lived.[1]

Furthermore, it is education, and especially Christian edu-

---

1. Cf. John Paul II, *Novo Millennio Ineunte*, n. 33.

cation, that shapes life based on God who is love (cf. 1 Jn 4:8, 16), and that has need of that closeness that is proper to love. Especially today, when isolation and loneliness are a widespread condition to which noise and group conformity is no real remedy, personal guidance becomes essential, giving those who are growing up the assurance that they are loved, understood, and listened to.

In practice this guidance must make tangible the fact that our faith is not something of the past—that it can be lived today, and that in living it we really find our good. Thus boys and girls and young people may be helped to free themselves from common prejudices and realize that the Christian way of life is possible and reasonable—indeed, is by far the most reasonable.

The entire Christian community, with all its many branches and components, is challenged by the important task of leading the new generations to the encounter with Christ; on this terrain, therefore, we must express and manifest particularly clearly our communion with the Lord and with one another, as well as our willingness and readiness to work together to "build a network," to achieve with an open and sincere mind every useful form of synergy, starting with the precious contribution of those women and men who have consecrated their lives to adoring God and interceding for their brethren.

However, it is very obvious that in educating and forming people in the faith the family has its own fundamental role and primary responsibility. Parents, in fact, are those through whom the child at the start of life has the first and crucial experience of love, of a love that is actually not only human, but also a reflection of God's love for him.

Therefore, the Christian family, the small "domestic Church," and the larger family of the Church must take care to develop the closest collaboration, especially with regard to the education of children.[2]

2. Cf. Second Vatican Council, Dogmatic Constituion *Lumen Gentium* (November 21, 1964), n. 11.

Everything that has matured in the three years in which our diocesan pastoral ministry has devoted special attention to the family should not only be implemented, but also further increased.

For example, the attempts to involve parents and even godparents more closely, before and after baptism, in order to help them understand and put into practice their mission as educators in the faith have already produced appreciable results and deserve to be continued and to become the common heritage of each parish. The same applies for the participation of families in catechesis and in the entire process of the Christian initiation of children and adolescents.

Of course, many families are unprepared for this task, and there is no lack of families that—if they are not actually opposed to it—do not seem to be interested in the Christian education of their own children; the consequences of the crisis in so many marriages are making themselves felt here.

Yet it is rare to meet parents who are wholly indifferent to the human and moral formation of their children, and consequently unwilling to be assisted in an educational task that they perceive as ever more difficult.

Therefore, an area of commitment and service opens up for our parishes, oratories, youth communities, and, above all, for Christian families themselves, called to be near other families to encourage and assist them in raising their children, thereby helping them to find the meaning and purpose of life as a married couple.

Let us now move on to other subjects concerning education in the faith.

As children gradually grow up, their inner desire for personal autonomy naturally increases. Especially in adolescence, this can easily lead to them taking a critical distance from their family. Here the closeness that can be guaranteed by the priest, religious, catechist, or other educators capable of making the friendly face of the Church and love of Christ concrete for the young person becomes particularly important.

If it is to produce positive effects that endure in time, our closeness must take into account that the education offered is a free encounter and that Christian education itself is formation in true freedom. Indeed, there is no real educational proposal, however respectful and loving it may be, that is not an incentive to making a decision, and the proposal of Christianity itself calls freedom profoundly into question, calling it to faith and conversion.

As I said at the Ecclesial Convention in Verona,

A true education must awaken the courage to make definitive decisions, which today are considered a mortifying bind to our freedom. In reality, they are indispensable for growth and in order to achieve something great in life—in particular, to cause love to mature in all its beauty, and therefore, to give consistency and meaning to freedom itself.[3]

When they feel that their freedom is respected and taken seriously, adolescents and young people, despite their changeability and frailty, are not in fact unwilling to let themselves be challenged by demanding proposals; indeed, they often feel attracted and fascinated by them.

They also wish to show their generosity in adhering to the great perennial values that constitute life's foundations. The authentic educator likewise takes seriously the intellectual curiosity that already exists in children and, as the years pass, is more consciously cultivated. Constantly exposed to, and often confused by, the multiplicity of information and by the contrasting ideas and interpretations presented to them, young people today nevertheless still have a great inner need for truth. They are consequently open to Jesus Christ, who, as Tertullian reminds us, "called himself truth, not custom."[4]

---

3. Benedict XVI, *Address to the Participants in the Fourth National Ecclesial Convention,* Pastoral Visit to Verona, October 19, 2006.
4. Tertullian, *De virginibus velandis* I.1.

It is up to us to seek to respond to the question of truth, fearlessly juxtaposing the proposal of faith with the reason of our time. In this way we will help young people to broaden the horizons of their intelligence, to open themselves to the mystery of God, in whom is found life's meaning and direction, and to overcome the conditioning of a rationality that trusts only what can be the object of experiment and calculation. Thus it is very important to develop what last year we called "the pastoral care of intelligence."

The task of education passes through freedom, but also requires authority. Therefore, especially when it is a matter of educating in faith, the figure of the witness and the role of witnessing are central. A witness of Christ does not merely transmit information, but is personally involved with the truth Christ proposes and, through the coherency of his own life, becomes a dependable reference point.

However, he does not refer to himself, but to Someone who is infinitely greater than he is, in whom he has trusted and whose trustworthy goodness he has experienced. The authentic Christian educator is therefore a witness who finds his model in Jesus Christ, the witness of the Father who said nothing about himself, but spoke as the Father had taught him (cf. Jn 8:28). This relationship with Christ and with the Father is for each one of us, dear brothers and sisters, the fundamental condition for being effective educators in the faith.

Our convention very rightly speaks of education not only in faith and discipleship, but also in witnessing to the Lord Jesus. Bearing an active witness to Christ does not, therefore, concern only priests, women religious, and lay people who as formation teachers have tasks in our communities, but children and young people themselves, and all who are educated in the faith.

Therefore, the awareness of being called to become witnesses of Christ is not a corollary, a consequence somehow external to Christian formation, such as, unfortunately, has often been thought and as today people continue to think. On the contrary, it is an intrinsic and essential dimension of education in the faith and discipleship, just as the Church is missionary by her very nature.[5]

If children, through a gradual process from the beginning of their formation, are to achieve permanent formation as Christian adults, the desire to be and the conviction of being sharers in the Church's missionary vocation in all the situations and circumstances of life must take root in the believers' souls. Indeed, we cannot keep to ourselves the joy of the faith. We must spread it and pass it on, and thereby also strengthen it in our own hearts.

If faith is truly the joy of having discovered truth and love, we inevitably feel the desire to transmit it, to communicate it to others. The new evangelization to which our beloved Pope John Paul II called us passes mainly through this process.

A concrete experience that will increase in the youth of the parishes and in the various ecclesial groups the desire to witness to their own faith is the "young people's mission" that you are planning, after the success of the great "city mission."

By educating in the faith, a very important task is entrusted to Catholic schools. Indeed, they must carry out their mission on the basis of an educational project that places the gospel at the center and keeps it as a decisive reference point for the person's formation and for the entire cultural program.

In convinced synergy with families and with the ecclesial community, Catholic schools should therefore seek to foster that unity between faith, culture, and life that is the fundamental goal of Christian education. State schools too can be sustained in their educational task in various ways by the presence of teachers who are believers—in the first place, but not exclusively, teachers of Catholic religion—and of students with a Christian formation, as well as by the collaboration of many families and of the Christian community itself.

5. Cf. Second Vatican Council, Decree *Ad Gentes* (December 7, 1965), n. 2.

The healthy secularism of schools, like that of the other state institutions, does not in fact imply closure to transcendence or a false neutrality with regard to those moral values that form the basis of an authentic formation of the person. A similar discourse naturally applies for universities, and it is truly a good omen that university ministry in Rome has been able to develop in all the athenaeums, among teachers as much as students, and that a fruitful collaboration has developed between the civil and pontifical academic institutions.

Today, more than in the past, the education and formation of the person are influenced by the messages and general climate spread by the great means of communication and that are inspired by a mindset and culture marked by relativism, consumerism, and a false and destructive exaltation, or rather, profanation, of the body and of sexuality.

Therefore, precisely because of the great "yes" that as believers in Christ we say to the man loved by God, we certainly cannot fail to take interest in the overall orientation of the society to which we belong, in the trends that motivate it, and in the positive or negative influence that it exercises on the formation of the new generations.

The very presence of the community of believers, its educational and cultural commitment, the message of faith, trust, and love it bears are in fact an invaluable service to the common good, and especially to the children and youth who are being trained and prepared for life.

Dear brothers and sisters, there is one last point to which I would like to draw your attention: it is supremely important for the Church's mission, and requires our commitment and first of all our prayer. I am referring to vocations to follow the Lord Jesus more closely in the ministerial priesthood and in the consecrated life.

In recent decades, the diocese of Rome has been gladdened by the gift of many priestly ordinations that have made it possible to bridge the gap in the previous period and to meet the requests of many sister Churches in need of clergy; but the most recent indications seem less favorable and prompt the whole of our diocesan community to renew to the Lord, with humility and trust, its request for laborers for his harvest (cf. Mt 9:37–38; Lk 10:2).

With delicacy and respect we must address a special, but clear and courageous invitation to follow Jesus to those young men and women who appear to be the most attracted and fascinated by friendship with him. In this perspective the diocese will designate several new priests specifically to the care of vocations, but we know well that prayer and the overall quality of our Christian witness, the example of life set by priests and consecrated souls, the generosity of the people called and of the families they come from, are crucial in this area.

The Church Is Not a Social, Philanthropic Organization

From *Address to Italian Pilgrims: On Church, Education, Family,* July 5, 2011

I am thankful to the Lord because your visit gives me the possibility to share with you a moment of the synodal journey of the Church that is in Altamura-Gravina-Acquaviva delle Fonti. The synod is an event that gives a concrete experience of being people of God on the way, of being Church, a pilgrim community in history [journeying] toward its eschatological fulfillment in God. This signifies recognizing that the Church does not possess in herself a life-giving principle, but depends on Christ, of whom she is the sign and effective instrument. In the relationship with the Lord Jesus she finds her own most profound identity: to be gift of God to humanity, prolonging the presence and work of salvation of the Son of God through the Holy Spirit. In this context we understand that the Church is essentially a mystery of love at the service of humanity in view of its sanctification.

On this point the Second Vatican Council stated, "God, however, does not make men holy and save them merely as individuals, without bond or link between one another. Rather has it pleased Him to bring men together as one people, a people that acknowledges Him in truth and serves Him in holiness."[6] We see here that the word of God has really created a people, a community; it has created a common joy, a common pilgrimage toward the Lord. Hence being Church does not happen only by our own human organizational strength, but finds its source and its real meaning in the communion of love of the Father, of the Son, and of the Holy Spirit: This eternal love is the source from which the Church springs, and the most holy Trinity is the model of unity in diversity and generates and molds the Church as a mystery of communion.

It is always necessary to start again and in a new way from this truth to understand and to live more intensely our being Church, people of God, body of Christ, Communion. Otherwise we run the risk of reducing the whole to a horizontal dimension, which alters the identity of the Church and the proclamation of the faith and would make our life and the life of the Church poorer. It is important to stress that the Church is not a social philanthropic organization, as so many others are: she is the community of God, the community that believes, that loves, that adores the Lord Jesus, and opens her sails to the breath of the Holy Spirit, and because of this, she is a community capable of evangelizing and humanizing. The profound relationship with Christ, lived and nourished by the Word and by the Eucharist, renders proclamation effective, motivates a commitment to catechesis, and animates the testimony of charity. Many men and women of our time are in need of encountering God, of encountering Christ, or of rediscovering the beauty of the close

---

6. Second Vatican Council, *Lumen Gentium*, n. 9.

God, of the God that in Jesus Christ has shown his face as Father and calls us to recognize the meaning and value of existence—to make it understood that it is good to live as man. The present historical moment is marked, we know it, by lights and shadows. We witness complex attitudes: withdrawal into oneself, narcissism, desire to possess and to consume, feelings and affections bereft of responsibility. Many are the causes of this disorientation, which manifests itself in a profound existential uneasiness, but behind all this one can perceive a negation of the transcendent dimension of man and of the fundamental relationship with God. Because of this it is decisive that Christian communities promote sound and demanding journeys of faith.

Dear friends, particular attention must be given to the way of considering education in Christian life, so that every person can follow an authentic path of faith, through the different ages of life; a path in which—like the Virgin Mary—the person receives profoundly the word of God and puts it into practice, becoming a witness of the gospel. In the declaration *Gravissimum Educationis* the Second Vatican Council stated, "Christian education has as its principal purpose this goal: that the baptized, while they are gradually introduced the knowledge of the mystery of salvation, become ever more aware of the gift of Faith they have received, ... and be conformed in their personal lives according to the new man created in justice and holiness of truth."[7]

In this educational effort the family remains the first responsible party. Dear parents, be the first witnesses of the faith! Do not be afraid of the difficulties amid which you are called to realize your mission. You are not alone! The Christian community is close to you and sustains you. Catechesis accompanies your children in their human and spiritual growth, but catechesis is a permanent formation, not limited to preparation to receive the sacraments; we must grow throughout our lives in knowledge of God, thus in knowledge of what it means to be a man.

7. Second Vatican Council, *Gravissimum Educationis,* n. 2.

Know how to draw strength and light from the liturgy; participation in the eucharistic celebration on the Day of the Lord is decisive for the family, for the whole community; it is the structure of our time. Let us remember always that in the sacraments, above all in the Eucharist, the Lord Jesus works for the transformation of men assimilating us to himself. It is precisely thanks to the encounter with Christ, to communion with him, that the Christian community can give a witness of communion, lending itself to service, receiving the poor and the little ones, recognizing the face of God in the sick and in every needy one. Hence I invite you, beginning from contact with the Lord in daily prayer and above all in the Eucharist, to appreciate adequately the educational proposals and the forms of volunteer work in dioceses, to form persons in solidarity, open and attentive to situations of spiritual and material hardship. In short, pastoral action should be geared to forming persons mature in the faith, able to live in contexts in which often God is ignored; persons coherent with the faith, so that the light of Christ will be taken to all environments; persons that live the faith with joy, to transmit the beauty of being Christians.

Finally, I wish to address a special thought to you, dear priests. Always be grateful for the gift received, so that you can serve with love and dedication the people of God entrusted to your care. Proclaim the gospel with courage and fidelity, be witnesses of the mercy of God and, guided by the Holy Spirit, be able to indicate the truth, not fearing dialogue with the culture and with those who are in search of God.

For Us God Is Not Some Abstract Hypothesis

From *Letter to Seminarians,* October 18, 2010

When in December 1944 I was drafted for military service, the company commander asked each of us what we planned to do in the future. I answered that I wanted to become a Catholic priest.

The lieutenant replied, "Then you ought to look for something else. In the new Germany priests are no longer needed." I knew that this "new Germany" was already coming to an end and that, after the enormous devastation that that madness had brought upon the country, priests would be needed more than ever. Today the situation is completely changed. In different ways, though, many people nowadays also think that the Catholic priesthood is not a "job" for the future, but one that belongs more to the past. You, dear friends, have decided to enter the seminary and to prepare for priestly ministry in the Catholic Church in spite of such opinions and objections. You have done a good thing. Because people will always have need of God, even in an age marked by technical mastery of the world and globalization; they will always need the God who has revealed himself in Jesus Christ, the God who gathers us together in the universal Church in order to learn with him and through him life's true meaning and in order to uphold and apply the standards of true humanity. Where people no longer perceive God, life grows empty; nothing is ever enough. People then seek escape in euphoria and violence; these are the very things that increasingly threaten young people. God is alive. He has created every one of us, and he knows us all. He is so great that he has time for the little things in our lives: "Every hair of your head is numbered." God is alive, and he needs people to serve him and bring him to others. It does make sense to become a priest; the world needs priests, pastors, today, tomorrow and always, until the end of time.

The seminary is a community journeying toward priestly ministry. I have said something very important here: one does not become a priest on one's own. The "community of disciples" is essential, the fellowship of those who desire to serve the greater Church. In this letter I would like to point out thinking back to my own time in the seminary several elements, which I consider important for these years of your journeying.

Anyone who wishes to become a priest must be first and

foremost a "man of God," to use the expression of St. Paul (1 Tim 6:11). For us God is not some abstract hypothesis; he is not some stranger who left the scene after the "Big Bang." God has revealed himself in Jesus Christ. In the face of Jesus Christ we see the face of God. In his words we hear God himself speaking to us. It follows that the most important thing in our path toward priesthood and during the whole of our priestly lives is our personal relationship with God in Jesus Christ. The priest is not the leader of a sort of association whose membership he tries to maintain and expand. He is God's messenger to his people. He wants to lead them to God, and in this way to foster authentic communion between all men and women. That is why it is so important, dear friends, that you learn to live in constant intimacy with God. When the Lord tells us to "pray constantly," he is obviously not asking us to recite endless prayers, but urging us never to lose our inner closeness to God. Praying means growing in this intimacy. So it is important that our day should begin and end with prayer; that we listen to God as the scriptures are read; that we share with him our desires and our hopes, our joys and our troubles, our failures and our thanks for all his blessings, and thus keep him ever before us as the point of reference for our lives. In this way we grow aware of our failings and learn to improve, but we also come to appreciate all the beauty and goodness, which we daily take for granted, and so we grow in gratitude. With gratitude comes joy for the fact that God is close to us and that we can serve him.

For us God is not simply Word. In the sacraments he gives himself to us in person, through physical realities. At the heart of our relationship with God and our way of life is the Eucharist. Celebrating it devoutly, and thus encountering Christ personally, should be the center of all our days. In St. Cyprian's interpretation of the gospel prayer, "Give us this day our daily bread," he says, among other things, that "our" bread, the bread that we receive as Christians in the Church, is the eucharistic Lord himself. In this petition of the Our Father, then, we pray that he may daily give us "our" bread; and that it may always nourish our lives; that the risen Christ, who gives himself to us in the Eucharist, may truly shape the whole of our lives by the radiance of his divine love. The proper celebration of the Eucharist involves knowing, understanding, and loving the Church's liturgy in its concrete form. In the liturgy we pray with the faithful of every age, the past, the present, and the future are joined in one great chorus of prayer. As I can state from personal experience, it is inspiring to learn how it all developed, what a great experience of faith is reflected in the structure of the Mass, and how it has been shaped by the prayer of many generations.

The sacrament of penance is also important. It teaches me to see myself as God sees me, and it forces me to be honest with myself. It leads me to humility. The Curé of Ars once said, "You think it makes no sense to be absolved today, because you know that tomorrow you will commit the same sins over again. Yet," he continues, "God instantly forgets tomorrow's sins in order to give you his grace today." Even when we have to struggle continually with the same failings, it is important to resist the coarsening of our souls and the indifference that would simply accept that this is the way we are. It is important to keep pressing forward, without scrupulosity, in the grateful awareness that God forgives us ever anew, yet also without the indifference that might lead us to abandon altogether the struggle for holiness and self-improvement. Moreover, by letting myself be forgiven, I learn to forgive others. In recognizing my own weakness, I grow more tolerant and understanding of the failings of my neighbor.

I urge you to retain an appreciation for popular piety, which is different in every culture, yet always remains very similar, for the human heart is ultimately one and the same. Certainly, popular piety tends toward the irrational and can at times be somewhat superficial. Yet it would be quite wrong to dismiss it. Through that piety the faith has entered human hearts and become part of the common patrimony of sentiments and customs, shaping the life and emotions of the community. Popular piety is thus one of the Church's great treasures. The faith has taken on flesh and blood. Certainly popular piety always needs to be purified and refocused, yet it is worthy of our love, and it truly makes us into the "people of God."

Above all your time in the seminary is also a time of study. The Christian faith has an essentially rational and intellectual dimension. Were it to lack that dimension, it would not be itself. Paul speaks of a "standard of teaching" to which we were entrusted in baptism (Rom 6:17). All of you know the words of St. Peter, which the medieval theologians saw as the justification for a rational and scientific theology: "Always be ready to make your defense to anyone who demands from you an 'accounting' (logos) for the hope that is in you" (1 Pet 3:15). Learning how to make such a defense is one of the primary responsibilities of your years in the seminary. I can only plead with you: Be committed to your studies! Take advantage of your years of study! You will not regret it. Certainly the subjects that you are studying can often seem far removed from the practice of the Christian life and the pastoral ministry. Yet it is completely mistaken to start questioning their practical value by asking, Will this be helpful to me in the future? Will it be practically or pastorally useful? The point is not simply to learn evidently useful things, but to understand and appreciate the internal structure of the faith as a whole, so that it can become a response to people's questions, which on the surface change from one generation to another, yet ultimately remain the same. For this reason it is important to move beyond the changing questions of the moment in order to grasp the real questions and so to understand how the answers are real answers. It is important to have a thorough knowledge of sacred scripture as a whole, in its unity as the Old and the New Testaments: the shaping of texts, their literary characteristics, the process by which they came to form the canon of sacred books, their dynamic inner unity, a unity that may not be immediately apparent, but that in fact gives the individual texts their full meaning. It is important to be familiar with the fathers and the great councils in which the Church appropriated, through faith-filled reflection, the essential statements of scripture. I could easily go on. What we call dogmatic theology is the understanding of the individual contents of the faith in their unity—indeed, in their ultimate simplicity: each single element is, in the end, only an unfolding of our faith in the one God who has revealed himself to us and continues to do so. I do not need to point out the importance of knowing the essential issues of moral theology and Catholic social teaching. The importance nowadays of ecumenical theology and of a knowledge of the different Christian communities is obvious, as is the need for a basic introduction to the great religions, to say nothing of philosophy: the understanding of that human process of questioning and searching to which faith seeks to respond. But you should also learn to understand and, dare I say it, to love canon law, appreciating how necessary it is and valuing its practical applications: a society without law would be a society without rights. Law is the condition of love. I will not go on with this list, but I simply say once more: love the study of theology and carry it out in the clear realization that theology is anchored in the living community of the Church, which, with her authority, is not the antithesis of theological science, but its presupposition. Cut off from the believing Church, theology would cease to be itself, and instead it would become a medley of different disciplines lacking inner unity.

Your years in the seminary should also be a time of growth toward human maturity. It is important for the priest, who is called to accompany others through the journey of life up to the threshold of death, to have the right balance of heart and mind, reason and feeling, body and soul, and to be humanly integrated. To the theological virtues the Christian tradition has always joined the cardinal virtues derived from human experience and philosophy and, more generally, from the sound ethical tradition of humanity. Paul makes this point very clearly to the Philippians: "Finally, brothers, whatever is true, whatever is honorable, whatever is just, whatever is pure, whatever is pleasing, whatever is commendable, if there is any excellence and if there is anything worthy of praise, think about these things" (4:8). This also involves the integration of sexuality into the whole personality. Sexuality is a gift of the Creator, yet it is also a task that relates to a person's growth toward human maturity. When it is not integrated within the person, sexuality becomes banal and destructive. Today we can see many examples of this in our society. Recently we have seen with great dismay that some priests disfigured their ministry by sexually abusing children and young people. Instead of guiding people to greater human maturity and setting them an example, their abusive behavior caused great damage, for which we feel profound shame and regret. As a result of all this, many people, perhaps even some of you, might ask whether it is good to become a priest—whether the choice of celibacy makes any sense as a truly human way of life. Yet even the most reprehensible abuse cannot discredit the priestly mission, which remains great and pure. Thank God, all of us know exemplary priests, men shaped by their faith, who bear witness that one can attain to an authentic, pure, and mature humanity in this state, and specifically in the life of celibacy. Admittedly, what has happened should make us all the more watchful and attentive, precisely in order to examine ourselves earnestly, before God, as we make our way toward priesthood, so as to understand whether this is his will for me. It is the responsibility of your confessor and your superiors to accompany you and help you along this path of discernment. It is an essential part of your journey to practice the fundamental human virtues, with your gaze fixed on the God who has revealed himself in Christ, and to let yourselves be purified by him ever anew.

The origins of a priestly vocation are nowadays more varied

and disparate than in the past. Today the decision to become a priest often takes shape after one has already entered upon a secular profession. Often it grows within the communities, particularly within the movements, that favor a communal encounter with Christ and his Church, spiritual experiences, and joy in the service of the faith. It also matures in very personal encounters with the nobility and the wretchedness of human existence. As a result, candidates for the priesthood often live on very different spiritual continents. It can be difficult to recognize the common elements of one's future mandate and its spiritual path. For this very reason, the seminary is important as a community that advances above and beyond differences of spirituality. The movements are a magnificent thing. You know how much I esteem them and love them as a gift of the Holy Spirit to the Church. Yet they must be evaluated by their openness to what is truly Catholic, to the life of the whole Church of Christ, which for all her variety still remains one. The seminary is a time when you learn with one another and from one another. In community life, which can at times be difficult, you should learn generosity and tolerance, not only bearing with, but also enriching one another, so that each of you will be able to contribute his own gifts to the whole, even as all serve the same Church, the same Lord. This school of tolerance, indeed, of mutual acceptance and mutual understanding in the unity of Christ's Body, is an important part of your years in the seminary.

Education: Growing in Friendship with God

From *Address of the Holy Father to Pupils of St. Mary's
University College,* Apostolic Journey to the United Kingdom,
Twickenham, September 17, 2010

It is not often that a pope, or indeed anyone else, has the opportunity to speak to the students of all the Catholic schools of England, Wales, and Scotland at the same time. And since I have the chance now, there is something I very much want to say to you. I hope that among those of you listening to me today there are some of the future saints of the twenty-first century. What God wants most of all for each one of you is that you should become holy. He loves you much more than you could ever begin to imagine, and he wants the very best for you. And by far the best thing for you is to grow in holiness.

Perhaps some of you have never thought about this before. Perhaps some of you think being a saint is not for you. Let me explain what I mean. When we are young, we can usually think of people that we look up to, people we admire, people we want to be like. It could be someone we meet in our daily lives that we hold in great esteem. Or it could be someone famous. We live in a celebrity culture, and young people are often encouraged to model themselves on figures from the world of sport or entertainment. My question for you is this: what are the qualities you see in others that you would most like to have yourselves? What kind of person would you really like to be?

When I invite you to become saints, I am asking you not to be content with second best. I am asking you not to pursue one limited goal and ignore all the others. Having money makes it possible to be generous and to do good in the world, but on its own, it is not enough to make us happy. Being highly skilled in some activity or profession is good, but it will not satisfy us unless we aim for something greater still. It might make us famous, but it will not make us happy. Happiness is something we all want, but one of the great tragedies in this world is that so many people never find it because they look for it in the wrong places. The key to it is very simple—true happiness is to be found in God. We need to have the courage to place our deepest hopes in God alone—not in money, in a career, in worldly success, or in our relationships with others, but in God. Only he can satisfy the deepest needs of our hearts.

Not only does God love us with a depth and an intensity

that we can scarcely begin to comprehend, but he invites us to respond to that love. You all know what it is like when you meet someone interesting and attractive, and you want to be that person's friend. You always hope he will find you interesting and attractive, and want to be your friend. God wants your friendship. And once you enter into friendship with God, everything in your life begins to change. As you come to know him better, you find you want to reflect something of his infinite goodness in your own life. You are attracted to the practice of virtue. You begin to see greed and selfishness and all the other sins for what they really are—destructive and dangerous tendencies that cause deep suffering and do great damage—and you want to avoid falling into that trap yourselves. You begin to feel compassion for people in difficulties, and you are eager to do something to help them. You want to come to the aid of the poor and the hungry, you want to comfort the sorrowful, you want to be kind and generous. And once these things begin to matter to you, you are well on the way to becoming saints.

In your Catholic schools, there is always a bigger picture over and above the individual subjects you study, the different skills you learn. All the work you do is placed in the context of growing in friendship with God, and all that flows from that friendship. So you learn not just to be good students, but good citizens, good people. As you move higher up the school, you have to make choices regarding the subjects you study; you begin to specialize with a view to what you are going to do later on in life. That is right and proper. But always remember that every subject you study is part of a bigger picture. Never allow yourselves to become narrow. The world needs good scientists, but a scientific outlook becomes dangerously narrow if it ignores the religious or ethical dimension of life, just as religion becomes narrow if it rejects the legitimate contribution of science to our understanding of the world. We need good historians and philosophers and economists, but if the account they give of human life within their particular field is too narrowly focused, they can lead us seriously astray.

A good school provides a rounded education for the whole person. And a good Catholic school, over and above this, should help all its students to become saints. I know that there are many non-Catholics studying in the Catholic schools in Great Britain, and I wish to include all of you in my words today. I pray that you too will feel encouraged to practice virtue and to grow in knowledge and friendship with God alongside your Catholic classmates. You are a reminder to them of the bigger picture that exists outside the school, and indeed, it is only right that respect and friendship for members of other religious traditions should be among the virtues learned in a Catholic school. I hope too that you will want to share with everyone you meet the values and insights you have learned through the Christian education you have received.

The "Yes" of God Abides With Men

From *Address to the Participants in the Fourth National Ecclesial Convention,* Pastoral Visit to Verona, October 19, 2006

This Fourth National Convention is a new step on the path of implementing the Vatican II directives, which the Italian Church has undertaken since the years immediately following the great council.

First of all, it is a path of communion with God the Father and with his Son Jesus Christ in the Holy Spirit, and therefore of communion among us in the unity of the one body of Christ (cf. 1 Jn 1:3; 1 Cor 12:12–13). It is a path directed toward evangelization, to keep the faith alive and strong in the Italian people. It is therefore a tenacious testimony of love for Italy and of active solicitude for the good of her children.

This journey of the Church in Italy has run in strict and constant union with the successor of Peter: I am happy to recall with

you the servant of God, Paul VI, who called the first convention
in now distant 1976, and John Paul II, with his fundamental interventions that we all remember at the conventions of Loreto
and Palermo, which have strengthened the confidence of the
Italian Church to work so that faith in Jesus Christ continues to
offer, also to the men and women of our time, the sense and the
orientation of [human] existence, and so has had "a leading role
and an effective drawing power" in the nation's journey toward
its future.[8]

RISEN LORD: CENTER OF LIFE

In the same spirit I have come to Verona today to pray to the Lord
with you, to share, even though briefly, in your work of these days,
and to propose my reflection to you on what appears of the first
importance for the Christian presence in Italy.

You have made a very appropriate choice, putting the risen
Jesus Christ at the center of the convention's attention and of all
the life and witness of the Church in Italy. The resurrection of
Christ is a fact that occurred in history, of which the apostles
were witnesses and certainly not its inventors. At the same time,
it was not simply a return to our earthly life. Instead, it is the
greatest "mutation" that ever occurred, the decisive "jump" toward a profoundly new dimension of life, the entry into a decidedly different order that regards above all Jesus of Nazareth, but
with him also us, the whole human family, history, and the entire
universe.

This is why the resurrection of Christ is the center of the
preaching and the Christian witness from the beginning and until the end of time. Certainly it is a great mystery, the mystery
of our salvation, which finds its fulfillment in the resurrection
of the incarnate Word and both anticipates and guarantees our
hope. But the mark of this mystery is love, and only in the logic

8. Cf. John Paul II, *Address at the Meeting with the Italian Church in Loreto*, April 11,
1985; *L'Osservatore Romano*, English edition, May 6, 1985.

of love can it be brought close and somehow understood: Jesus Christ risen from the dead, because all of his being is perfectly and intimately united with God who is love, which is truly stronger than death.

He was one with indestructible life, and therefore he could give his own life, letting himself be killed, but he could not succumb to death definitively: at the Last Supper he concretely anticipated and accepted out of love his own death on the cross, thus transforming it into the gift of himself, that gift that gives us life, liberty, and salvation.

His resurrection, therefore, has been like an explosion of light, an explosion of love that melts the chains of sin and death. It inaugurated a new dimension of life and reality, from which the new world comes forth, which continuously penetrates our world, transforming it and drawing it to himself.

All of this concretely happens through the life and witness of the Church; rather, the Church herself constitutes the first fruits of this transformation, which is God's work and not ours. It comes to us through faith and the sacrament of baptism, which is really death and resurrection, rebirth, transformation to a new life. It is what St. Paul reveals in the Letter to the Galatians: "It is no longer I who live, but Christ who lives in me" (2:20). Hence, the essential identity of my life is changed through baptism, and I continue to exist only in this changed state.

My own self is taken away and I am filled with a new and greater subject, in which my "I" is still there, but transformed, purified, "open" through the insertion into the other, who acquires new space in my existence. Thus, we become "one in Christ" (Gal 3:28), a unique new subject, and our "I" is freed from its isolation.

"I, but no longer I": this is the formula of Christian existence established in baptism, the formula of the resurrection in time, the formula of the Christian "novelty" called to transform the world.

Here lies our Paschal joy. Our vocation and our Christian

duty consist in cooperating so that they reach effective fulfillment in the daily reality of our life, what the Holy Spirit accomplishes in us with baptism. In fact, we are called to become new women and men, to be able to be true witnesses of the Risen One and thus bearers of Christian joy and hope in the world, concretely in that community of men and women in which we live.

CHURCH OF ITALY'S SERVICE

So, from this fundamental message of the resurrection present in us and in our daily work, I come to the theme of the Church in Italy's service to the nation, to Europe, and to the world.

The Italy of today presents itself to us as a profoundly needy land and at the same time a very favorable place for such a witness.

It is profoundly needy because it participates in the culture that predominates in the West and seeks to present itself as universal and self-sufficient, generating a new custom of life. From this a new wave of illuminism and laicism is derived, by which only what is experiential and calculable would be rationally valid, while on the level of praxis, individual freedom is held as a fundamental value to which all others must be subject.

Therefore, God remains excluded from culture and from public life, and faith in him becomes more difficult, also because we live in a world that almost always appears to be of our making, in which, so to speak, God no longer appears directly, but seems to have become superfluous, even out of place.

In strict relationship with all of this, a radical reduction of man has taken place, in which man is considered a simple product of nature and as such not really free, and is in himself susceptible to be treated like any other animal. Thus an authentic overturning of the point of departure of this culture has come about, which started as a claim of the centrality of man and his freedom.

Along the same lines, ethics is brought within the confines of relativism and utilitarianism with the exclusion of every moral principle that is valid and in itself binding.

It is not difficult to see how this type of culture represents a radical and profound break, not only with Christianity, but in general with the religious and moral traditions of humanity. It is therefore not able to establish a true dialogue with other cultures in which the religious dimension is strongly present or to respond to the fundamental questions on the sense and direction of our life.

Therefore this culture is marked by a deep privation, but also by a great and poorly hidden need of hope.

As I mentioned, however, Italy at the same time constitutes a land favorable for Christian witness. Here, in fact, the Church is a lively reality—and we see it!—that conserves a capillary presence in the midst of people of every age and level.

Christian traditions often continue to be rooted and to produce fruit, while a great effort of evangelization and catechesis is taking place, addressed particularly to the new generations, but now even more so to families. Besides, with growing clarity, the insufficiency of a rationality closed in on itself and an overly individualistic ethic are felt; in practice, the grave risk of detaching itself from the Christian roots of our society is sensed.

This sensation, diffused in the Italian people, is expressly and strongly formulated by many important cultural figures, including among those who do not share, or at least who do not practice, our faith.

The Church and Catholic Italians are called, therefore, to welcome this great opportunity, and above all to be aware of it. Consequently, our attitude must never be renunciatory or closed in on ourselves. Instead, we must keep alive and if possible increase our dynamism, trustingly open to new relationships, without wasting any energy that can contribute to the cultural and moral growth of Italy.

It is up to us, in fact, not with our poor resources, but with the strength that comes from the Holy Spirit, to give positive and convincing responses to the longings and questions of our people.

If we can do it, the Church in Italy will render a great service not only to this nation, but also to Europe and to the world, because the trap of secularism is present everywhere, and the need for a faith lived in relation to the challenges of our time is likewise universal.

SHOWING THE "YES" OF FAITH

Dear brothers and sisters, now we must ask ourselves: how, and on what foundations, can we accomplish such a task? In this convention you have rightly held it indispensable to give concrete, practicable content to Christian witness, examining how it can be carried out and developed in each of the great areas of human experience.

We will therefore be helped by not losing sight in our pastoral activity of the link between faith and daily life, between the gospel proposition and the preoccupations and aspirations that most people have at heart.

Thus in these days you have reflected on the affective life and on the family, on work and on holidays, on education and the culture, on situations of poverty and illness, on the duties and responsibilities of social and political life.

Above all, I would like to emphasize, for my part, how, through this multiform witness, that great "yes" must emerge that God, through Jesus Christ, has said to man and to his life, to human love, to our freedom and our intelligence; how, therefore, faith in the God with a human face brings joy to the world.

Indeed, Christianity is open to all in cultures and society that are just, true, and pure, to that which gladdens, consoles, and strengthens our existence. St. Paul, in the Letter to the Philippians, wrote, "Whatever is true, whatever is honorable, whatever is just, whatever is pure, whatever is lovely, whatever is gracious, if there is any excellence, if there is anything worthy of praise, think about these things" (Phil 4:8).

So the disciples of Christ recognize and gladly welcome the authentic values of the culture of our time, such as scientific knowledge and technological advancement, human rights, religious freedom, democracy. They do not overlook or undervalue, however, that dangerous fragility of human nature that is a threat for man's advancement in every historical context; in particular, they do not neglect the interior tensions and contradictions of our age.

Therefore, the work of evangelization is never a simple adaptation to culture, but it is always also a purification, a courageous break that leads to maturation and healing, an openness that brings to birth that "new creation" (2 Cor 5:17; Gal 6:15) that is the fruit of the Holy Spirit.

As I wrote in the encyclical *Deus Caritas Est,* at the origin of the Christian being—and therefore at the origin of our witness as believers—there is no ethical decision or great idea, but the encounter with the Person of Jesus Christ, "which gives life a new horizon and a decisive direction."[9]

The fruitfulness of this encounter is also manifest in a peculiar and creative manner in the actual human and cultural context, above all in relation to reason, which has given life to modern science and to the related technologies. A fundamental characteristic of the latter is, in fact, the systematic employment of mathematical instruments to be able to work with nature to harness its immense energies for our service.

Mathematics as such is a creation of our intelligence: the correspondence between its structures and the real structures of the universe—which is the presupposition of all modern scientific and technological developments, already expressly formulated by Galileo Galilei with the famous affirmation that the book of

9. Benedict XVI, *Deus Caritas Est,* n. 1.

nature is written in mathematical language—arouses our admiration and raises a big question.

It implies, in fact, that the universe itself is structured in an intelligent manner, such that a profound correspondence exists between our subjective reason and the objective reason in nature.

It then becomes inevitable to ask oneself if there might not be a single original intelligence that is the common font of them both.

Thus precisely the reflection on the development of science brings us toward the Creator *Logos.* The tendency to give irrationality, chance and necessity, the primacy is overturned together with the tendency to lead our intelligence and our freedom back to it. Upon these bases it again becomes possible to enlarge the area of our rationality, to reopen it to the larger questions of the truth and the good, to link theology, philosophy, and science between them in full respect for the methods proper to them and of their reciprocal autonomy, but also in the awareness of the intrinsic unity that holds them together.

This is the task that is before us, a fascinating adventure that is worth our effort, to give a new thrust to the culture of our time and to restore the Christian faith to full citizenship in it.

The "cultural project" of the Church in Italy, with this object in view, is without doubt a happy intuition and can make a very important contribution.

THE HUMAN PERSON: REASON, INTELLIGENCE, LOVE

The human person is not, on the other hand, only reason and intelligence, although they are constitutive elements. He bears within himself, written in the most profound depths of his being, the need for love, to be loved and in turn to love. Therefore, he questions himself and often feels lost before the harshness of life, the evil that exists in the world and that appears so strong and at the same time radically devoid of sense.

Particularly in our age, notwithstanding all the progress made, evil has certainly not been overcome. Indeed, its power seems reinforced, and all the attempts to hide it are quickly unveiled, as both daily experience and great historical events demonstrate.

The recurring questions therefore return: can there be a safe space in our life for authentic love? In the final analysis, is the world truly the work of God's wisdom? Here, much more than any human reason, the upsetting novelty of biblical revelation comes to our aid: the Creator of Heaven and earth, the one God who is the source of every being, the sole Creator *Logos,* this creative reason knows how to love man personally, or rather, loves him passionately and wants to be loved in his turn. This creative Reason, who at the same time loves, therefore gives life to a history of love with Israel, his people; and in this affair, in the face of the betrayal of the people, his love shows itself rich in inexhaustible fidelity and mercy. It is a love that forgives beyond all limits.

In Jesus Christ such an attitude reaches an extreme, unheard-of, and dramatic level; in him, in fact, God makes himself one of us, our brother in humanity, and what is more, sacrifices his life for us.

Through death on the cross, apparently the greatest evil in history, is brought about "that turning of God against himself in which he gives himself in order to raise man up and save him. This is love in its most radical form,"[10] in which is made manifest what "God is love" means (1 Jn 4:8), and in which one also understands how authentic love must be defined.[11]

Precisely because he truly loves us, God respects and saves our freedom. He does not counter the power of evil and sin with a greater power, but—as our beloved Pope John Paul II told us in the encyclical *Dives in Misericordia,* and later in the book *Memory and Identity,* his true spiritual testament—he prefers to

10. Benedict XVI, *Deus Caritas Est,* n. 12.
11. Cf. Benedict XVI, *Deus Caritas Est,* nn. 9–10, 12.

put a limit on his patience and his mercy, that limit that is, in fact, the suffering of God's Son. In this way our suffering is also transformed from within, appears in the dimension of love, and contains a promise of salvation.

Dear brothers and sisters, all this John Paul II not only thought, and even not only believed with an abstract faith; he understood it and lived it with a faith matured in suffering. Upon this road, as Church, we are called to follow him, in the way and in the measure that God sets for each one of us.

Rightly, the cross causes us fear, as it provoked fear and anguish in Jesus Christ (cf. Mk 14:33–36); but it is not a negation of life, of which in order to be happy it is necessary to rid oneself.

It is rather the extreme "yes" of God to man, the supreme expression of his love and the source of full and perfect life. It therefore contains the most convincing invitation to follow Christ on the way of gift of self.

Here I would like to address a special affectionate thought to the suffering members of the body of the Lord. In Italy, as in every part of the world, they complete what is lacking in the sufferings of Christ in their own flesh (cf. Col 1:24), and so they contribute in the most effective manner to everyone's salvation. They are the most convincing witnesses of the joy that comes from God and that gives strength to accept the cross in love and in perseverance.

We know well that this choice of faith and of following Christ is never easy. Instead, it is always opposed and controversial. The Church remains, therefore, a "sign of contradiction" in the footsteps of her Master (cf. Lk 2:34), even in our time.

But we do not lose heart because of this. On the contrary, we must always be ready to give a response (*apo-logia*) to whoever asks us the reason (*logos*) for our hope, as the First Letter of St. Peter (3:15) invites us, which you have chosen very opportunely as a biblical guide for the itinerary of this convention. We must answer "with gentleness and reverence," with a "clear conscience" (3:15–16), with that gentle power that comes from union with Christ.

We must do it fulltime, on the level of thought and action, of personal behavior and public witness. The strong unity that was present in the Church of the first centuries, between a faith that befriends intelligence and a life praxis characterized by reciprocal love and caring attention to the poor and suffering, made the great missionary expansion of Christianity in the Hellenistic Roman world possible. So it also happened later, in the different cultural contexts and historical situations.

This continues to be the high road for evangelization. May the Lord guide us to live this unity between truth and love in the conditions proper to our time, for the evangelization of Italy and of the world today. And so I come to an important and fundamental point: education.

EDUCATION

Basically, in order for the experience of Christian faith and love to be welcomed and lived and transmitted from one generation to the next, there is the fundamental and decisive question of the education of the person. The formation of his mind must be a concern, without neglecting his freedom and capacity to love. This is why recourse to the help of grace is necessary.

Only in this way can that risk for the fate of the human family be effectively opposed, which is represented by the imbalance between the very rapid growth of our technological power and the more laborious growth of our moral resources.

A true education must awaken the courage to make definitive decisions, which today are considered a mortifying bind to our freedom. In reality, they are indispensable for growth and in order to achieve something great in life—in particular, to cause love to mature in all its beauty, and therefore, to give consistency and meaning to freedom itself.

From this solicitude for the human person and his formation comes our "no" to weak and deviant forms of love and to the counterfeiting of freedom, seen also in the reduction of reason to only what is calculable or manipulatable. In truth, these "nos" are rather "yeses" to authentic love, to the reality of man as he has been created by God.

I want to express here my wholehearted appreciation for the great formative and educative work that the single Churches never tire of carrying out in Italy by their pastoral attention to the new generations and to families; thank you for this attention!

Among the multiple forms of this commitment, I cannot but think of Catholic schools in particular, because in their regard there still exists, in some measure, antiquated prejudices that cause damaging delays and are no longer justifiable in recognizing their function and in permitting their concrete work.

WITNESSES OF CHARITY

Jesus told us that whatever we would have done to the least of the brethren we would have done it to him (cf. Mt 25:40). Therefore, the authenticity of our adherence to Christ is verified especially in the concrete love and solicitude for the weakest and poorest, those most threatened and in serious difficulty.

The Church in Italy has a great tradition of closeness, help, and solidarity toward the needy, the sick, and the marginalized that finds its highest expression in a wonderful succession of "saints of charity." This tradition still continues today, and it deals with the many new forms of moral and material poverty through *Caritas,* volunteer organizations, the often hidden works of many parishes, religious communities, associations, and groups, individual people moved by love of Christ and neighbor.

What is more, the Church in Italy shows extraordinary solidarity toward the immense multitudes of poor on the earth. Therefore, it is very important that all these witnesses of charity always keep their specific profile aloft and alight, nourishing itself on humility and trust in the Lord, keeping itself free from ideological suggestions and party sympathies, and above all measuring its own vision on the vision of Christ. The practical work is important, therefore, but the personal sharing with the needy and with the suffering of one's neighbor counts even more.

Thus, dear brothers and sisters, the Church's charity makes visible God's love in the world and so makes our faith in the incarnate, crucified, and risen God convincing.

CIVIL AND POLITICAL RESPONSIBILITY OF CATHOLICS

Your convention has rightly considered the theme of citizenship—that is, the question of the civil and political responsibility of Catholics. Christ has come to save the real, concrete man who lives in history and in the community, and so Christianity and the Church have had a public dimension and value from the beginning.

As I wrote in the encyclical *Deus Caritas Est* on the relationship between religion and politics,[12] Jesus Christ brought a substantial novelty, opening the way toward a more human, freer world through the reciprocal distinction and autonomy of the state and the Church—that is, between what belongs to Caesar and what belongs to God (cf. Mt 22:21).

The very religious freedom that we hold as a universal value, particularly necessary in the world today, has its historical roots here. The Church, therefore, is not and does not intend to be a political agent. At the same time she has a profound interest in the good of the political community, whose soul is justice, and offers it her specific contribution at a double level.

Indeed, Christian faith purifies reason and helps it to be better; as a result, with its social doctrine whose argument begins from what is conformed to the nature of every human being, the

---

12. Cf. Benedict XVI, *Deus Caritas Est,* nn. 28–29.

Church's contribution is to enable whatever is just to be effectively recognized and then also accomplished. To this end, moral and spiritual energies are clearly indispensable, as they ensure that the demands of justice are put before personal interests, a social category, or even a state. For the Church, here again, there is ample space to root these energies in the conscience, to nourish them and fortify them.

The immediate duty to act in the political sphere to build a just order in society is not the Church's task as such, but that of the lay faithful, who work as citizens under their own responsibility. This is a duty of great importance, to which Italian lay Christians are called to dedicate themselves with generosity and courage, illuminated by faith and by the magisterium of the Church and animated by the charity of Christ.

Special attention and extraordinary commitment are demanded today by those great challenges that endanger vast portions of the human family: war and terrorism, hunger and thirst, some terrible epidemics. But it is also necessary to face, with equal determination and clear policies, the risks of political and legislative choices that contradict fundamental values and anthropological principles and ethics rooted in the nature of the human being, in particular, regarding the guardianship of human life in all its stages, from conception to natural death, and to the promotion of the family founded on marriage, avoiding the introduction in the public order of other forms of union that would contribute to destabilizing it, obscuring its particular character and its irreplaceable role in society.

The open and courageous testimony that the Church and Italian Catholics have given and are giving in this regard is a precious service to Italy, useful and stimulating also for many other nations. This commitment and this witness are certainly part of that great "yes" that as believers in Christ we say to man loved by God.

TO BE UNITED TO CHRIST

Dear brothers and sisters, the duties and the responsibilities that this ecclesial convention is highlighting are certainly great and multiple. We are encouraged to keep ever in mind that we are not alone in carrying the burden. In fact, we support one another, and the Lord himself above all guides and sustains the fragile boat of the Church.

Hence we return to the point of departure: our being united in him is decisive, and therefore among ourselves, to be with him to be able to go out in his name (cf. Mk 3:13–15).

Thus our true strength is to nourish ourselves on his Word and his body, to unite ourselves to his offering for us, as we will do in the [eucharistic] celebration this afternoon, adore him present in the Eucharist; in fact, adoration must precede our every activity and program, that it may render us truly free and that we may be given the criteria for our action.

May the Virgin Mary, so loved and venerated in every part of Italy, precede and guide us in our union with Christ. In her we meet, pure and undeformed, the true essence of the Church, and so through her we learn to know and love the mystery of the Church that lives in history; we deeply feel a part of it, and in our turn we become "ecclesial souls"; we learn to resist that "internal secularization" that threatens the Church of our time, a consequence of the secularization process that has profoundly marked European civilization.

True Solidarity Is to Give One's Life

From *Address to the Participants in the 14th Session of the Pontifical Academy of Social Sciences,* May 3, 2008

In choosing the theme "Pursuing the Common Good: How Solidarity and Subsidiarity Can Work Together," you have decided to examine the interrelationships between four fundamental principles of Catholic social teaching: the dignity of the human person, the common good, subsidiarity, and solidarity.[13] These key realities, which emerge from the living contact between the gospel and concrete social circumstances, offer a framework for viewing and addressing the imperatives facing mankind at the dawn of the twenty-first century, such as reducing inequalities in the distribution of goods, expanding opportunities for education, fostering sustainable growth and development, and protecting the environment.

How can solidarity and subsidiarity work together in the pursuit of the common good in a way that not only respects human dignity, but allows it to flourish? This is the heart of the matter that concerns you. As your preliminary discussions have already revealed, a satisfactory answer can only surface after careful examination of the meaning of the terms.[14] *Human dignity* is the intrinsic value of a person created in the image and likeness of God and redeemed by Christ. The totality of social conditions allowing persons to achieve their communal and individual fulfillment is known as the *common good*. *Solidarity* refers to the virtue enabling the human family to share fully the treasure of material and spiritual goods, and *subsidiarity* is the coordination of society's activities in a way that supports the internal life of the local communities.

Yet definitions are only the beginning. What is more, these definitions are adequately grasped only when linked organically to one another and seen as mutually supportive of one another. We can initially sketch the interconnections among these four principles by placing the dignity of the person at the intersection of two axes: one horizontal, representing "solidarity" and "subsidiarity," and one vertical, representing the "common good." This creates a field upon which we can plot the various points

---

13. Cf. *Compendium of the Social Doctrine of the Church* (2004), nn. 160–63.
14. Cf. *Compendium of the Social Doctrine of the Church,* chap. 4.

of Catholic social teaching that give shape to the common good.

Though this graphic analogy gives us a rudimentary picture of how these fundamental principles imply one another and are necessarily interwoven, we know that the reality is much more complex. Indeed, the unfathomable depths of the human person and mankind's marvelous capacity for spiritual communion—realities that are fully disclosed only through divine revelation—far exceed the capacity of schematic representation. The solidarity that binds the human family, and the subsidiary levels reinforcing it from within, must however always be placed within the horizon of the mysterious life of the triune God (cf. Jn 5:26; 6:57), in whom we perceive an ineffable love shared by equal, though nonetheless distinct, persons.[15]

My friends, I invite you to allow this fundamental truth to permeate your reflections, not only in the sense that the principles of solidarity and subsidiarity are undoubtedly enriched by our belief in the Trinity, but particularly in the sense that these principles have the potential to place men and women on the path to discovering their definitive, supernatural destiny. The natural human inclination to live in community is confirmed and transformed by the "oneness of spirit" that God has bestowed upon his adopted sons and daughters (cf. Eph 4:3; 1 Pet 3:8). Consequently, the responsibility of Christians to work for peace and justice, their irrevocable commitment to build up the common good, is inseparable from their mission to proclaim the gift of eternal life to which God has called every man and woman. In this regard, the *tranquillitas ordinis* of which St. Augustine speaks refers to "*all* things"—that is to say, both "civil peace," which is a "concord among citizens," and the "peace of the heavenly city," which is the "perfectly ordered and harmonious enjoyment of God, and of one another in God."[16]

---

15. Cf. Thomas Aquinas, *Summa Theologiae* I, q. 42.
16. Augustine, *De Civitate Dei* XIX.13.

The eyes of faith permit us to see that the heavenly and earthly cities interpenetrate and are intrinsically ordered to one another, inasmuch as they both belong to God the Father, who is "above all and through all and in all" (Eph 4:6). At the same time, faith places into sharper focus the due autonomy of earthly affairs insofar as they are "endowed with their own stability, truth, goodness, proper laws and order."[17] Hence you can be assured that your discussions will be of service to all people of good will, while simultaneously inspiring Christians to embrace more readily their obligation to enhance solidarity with and among their fellow citizens, and to act upon the principle of subsidiarity by promoting family life, voluntary associations, private initiative, and a public order that facilitates the healthy functioning of society's most basic communities.[18]

When we examine the principles of solidarity and subsidiarity in the light of the gospel, we realize that they are not simply "horizontal": they both have an essentially vertical dimension. Jesus commands us to do unto others as we would have them do unto us (cf. Lk 6:31); to love our neighbor as ourselves (cf. Mt 22:35). These laws are inscribed by the Creator in man's very nature.[19] Jesus teaches that this love calls us to lay down our lives for the good of others (cf. Jn 15:12–13). In this sense, true solidarity—though it begins with an acknowledgment of the *equal* worth of the other—comes to fulfillment only when I willingly place my life at the service of the other (cf. Eph 6:21). Herein lies the "vertical" dimension of solidarity: I am moved to make myself *less* than the other so as to minister to his or her needs (cf. Jn 13:14–15), just as Jesus "humbled himself" so as to give men and women a share in his divine life with the Father and the Spirit (cf. Phil 2:8; Mt 23:12).

Similarly, subsidiarity—which encourages men and women

17. Second Vatican Council, *Gaudium et Spes,* n. 36.
18. Cf. *Compendium of the Social Doctrine of the Church,* n. 187.
19. Cf. Benedict XVI, *Deus Caritas Est,* n. 31.

to enter freely into life-giving relationships with those to whom they are most closely connected and upon whom they most immediately depend and demands of higher authorities respect for these relationships—manifests a vertical dimension pointing toward the Creator of the social order (cf. Rom 12:16, 18). A society that honors the principle of subsidiarity liberates people from a sense of despondency and hopelessness, granting them the freedom to engage with one another in the spheres of commerce, politics, and culture.[20] When those responsible for the public good attune themselves to the natural human desire for self-governance based on subsidiarity, they leave space for individual responsibility and initiative, but most importantly, they leave space for *love*,[21] which always remains "the most excellent way" (cf. 1 Cor 12:31).

In revealing the Father's love, Jesus has taught us not only how to live as brothers and sisters here on earth; he has shown us that he himself is the way to perfect communion with one another and with God in the world to come, since it is through him that "we have access in one Spirit to the Father" (cf. Eph 2:18). As you strive to articulate the ways in which men and women can best promote the common good, I encourage you to survey both the "vertical" and "horizontal" dimensions of solidarity and subsidiarity. In this way you will be able to propose more effective ways of resolving the manifold problems besetting mankind at the threshold of the third millennium, while also bearing witness to the primacy of love, which transcends and fulfills justice as it draws mankind into the very life of God.[22]

20. Cf. Pope Pius XI, Encyclical Letter *Quadragesimo Anno* (May 15, 1931), n. 80.
21. Cf. Rom 13:8; Benedict XVI, *Deus Caritas Est*, n. 28.
22. Cf. John Paul II, *Message for the 2004 World Day of Peace*, January 1, 2004.

Peter Damien: The University Is Not
Isolated from Society

From *Address to Lecturers and Students of the University
of Parma,* December 1, 2008

As you know, the university was my area of work for a number of years, and even after leaving it I have never stopped keeping up with it and feeling spiritually attached to it. I have often had the opportunity to speak at various athenaeums, and I also clearly remember coming to Parma in 1990, when I gave a reflection on the "ways of the faith" in the midst of the changes of the present time.[23] Today I would like briefly to consider with you the "lesson" that St. Peter Damian has bequeathed to us, taking up several of his ideas that are particularly relevant to the university environment of our day.

Last year, on the occasion of the liturgical memorial of the Great Hermit, February 20, I sent a Letter to the Order of Camaldolese Hermits in which I shed light on how especially applicable the central feature of his personality is to our time: in other words, the felicitous synthesis between the eremitical life and pastoral activity, the harmon-ious tension between the two fundamental poles of human existence: solitude and communion.[24] Those who, like you, dedicate their time to advanced studies for their whole life or in their youth cannot fail to be sensitive to this spiritual heritage of St. Peter Damian. Due mainly to the spread of the new computer technologies, the young generations are increasingly exposed to a double risk: on the one hand, the danger of seeing the capacity for concentration and mental application at the personal level progressively reduced; on the other, that of individual isolation into a reality that is increasingly virtual. Thus the social dimension has been shattered

23. Cf. Joseph Ratzinger, *Svolta per l'Europa?* (Milan: Pauline Press 1991), 65–89.
24. Benedict XVI, *Message to Fr. Guido Innocenzo Gargano, OSB Cam., for the Centenary of the Birth of St. Peter Damian,* February 20, 2007.

into smithereens, while the personal dimension withdraws into the self and tends to be closed to constructive relations with others or with those who are different. Instead, the university, by its very nature, lives precisely the fine balance between the individual moment and that of the community, between the research and reflection of each one and sharing and exchange that is open to others in a tendentially universal dimension.

Like that of Peter Damian, our epoch is also marked by forms of particularism and uncertainty, by the lack of unifying principles.[25] Academic studies must undoubtedly contribute to qualify the formative level of society, not only at the level of scientific research, strictly speaking, but also, more in general, offering youth the possibility to mature intellectually, morally, and civilly with the important questions that challenge the conscience of contemporary man.

History lists Peter Damian among the great "reformers" of the Church after the year 1000. We can call him the soul of the Gregorian reform that took its name from Pope St. Gregory VII, Hildebrand of Soana, whose close collaborator Peter Damian had been since the time when, before he was elected bishop of Rome, he was archdeacon of this Church.[26] However, what is the genuine concept of reform? One fundamental aspect that we may find in the writings and especially in the personal witness of Peter Damian is that every authentic reform must first of all be spiritual and moral; in other words, it must be born in the conscience. Today, in Italy too, there is often talk of university reform. I think, having duly weighed the pros and cons, that this teaching always remains valid. Structural and technical modifications are effectively efficient if they are accompanied by a serious examination of conscience on the part of those in charge at all levels, but more generally of each teacher, each student, each member of the technical and administrative personnel. We

25. Cf. Benedict XVI, *Message to Fr. Guido Innocenzo Gargano*.
26. Cf. Benedict XVI, *Message to Fr. Guido Innocenzo Gargano*.

know that Peter Damian was very strict with himself and his monks—very demanding in discipline. If one wants a human milieu to improve in quality and effectiveness, it is first necessary that each one start by reforming himself, correcting anything that may damage the common good or hinder it in some way.

In connection with the concept of reform, I would also like to highlight that of freedom. In fact, the goal of St. Peter Damian and his contemporaries' reforming endeavors was to ensure that the Church might become freer, first of all at the spiritual level, but then also historically speaking.

Likewise, the validity of a university reform can only be proven by its freedom: freedom in teaching, freedom in research, the academic institution's freedom from the economic and political authorities. This does not imply the university's isolation from society, nor self-reference, nor even less the use of public funds to pursue private interests. This is certainly not Christian freedom! Truly free, according to the gospel and the tradition of the Church, are the person, community, and institution that fully respond to their nature and aims, and the vocation of the university is people's scientific and cultural training for the development of the social and civil community as a whole.

Dear friends, I thank you, because with your visit, in addition to the pleasure of meeting you, you have given me an opportunity to reflect on the timeliness of St. Peter Damian at the end of the millennial celebrations in his honor. I wish you all the best for the scientific and pedagogical activities of your athenaeum, and I pray that, despite its now considerable size, it may always strive to be a *universitas studiorum* in which each one may recognize and express himself as a person, taking part in the "symphonic" search for the truth. To this end I encourage the university's present pastoral initiatives, as they are always a precious service to the human and spiritual formation of youth. And in this context I also hope that the historic Church of St. Francesco al Prato may soon be reopened for worship for the benefit of the university and the whole city.

Erik Peterson: Educator Through Christian Witness

From *Address to Participants in the International Symposium on Erik Peterson*, October 25, 2010

[Erik Peterson] lived in Rome with his family for several periods from 1930, and then settled here in 1933. He first lived on the Aventine near Sant'Anselmo, and later in the Vatican district in a house facing Porta Sant'Anna. Thus it gives me special joy to be able to greet the Peterson family who are with us here, his esteemed daughters and his son, with their respective families.

In 1990, together with Cardinal Lehmann, in the apartment you shared, on the occasion of her eightieth birthday I was able to give your mother an autograph with a picture of Bl. Pope John Paul II, and I recall this meeting with you with pleasure.

"Here we have no lasting city, but we seek the city which is to come" (Heb 13:14).

This citation from the Letter to the Hebrews could sum up Erik Peterson's life. In fact, he never found in his life a true place where he could obtain recognition and a permanent home.

He began his scientific work in a period of upheaval in Germany after the First World War. The monarchy had fallen. The civil order seemed to be at risk, given the political and social turmoil. This was also reflected in the religious sphere and, in a particular way, in German Protestantism.

The open theology predominant until then, with its optimism and progress, had entered a crisis and was giving way to new and clashing theological trends. The contemporary situation posed an existential problem to young Peterson. With an interest in both history and theology, he had already chosen the subject he was to study, as he says, in accordance with the perspective that "when we are left alone with human history, we find ourselves facing a meaningless enigma."[27]

27. Erik Peterson, "Eintrag in das Bonner 'Album Professorum' 1926/27," in *Aus-*

Peterson—I quote him again—decided "to work in the historical field and especially to address the problems of the history of religions," because in the evangelical theology of the time he had not managed "to make headway, hindered by numerous opinions, even things in themselves."[28] On this path he came ever closer to the certainty that no history is detached from God, and that in this history the Church has a special place and finds her meaning. I cite him further: "That the Church exists and is constituted in a quite particular way strictly depends on the fact that ... there is a well-defined, specifically theological history."[29]

The Church receives from God the mandate to lead men and women from their limited and isolated existence to universal communion, from the natural to the supernatural, from transience to the end of time. In his work on angels Peterson says in this regard, "The Church's journey leads from the earthly to the heavenly Jerusalem ... to the city of Angels and of Saints."[30] The starting point of this journey is the binding character of sacred scripture. According to Peterson, sacred scripture becomes binding and is binding to the extent that it is not only in itself, but in the hermeneutic of apostolic tradition that, in turn, is brought about in the apostolic succession. Hence the Church preserves scripture in a living present and at the same time interprets it. Through the bishops, who are in the apostolic succession, the testimony of scripture remains alive in the Church and constitutes the foundation for the ever valid convictions of the Church's faith that we find first of all in the creed and in dogma.

These convictions are continuously developed in the liturgy as a living space of the Church for praise of God. The divine

---

gewählte Schriften [Selected Writings], special volume, edited by Barbara Nichtweiss, Karl Lehmann, and Hans-Ulrich Weidemann, III (Würzburg: Echter, 2010)

28. Peterson, "Eintrag."

29. Peterson, Vorlesung, "Geschichte der Alten Kirche Bonn 1928," Ausgewählte Schriften, special volume, 88.

30. Peterson, Einleitung, Buch von den Engeln (Leipzig: Hegner, 1935).

office celebrated on earth therefore has an indissoluble relationship with the heavenly Jerusalem; it is there that the true and eternal sacrifice of praise, whose earthly celebration is only an image, is offered to God and to the Lamb.

Those who take part in holy Mass stand almost on the threshold of the heavenly sphere from which they contemplate the worship of the angels and saints. Wherever the earthly Church intones her eucharistic praise, she is united with the festive, heavenly assembly in which, in the saints, a part of her has already arrived and gives hope to all on this earth who are still journeying on toward the eternal fulfillment.

Perhaps at this point I should make a personal reflection. I discovered the figure of Erik Peterson for the first time in 1951. I was then chaplain at Bogenhausen. Mr. Wild, director of Kosel, the local publishing house, gave me the recently published book *Theologische Traktate* [Theological Treatises]. I read the book with increasing curiosity and let myself be truly impassioned by it, because in it I found the theology I was seeking: it is a theology that uses all the seriousness of history to understand and study texts; it analyzes them with the full gravity of historical research and does not relegate them to the past.

Indeed, in his research, the author participates in the self-surmounting of the letter, enters into this self-surmounting, and lets himself be guided by it. Thus he comes into contact with the One from whom theology itself derives: the living God.

In this way the discrepancy between the past, which philology analyzes, today is surmounted in and of itself, because the word leads to the encounter with reality and the entire timeliness of what is written, which transcends itself toward reality and becomes alive and active. Thus I learned from him, in a most essential and profound way, what theology really is. And I even felt admiration, because here he does not only say what he thinks, but this book is an expression of a quest that was the passion of his life.

Paradoxically, the exchange of letters with Harnack is the maximum expression of the unexpected attention that Peterson was receiving. Harnack confirmed—indeed, he had already written previously and independently—that the Catholic formal principle that holds that "scripture lives in tradition and tradition lives in the living form of the succession"—is the original and objective principle, and that "scripture by itself" does not function.

Peterson grasped the full seriousness of this affirmation of the open theologian and let himself be shaken, overwhelmed, bent, and transformed by it. In this way he found the path to conversion and with it truly took a step, like Abraham, as we heard at the beginning of the Letter to the Hebrews: "Here we have no lasting city."

He went from the security of a chair to uncertainty, to having no dwelling place, and throughout his life he lacked a sure base, a real homeland; he was truly journeying with faith and for faith, confident that by journeying on and possessing no home he was at home in a different way and was drawing ever closer to the heavenly liturgy that had impressed him.

From all this one realizes that many of the things Peterson thought and wrote remained fragmented because of this precarious mode of life, following the loss of his teaching post because of his conversion. Yet, although he had to live without the security of a fixed salary, he married here in Rome and founded a family. By so doing he expressed in practice his inner conviction that we, though foreigners—and he was so in a special way—nevertheless find support in the communion of love, and that in love itself there is something that lasts for eternity.

He experienced this foreignness of the Christian. He had become a foreigner in evangelical theology and remained a foreigner in Catholic theology, too, as it was then.

Today we know that he belonged to both, and that from him both must learn the whole drama, the realism and the existential and human need of theology.

Erik Peterson, as Cardinal Lehmann said, was certainly appreciated and loved by many, an author recommended in a narrow circle, but who did not receive the scientific recognition he deserved. It would have been, in a certain way, too soon. As I said, he was both here and there [in Catholic and in evangelical theology] a foreigner.

Cardinal Lehmann cannot be sufficiently praised for having taken the initiative in publishing a magnificent complete edition of Peterson's works, nor can Mrs. Nichtweiss, to whom he has entrusted this task that she carries out with admirable competence.

Thus the attention given to him in this publication is more than deserved, given that various works have now also been translated into Italian, French, Spanish, English, Hungarian, and even Chinese. I hope this will ensure that Peterson's thought, which does not stop at details, but always has a vision of the whole of theology, will be more widely disseminated.

Guardini: Reaching for That Which Is Primary and Essential

From *Address to the Guardini Foundation's Congress on*
"The Spiritual and Intellectual Legacy of Romano Guardini,"
October 29, 2010

In his speech of thanks on the occasion of his eightieth birthday in February 1965, at the "Ludwig-Maximilian" University in Munich, Guardini described his life's work, as he understood it, as a method of questioning himself in a continuous spiritual exchange on the meaning of the Christian *Weltanschauung* [vision of the world].[31] For Guardini this vision, this comprehensive survey of the world, was not an external survey like a simple matter of research. Nor did he mean the perspective of the history

---

31. Guardini, *Stationen und Rückblicke* (Würzburg: Echter, 1965), 41.

of the spirit that examines and ponders what others have said or written on the religious form of an epoch. In Guardini's opinion all these points of view were insufficient.

In the notes on his life he affirmed, "what was of immediate interest to me was not the question of what someone had said about Christian truth, but of what was true."[32] And it was this line of his teaching that impressed us as young men, because we were not interested in witnessing a "firework display" of opinions to be found within Christianity or outside it. We wanted to know "what it is." And here was a man who, fearlessly but at the same time with all the seriousness of critical thought, asked this question and helped us think together. Guardini did not want to know one thing or many things; he aspired to the truth of God and to the truth about man. For him the means of approaching this truth was the *Weltanschauung*—as it was then called—which is achieved in a living exchange with the world and with men. The specific Christian principle lies in the fact that man knows he stands in a relationship to God that precedes him, and from which he cannot withdraw.

The principle that establishes the yardstick is not our own thought, but God who surpasses our units of measurement and cannot be reduced to any entity that we may create. God reveals himself as the truth, not an abstract truth, but rather one to be found in the living and the concrete, ultimately in the form of Jesus Christ.

Anyone who desires to see Jesus, the truth, however, must "change course," must leave behind the autonomy of arbitrary thought and move toward the willingness to listen, which accepts "what is." And this journey backward, which Guardini made during his conversion, shaped his whole thought and his whole life as a continuous departure from autonomy to turn toward listening, toward receiving. However, even in an authentic

---

32. Guardini, *Berichte über mein Leben* (Düsseldorf: Patmos, 1984), 24.

relationship with God, man does not always comprehend what God says. He needs interpretation, and this consists in an exchange with others that down the ages has found its most reliable form in the living Church that unites all people.

Guardini was a man of dialogue. His works, almost without exception, were born from dialogue, even if only an inner one. The lessons of the professor of the philosophy of religion and of Christian *Weltanschauung* at the University of Berlin in the 1920s represented above all meetings with great thinkers of the past. Guardini read the works of these authors, listened to them, learned from them how they saw the world and entered into dialogue in order to develop through dialogue with them what he, as a Catholic thinker, had to say to them regarding their thoughts. He pursued this habit in Munich, and this was the particular style of his teaching—the fact that he was in dialogue with the thinkers.

His key words were, "you see," because he wanted to guide us to "seeing," while he himself was in a common inner dialogue with his listeners. This was the innovation in comparison with the rhetoric of the old days: rather that, far from seeking rhetoric, he talked to us in a totally simple way, and at the same time spoke of truth and led us to dialogue with the truth. And there was a broad spectrum of "dialogues" with authors such as Socrates, St. Augustine, Pascal, Dante, Hölderlin, Mörike, Rilke, and Dostoyevsky. He saw them as living mediators who reveal the present in a word from the past, allowing us to see and live it in a new way. They give us a strength that can lead us once again back to ourselves.

Guardini held that when we open ourselves to the truth, an *ethos*—a basis for our moral behavior to our neighbor—follows as a requirement of our existence. Since man can encounter God, he can also behave well. This primacy of ontology over ethos applies to him. Upright conduct therefore derives from the being, from the very being of God correctly understood and listened to. Guardini used to say, "authentic praxis, that is, correct behavior, stems from the truth and it is necessary to fight for it."[33]

It was first and foremost among the young that Guardini noted this yearning for the truth, this reaching for what is primary and essential. In his dialogues with young people, particularly at Rothenfels Castle, which, thanks to him, had by then become the center of the Catholic Youth Movement, the priest and educator promoted the ideals of the youth movement, such as self-determination, personal responsibility, and an inner disposition for the truth; he purified and deepened these ideals. Freedom. Yes, but the only person who is really free, he used to tell us, is the one who is "completely what he should be, in accordance with his own nature.... Freedom is truth."[34] The truth of man, for Guardini, is essentiality and conformity to being. Man's journey leads to truth when he practices "the obedience of our being in relation to the being of God."[35] This takes place ultimately in worship, which Guardini considers belongs to the sphere of thought.

In guiding the young, Guardini also discovered a new approach to the liturgy. For him the rediscovery of the liturgy was a rediscovery of the oneness of spirit and flesh in the totality of the single human being, since liturgical action is always at the same time both bodily and spiritual. Prayer is extended through physical and community action, hence the oneness of reality as a whole is revealed. The liturgy is symbolic action. The symbol as the quintessence of the oneness of the spiritual and the material is lost when these separate, when the world is split in half, into spirit and flesh, into subject and object. Guardini was profoundly convinced that man is *spirit in flesh and flesh in spirit* and that the liturgy and the symbol therefore lead him to the essence of himself and ultimately, through worship, to the truth.

---

33. Guardini, *Berichte über mein Leben,* 111.
34. Guardini, *Auf dem Wege* (Mainz: Matthias Grünewald, 1923), 20.
35. Guardini, *Auf dem Wege,* 21.

Among Guardini's great themes of life, the relationship between faith and the world is constantly in the forefront. Guardini saw the university above all as a place for seeking truth.
The university, however, can only be such when it is free from
all exploitation for political advantage or other ends. Today, in
our globalized but fragmented world, it is more important than
ever to fulfill this intention that the Guardini Foundation has
very much at heart and for the realization of which the Guardini
chair was created.

Vocation to Holiness

From *Address to the Community of the Pontifical Ethiopian
College in the Vatican,* January 29, 2011

I would now like to reflect on the luminous figure of St. Justin De
Jacobis, whose important anniversary you celebrated last July 31. A
praiseworthy son of St. Vincent de Paul, St. Justin lived exemplar-
ily, "making himself all things to all people," especially in service
to the Abyssinian people. At the age of thirty-eight he was sent
by Cardinal Franzoni, the then prefect of Propaganda Fide, as a
missionary to Tigrai, Ethiopia. He worked first in Adua and then
in Guala, where he immediately thought of forming Ethiopian
priests, and founded a seminary called "College of the Immacu-
late Virgin." In his zealous ministry he worked tirelessly to ensure
that this portion of the people of God might rediscover the original fervor of faith, sown by the first evangelizer, St. Frumentius.[36]
With farsightedness Justin perceived that attention to the cultural
context must be a privileged path on which the Lord's grace would
form new generations of Christians. Learning the local language
and encouraging the age-old liturgical tradition of the rite of those
communities, his approach was effectively ecumenical. For more
than twenty years his generous priestly, then episcopal ministry

36. Cf. *PL* 21, 473–80.

benefited all those he met and loved as living members of the people entrusted to his care.

Because of his enthusiasm for education, especially for forming priests, he may rightly be considered your college's patron; indeed, this praiseworthy institution still accepts priests and candidates to the priesthood today, supporting them in their commitment to theological, spiritual, and pastoral training.

On returning to your original communities or accompanying your compatriots who have emigrated, may you be able to inspire in each one love for God and for the Church, following the example of St. Justin De Jacobis. He crowned his fruitful contribution to the religious and civil life of the Abyssinian peoples with the gift of his life, silently given back to God after much suffering and persecution. He was beatified by the venerable Pius XII on June 25, 1939 and canonized by the servant of God Paul VI on October 26, 1975.

Dear priests and seminarians, the way of holiness is marked out for you, too! Christ continues to be present in the world and to reveal himself through those who, like St. Justin De Jacobis, allow themselves to be enlivened by his Spirit. The Second Vatican Council reminds us of this, saying, among other things, "God shows to men, in a vivid way, his presence and his face in the lives of those companions of ours in the human condition who are more perfectly transformed into the image of Christ (cf. 2 Cor 3:18). He speaks to us in them and offers us a sign of this Kingdom."[37]

Christ, the eternal priest of the New Covenant, who with his special vocation to the priestly ministry has "conquered" our life, does not suppress the characteristic qualities of the person; on the contrary, he uplifts them, he ennobles them and, making them his own, calls them to serve his mystery and his work. God also needs each one of us so that "in the coming ages he might show the immeasurable riches of his grace in kindness toward us in Christ Jesus" (Eph 2:7).

---

37. Second Vatican Council, *Lumen Gentium*, n. 50.

Despite the individual character of each one's vocation, we are not separated from each other; on the contrary, we are in solidarity, in communion within a single spiritual body. We are called to form the total Christ, a unity recapitulated in the Lord, enlivened by his Sprit to become his "pleroma" and to enrich the canticle of praise that he raises to the Father.

Christ is inseparable from the Church that is his body. It is in the Church that Christ most closely gathers round him the baptized and, nourishing them with his own body and his blood—makes them partakers in his own glorious life.[38]

Holiness is therefore placed in the very heart of the ecclesial mystery and is the vocation to which we are all called. The saints are not external ornaments that adorn the Church, but are like the blossom of a tree that reveals the inexhaustible vitality of the sap that rises in it. It is thus beautiful to contemplate the Church, ascending toward the fullness of the *Vir perfectus* in continuous, demanding, and gradual maturation, dynamically impelled toward complete fulfillment in Christ.

Dear priests and seminarians of the Pontifical Ethiopian College, live with joy and dedication this important period of your formation in the shadow of the dome of St. Peter's. May you walk with determination on the path of holiness. You are a sign of hope, especially for the Church in your native countries. I am sure that the experience of communion you have lived here in Rome will help you also to make a precious contribution to the growth and peaceful coexistence of your beloved nations.

Lex Naturalis

From Address to the Participants in the International Congress
on Natural Moral Law, *February 12, 2007*

There is no doubt that we are living in a moment of extraordinary development in the human capacity to decipher the rules

---

38. Second Vatican Council, *Lumen Gentium,* n. 48.

and structures of matter, and in the consequent dominion of man over nature.

We all see the great advantages of this progress, and we see more and more clearly the threat of destruction of nature by what we do.

There is another, less visible danger, but no less disturbing: the method that permits us to know ever more deeply the rational structures of matter makes us ever less capable of perceiving the source of this rationality—creative reason. The capacity to see the laws of material being makes us incapable of seeing the ethical message contained in being, a message that tradition calls *lex naturalis,* natural moral law.

This word for many today is almost incomprehensible due to a concept of nature that is no longer metaphysical, but only empirical. The fact that nature, being itself, is no longer a transparent moral message creates a sense of disorientation that renders the choices of daily life precarious and uncertain.

Naturally the disorientation strikes the younger generations, who must in this context find the fundamental choices for their lives, in a particular way.

It is precisely in the light of this contestation that all the urgency of the necessity to reflect upon the theme of natural law and to rediscover its truth common to all men appears. The said law, to which the Apostle Paul refers (cf. Rom 2:14–15), is written on the heart of man and is consequently, even today, accessible.

This law has as its first and general principle, "to do good and to avoid evil." This is a truth that by its very evidence immediately imposes itself on everyone. From it flow the other, more particular principles that regulate ethical justice on the rights and duties of everyone.

So does the principle of respect for *human life* from its conception to its natural end, because this good of life is not man's property, but the free gift of God. Beside this is the duty *to seek the truth* as the necessary presupposition of every authentic personal maturation.

Another fundamental application of the subject is *freedom*. Yet taking into account the fact that human freedom is always a freedom shared with others, it is clear that the harmony of freedom can be found only in what is common to all: the truth of the human being, the fundamental message of being itself, exactly the *lex naturalis*.

And how can we not mention, on one hand, the demand of *justice* that manifests itself in giving *unicuique suum* and, on the other, the expectation of *solidarity* that nourishes in everyone, especially if they are poor, the hope of the help of the more fortunate?

In these values are expressed unbreakable and contingent norms that do not depend on the will of the legislator, and not even on the consensus that the state can and must give. They are, in fact, norms that precede any human law; as such, they are not subject to modification by anyone.

The natural law, together with fundamental rights, is the source from which ethical imperatives also flow, which it is only right to honor.

In today's ethics and philosophy of law, petitions of juridical positivism are widespread. As a result, legislation often becomes only a compromise between different interests seeking to transform private interests or wishes into law that conflict with the duties deriving from social responsibility.

In this situation it is opportune to recall that every juridical methodology, be it on the local or international level, ultimately draws its legitimacy from its rooting in the natural law, in the ethical message inscribed in the actual human being.

Natural law is, definitively, the only valid bulwark against the arbitrary power or the deception of ideological manipulation. The knowledge of this law inscribed on the heart of man increases with the progress of the moral conscience.

The first duty for all, and particularly for those with public responsibility, must therefore be to promote the maturation of the moral conscience. This is the fundamental progress without which all other progress proves nonauthentic.

The law inscribed in our nature is the true guarantee offered to everyone in order to be able to live in freedom and to be respected in his or her own dignity.

What has been said up to this point has very concrete applications if one refers to the family—that is, to "the intimate partnership of life and the love which constitutes the married state ... established by the Creator and endowed by him with its own proper laws."[39]

Concerning this, the Second Vatican Council has opportunely recalled that the institution of marriage has been "confirmed by the divine law," and therefore "this sacred bond ... for the good of the partner, of the children and of society no longer depends on human decision alone."[40]

Therefore, no law made by man can override the norm written by the Creator without society becoming dramatically wounded in what constitutes its basic foundation. To forget this would mean to weaken the family, penalizing the children and rendering the future of society precarious.

Lastly, I feel the duty to affirm yet again that not all that is scientifically possible is also ethically licit.

Technology, when it reduces the human being to an object of experimentation, results in abandoning the weak subject to the arbitration of the stronger. To blindly entrust oneself to technology as the only guarantee of progress, without offering at the same time an ethical code that penetrates its roots in that same reality under study and development, would be equal to doing violence to human nature, with devastating consequences for all.

The contribution of scientists is of primary importance. Together with the progress of our capacity to dominate nature, sci-

39. Second Vatican Council, *Gaudium et Spes*, n. 48.
40. Second Vatican Council, *Gaudium et Spes*, n. 48.

entists must also contribute to help understand the depth of our responsibility for man and for nature entrusted to him.

On this basis it is possible to develop a fruitful dialogue between believers and nonbelievers, between theologians, philosophers, jurists, and scientists—a dialogue that can offer to legislation as well precious material for personal and social life.

Therefore, I hope these days of study will bring not only a greater sensitivity of the learned with regard to the natural moral law, but will also serve to create conditions so that this theme may reach an ever fuller awareness of the inalienable value that the *lex naturalis* possesses for a real and coherent progress of private life and the social order.

Religion: Vital Contributor to the National Conversation

From *Address to Representatives of British Society, Including the Diplomatic Corps, Politicians, Academics, and Business Leaders,* Apostolic Journey to the United Kingdom, Westminster, September 17, 2010

As I address you, I am conscious of the privilege afforded me to speak to the British people and their representatives in Westminster Hall, a building of unique significance in the civil and political history of the people of these islands. Allow me also to express my esteem for the Parliament that has existed on this site for centuries and that has had such a profound influence on the development of participative government among the nations, especially in the Commonwealth and the English-speaking world at large. Your common law tradition serves as the basis of legal systems in many parts of the world, and your particular vision of the respective rights and duties of the state and the individual, and of the separation of powers, remains an inspiration to many across the globe.

As I speak to you in this historic setting, I think of the countless men and women down the centuries who have played their part in the momentous events that have taken place within these walls and have shaped the lives of many generations of Britons, and others besides. In particular, I recall the figure of St. Thomas More, the great English scholar and statesman, who is admired by believers and nonbelievers alike for the integrity with which he followed his conscience, even at the cost of displeasing the sovereign whose "good servant" he was, because he chose to serve God first. The dilemma that faced More in those difficult times, the perennial question of the relationship between what is owed to Caesar and what is owed to God, allows me the opportunity to reflect with you briefly on the proper place of religious belief within the political process.

This country's parliamentary tradition owes much to the national instinct for moderation, to the desire to achieve a genuine balance between the legitimate claims of government and the rights of those subject to it. While decisive steps have been taken at several points in your history to place limits on the exercise of power, the nation's political institutions have been able to evolve with a remarkable degree of stability. In the process, Britain has emerged as a pluralist democracy that places great value on freedom of speech, freedom of political affiliation, and respect for the rule of law, with a strong sense of the individual's rights and duties, and of the equality of all citizens before the law. While couched in different language, Catholic social teaching has much in common with this approach in its overriding concern to safeguard the unique dignity of every human person, created in the image and likeness of God, and in its emphasis on the duty of civil authority to foster the common good.

And yet the fundamental questions at stake in Thomas More's trial continue to present themselves in ever-changing terms as new social conditions emerge. Each generation, as it seeks to advance the common good, must ask anew: what are the requirements that governments may reasonably impose upon citizens, and how far do they extend? By appeal to what authority can moral dilemmas be resolved? These questions take us directly to the ethical foundations of civil discourse. If the moral principles underpinning the democratic process are themselves determined by nothing more solid than social consensus, then the fragility of the process becomes all too evident—herein lies the real challenge for democracy.

The inadequacy of pragmatic, short-term solutions to complex social and ethical problems has been illustrated all too clearly by the recent global financial crisis. There is widespread agreement that the lack of a solid ethical foundation for economic activity has contributed to the grave difficulties now being experienced by millions of people throughout the world. Just as "every economic decision has a moral consequence,"[41] so too in the political field, the ethical dimension of policy has far-reaching consequences that no government can afford to ignore. A positive illustration of this is found in one of the British Parliament's particularly notable achievements—the abolition of the slave trade. The campaign that led to this landmark legislation was built upon firm ethical principles, rooted in the natural law, and it has made a contribution to civilization of which this nation may be justly proud.

The central question at issue, then, is this: where is the ethical foundation for political choices to be found? The Catholic tradition maintains that the objective norms governing right action are accessible to reason, prescinding from the content of revelation. According to this understanding, the role of religion in political debate is not so much to supply these norms, as if they could not be known by nonbelievers—still less to propose concrete political solutions, which would lie altogether outside the competence of religion—but rather to help purify and shed light upon the application of reason to the discovery of objective moral principles. This "corrective" role of religion vis-à-vis

41. Benedict XVI, *Caritas in Veritate*, n. 37.

reason is not always welcomed, though, partly because distorted forms of religion, such as sectarianism and fundamentalism, can be seen to create serious social problems themselves. And in their turn, these distortions of religion arise when insufficient attention is given to the purifying and structuring role of reason within religion. It is a two-way process. Without the corrective supplied by religion, though, reason too can fall prey to distortions, as when it is manipulated by ideology or applied in a partial way that fails to take full account of the dignity of the human person. Such misuse of reason, after all, was what gave rise to the slave trade in the first place and to many other social evils, not least the totalitarian ideologies of the twentieth century. This is why I would suggest that the world of reason and the world of faith—the world of secular rationality and the world of religious belief—need one another and should not be afraid to enter into a profound and ongoing dialogue for the good of our civilization.

Religion, in other words, is not a problem for legislators to solve, but a vital contributor to the national conversation. In this light I cannot but voice my concern at the increasing marginalization of religion, particularly of Christianity, that is taking place in some quarters, even in nations that place a great emphasis on tolerance. There are those who would advocate that the voice of religion be silenced, or at least relegated to the purely private sphere. There are those who argue that the public celebration of festivals such as Christmas should be discouraged, in the questionable belief that it might somehow offend those of other religions or none. And there are those who argue—paradoxically with the intention of eliminating discrimination—that Christians in public roles should be required at times to act against their conscience. These are worrying signs of a failure to appreciate not only the rights of believers to freedom of conscience and freedom of religion, but also the legitimate role of religion in the public square. I would invite all of you, therefore, within your respective spheres of influence, to seek ways of promoting and encouraging dialogue between faith and reason at every level of national life.

Your readiness to do so is already implied in the unprecedented invitation extended to me today. And it finds expression in the fields of concern in which your government has been engaged with the Holy See. In the area of peace there have been exchanges regarding the elaboration of an international arms trade treaty; regarding human rights, the Holy See and the United Kingdom have welcomed the spread of democracy, especially in the last sixty-five years; in the field of development, there has been collaboration on debt relief, fair trade, and financing for development, particularly through the International Finance Facility, the International Immunization Bond, and the Advanced Market Commitment. The Holy See also looks forward to exploring with the United Kingdom new ways to promote environmental responsibility, to the benefit of all.

I also note that the present government has committed the United Kingdom to devoting 0.7 percent of national income to development aid by 2013. In recent years it has been encouraging to witness the positive signs of a worldwide growth in solidarity toward the poor. But to turn this solidarity into effective action calls for fresh thinking that will improve life conditions in many important areas, such as food production, clean water, job creation, education, support to families, especially migrants, and basic healthcare. Where human lives are concerned, time is always short; yet the world has witnessed the vast resources that governments can draw upon to rescue financial institutions deemed "too big to fail." Surely the integral human development of the world's peoples is no less important: here is an enterprise, worthy of the world's attention, that is truly "too big to fail."

This overview of recent cooperation between the United Kingdom and the Holy See illustrates well how much progress has been made, in the years that have passed since the establish-

ment of bilateral diplomatic relations, in promoting throughout the world the many core values that we share. I hope and
pray that this relationship will continue to bear fruit, and that
it will be mirrored in a growing acceptance of the need for dialogue and respect at every level of society between the world of
reason and the world of faith. I am convinced that, within this
country, too, there are many areas in which the Church and the
public authorities can work together for the good of citizens,
in harmony with this parliament's historic practice of invoking
the Spirit's guidance upon those who seek to improve the conditions of all mankind. For such cooperation to be possible,
religious bodies—including institutions linked to the Catholic
Church—need to be free to act in accordance with their own
principles and specific convictions, based upon the faith and the
official teaching of the Church. In this way, such basic rights as
religious freedom, freedom of conscience, and freedom of association are guaranteed. The angels looking down on us from the
magnificent ceiling of this ancient hall remind us of the long tradition from which British parliamentary democracy has evolved.
They remind us that God is constantly watching over us to guide
and protect us. And they summon us to acknowledge the vital
contribution that religious belief has made and can continue to
make to the life of the nation.

The Listening Heart: Reflections on
the Foundations of Law

From *Address to the Bundestag,* Apostolic Journey to Germany,
Berlin, September 22, 2011

It is an honor and a joy for me to speak before this distinguished
house, before the parliament of my native Germany, which meets
here as a democratically elected representation of the people, in
order to work for the good of the Federal Republic of Germany.
I should like to thank the president of the *Bundestag,* both for

his invitation to deliver this address and for the kind words of greeting and appreciation with which he has welcomed me. At this moment I turn to you, distinguished ladies and gentlemen, not least as your fellow countryman, who for all his life has been conscious of close links to his origins, and has followed the affairs of his native Germany with keen interest. But the invitation to give this address was extended to me as pope, as the bishop of Rome, who bears the highest responsibility for Catholic Christianity. In issuing this invitation you are acknowledging the role that the Holy See plays as a partner within the community of peoples and states. Setting out from this international responsibility that I hold, I should like to propose to you some thoughts on the foundations of a free state of law.

Allow me to begin my reflections on the foundations of law [*Recht*] with a brief story from sacred scripture. In the First Book of the Kings, it is recounted that God invited the young King Solomon, on his accession to the throne, to make a request. What will the young ruler ask for at this important moment? Success—wealth—long life—destruction of his enemies? He chooses none of these things. Instead, he asks for a listening heart so that he may govern God's people and discern between good and evil (cf. 1 Kings 3:9). Through this story the Bible wants to tell us what should ultimately matter for a politician. His fundamental criterion and the motivation for his work as a politician must not be success, and certainly not material gain. Politics must be a striving for justice, and hence it has to establish the fundamental preconditions for peace. Naturally a politician will seek success, without which he would have no opportunity for effective political action at all. Yet success is subordinated to the criterion of justice, to the will to do what is right, and to the understanding of what is right. Success can also be seductive, and thus can open up the path toward the falsification of what is right, toward the destruction of justice. "Without justice—what else is the state but a great band of robbers?" as St. Augustine once said. We Germans know from our own experience that these words are no empty specter. We have seen how power became divorced from right, how power opposed right and crushed it, so that the state became an instrument for destroying right—a highly organized band of robbers, capable of threatening the whole world and driving it to the edge of the abyss. To serve right and to fight against the dominion of wrong is and remains the fundamental task of the politician. At a moment in history when man has acquired previously inconceivable power, this task takes on a particular urgency. Man can destroy the world. He can manipulate himself. He can, so to speak, make human beings, and he can deny them their humanity. How do we recognize what is right? How can we discern between good and evil, between what is truly right and what may appear right? Even now, Solomon's request remains the decisive issue facing politicians and politics today.

For most of the matters that need to be regulated by law, the support of the majority can serve as a sufficient criterion. Yet it is evident that, for the fundamental issues of law, in which the dignity of man and of humanity is at stake, the majority principle is not enough; everyone in a position of responsibility must personally seek out the criteria to be followed when framing laws. In the third century the great theologian Origen provided the following explanation for the resistance of Christians to certain legal systems: "Suppose that a man were living among the Scythians, whose laws are contrary to the divine law, and was compelled to live among them ... such a man for the sake of the true law, though illegal among the Scythians, would rightly form associations with like-minded people contrary to the laws of the Scythians."[42]

This conviction was what motivated resistance movements to

42. Origen of Alexandria, *Contra Celsum*, bk 1, chap. 1; cf. Alfons Fürst, "Monotheismus und Monarchie. Zum Zusammenhang von Heil und Herrschaft in der Antike," *Theologie und Philosophie* 81 (2006): 321–38, quoted on 336; cf. also Ratzinger, *Die Einheit der Nationen: Eine Vision der Kirchenväter* (Salzburg and Munich: Pustet, 1971), 60.

act against the Nazi regime and other totalitarian regimes, thereby doing a great service to justice and to humanity as a whole. For these people it was indisputably evident that the law in force was actually unlawful. Yet when it comes to the decisions of a democratic politician, the question of what now corresponds to the law of truth, what is actually right and may be enacted as law, is less obvious. In terms of the underlying anthropological issues, what is right and may be given the force of law is in no way simply self-evident today. The question of how to recognize what is truly right and thus to serve justice when framing laws has never been simple, and today, in view of the vast extent of our knowledge and our capacity, it has become still harder.

How do we recognize what is right? In history, systems of law have almost always been based on religion; decisions regarding what was to be lawful among men were taken with reference to the divinity. Unlike other great religions, Christianity has never proposed a revealed law to the state and to society—that is to say, a juridical order derived from revelation. Instead, it has pointed to nature and reason as the true sources of law—and to the harmony of objective and subjective reason, which naturally presupposes that both spheres are rooted in the creative reason of God. Christian theologians thereby aligned themselves with a philosophical and juridical movement that began to take shape in the second century B.C. In the first half of that century, the social natural law developed by the Stoic philosophers came into contact with leading teachers of Roman law.[43] Through this encounter the juridical culture of the West was born, which was and is of key significance for the juridical culture of mankind. This pre-Christian marriage between law and philosophy opened up the path that led via the Christian Middle Ages and the juridical developments of the age of Enlightenment all the way to the Declaration of Human Rights and to our German Ba-

43. Cf. Wolfgang Waldstein, *Ins Herz geschrieben: Das Naturrecht als Fundament einer menschlichen Gesellschaft* (Augsburg: Sankt Ulrich Verlag, 2010), 11ff., 31–61.

sic Law of 1949, with which our nation committed itself to "inviolable and inalienable human rights as the foundation of every human community, and of peace and justice in the world."

For the development of law and for the development of humanity, it was highly significant that Christian theologians aligned themselves against the religious law associated with polytheism and on the side of philosophy, and that they acknowledged reason and nature in their interrelation as the universally valid source of law. This step had already been taken by St. Paul in the Letter to the Romans when he said, "When Gentiles who have not the Law [the Torah of Israel] do by nature what the law requires, they are a law to themselves ... they show that what the law requires is written on their hearts, while their conscience also bears witness" (Rom 2:14f). Here we see the two fundamental concepts of nature and conscience, where conscience is nothing other than Solomon's listening heart, reason that is open to the language of being. If this seemed to offer a clear explanation of the foundations of legislation up to the time of the Enlightenment, up to the time of the Declaration on Human Rights after the Second World War and the framing of our Basic Law, there has been a dramatic shift in the situation in the last half century. The idea of natural law is today viewed as a specifically Catholic doctrine, not worth bringing into the discussion in a non-Catholic environment, so that one feels almost ashamed even to mention the term. Let me outline briefly how this situation arose. Fundamentally it is because of the idea that an unbridgeable gulf exists between "is" and "ought." An "ought" can never follow from an "is," because the two are situated on completely different planes. The reason for this is that in the meantime, the positivist understanding of nature has come to be almost universally accepted. If nature—in the words of Hans Kelsen—is viewed as "an aggregate of objective data linked together in terms of cause and effect," then indeed no ethical indication of any kind can be derived from it.[44] A positivist conception of na-

44. Cf. Waldstein, *Ins Herz geschrieben*, 15–21.

ture as purely functional, as the natural sciences consider it to be, is incapable of producing any bridge to ethics and law, but once again yields only functional answers. The same also applies to reason, according to the positivist understanding that is widely held to be the only genuinely scientific one. Anything that is not verifiable or falsifiable, according to this understanding, does not belong to the realm of reason strictly understood. Hence ethics and religion must be assigned to the subjective field, and they remain extraneous to the realm of reason in the strict sense of the word. Where positivist reason dominates the field to the exclusion of all else—and that is broadly the case in our public mindset—then the classical sources of knowledge for ethics and law are excluded. This is a dramatic situation that affects everyone, and on which a public debate is necessary. Indeed, an essential goal of this address is to issue an urgent invitation to launch one.

The positivist approach to nature and reason, the positivist worldview in general, is a most important dimension of human knowledge and capacity that we may in no way dispense with. But in and of itself it is not a sufficient culture corresponding to the full breadth of the human condition. Where positivist reason considers itself the only sufficient culture and banishes all other cultural realities to the status of subcultures, it diminishes man—indeed, it threatens his humanity. I say this with Europe specifically in mind, where there are concerted efforts to recognize only positivism as a common culture and a common basis for lawmaking, reducing all the other insights and values of our culture to the level of subculture, with the result that Europe vis-à-vis other world cultures is left in a state of culturelessness at the same time that extremist and radical movements emerge to fill the vacuum. In its self-proclaimed exclusivity, the positivist reason that recognizes nothing beyond mere functionality resembles a concrete bunker with no windows, in which we ourselves provide lighting and atmospheric conditions, being no longer willing to obtain either from God's wide world. And yet we cannot hide from ourselves the fact that even in this artificial world, we are still covertly drawing upon God's raw materials, which we refashion into our own products. The windows must be flung open again; we must see the wide world, the sky, and the earth once more and learn to make proper use of all this.

But how are we to do this? How do we find our way out into the wide world, into the big picture? How can reason rediscover its true greatness, without being sidetracked into irrationality? How can nature reassert itself in its true depth, with all its demands, with all its directives? I would like to recall one of the developments in recent political history, hoping that I will neither be misunderstood nor provoke too many one-sided polemics. I would say that the emergence of the ecological movement in German politics since the 1970s, while it has not exactly flung open the windows, nevertheless was and continues to be a cry for fresh air that must not be ignored or pushed aside, just because too much of it is seen to be irrational. Young people had come to realize that something is wrong in our relationship with nature, that matter is not just raw material for us to shape at will, but that the earth has a dignity of its own and that we must follow its directives. In saying this, I am clearly not promoting any particular political party—nothing could be further from my mind. If something is wrong in our relationship with reality, then we must all reflect seriously on the whole situation, and we are all prompted to question the very foundations of our culture. Allow me to dwell a little longer on this point. The importance of ecology is no longer disputed. We must listen to the language of nature, and we must answer accordingly. Yet I would like to underline a point that seems to me to be neglected, today as in the past: there is also an ecology of man. Man too has a nature that he must respect and that he cannot manipulate at will. Man is not merely self-creating freedom. Man does not create himself. He is intellect and will, but he is also nature, and his will is rightly ordered if he respects his nature, listens to it, and accepts himself for who he is, as one who did not create himself. In this way, and in no other, is true human freedom fulfilled.

Let us come back to the fundamental concepts of nature and reason, from which we set out. The great proponent of legal positivism, Kelsen, at the age of eighty-four—in 1965—abandoned the dualism of "is" and "ought." (I find it comforting that rational thought is evidently still possible at the age of 84!) Previously he had said that norms can only come from the will. Nature therefore could only contain norms, he adds, if a will had put them there. But this, he says, would presuppose a Creator God, whose will had entered into nature. "Any attempt to discuss the truth of this belief is utterly futile," he observed.[45] Is it really?—I find myself asking. Is it really pointless to wonder whether the objective reason that manifests itself in nature does not presuppose a creative reason, a *Creator Spiritus?*

At this point Europe's cultural heritage ought to come to our assistance. The conviction that there is a Creator God is what gave rise to the idea of human rights, the idea of the equality of all people before the law, the recognition of the inviolability of human dignity in every single person, and the awareness of people's responsibility for their actions. Our cultural memory is shaped by these rational insights. To ignore it or dismiss it as a thing of the past would be to dismember our culture totally and to rob it of its completeness. The culture of Europe arose from the encounter between Jerusalem, Athens, and Rome—from the encounter between Israel's monotheism, the philosophical reason of the Greeks, and Roman law. This three-way encounter has shaped the inner identity of Europe. In the awareness of man's responsibility before God and in the acknowledgment of the inviolable dignity of every single human person, it has established criteria of law; it is these criteria that we are called to defend at this moment in our history.

45. Cf. Waldstein, *Ins Herz geschrieben,* 19.

As he assumed the mantle of office, the young King Solomon was invited to make a request. How would it be if we, the lawmakers of today, were invited to make a request? What would we ask for? I think that, even today, there is ultimately nothing else we could wish for but a listening heart—the capacity to discern between good and evil, and thus to establish true law, to serve justice and peace. I thank you for your attention!

6. CULTURE AND THE UNIVERSITY

Quaerere Deum

From *Address to Representatives from the World of Culture at the "Collège des Bernardins" in Paris,* Apostolic Journey to France, Paris, September 12, 2008

I would like to speak with you this evening of the origins of Western theology and the roots of European culture. I began by recalling that the place in which we are gathered is in a certain way emblematic. It is in fact a place tied to monastic culture, insofar as young monks came to live here in order to learn to understand their vocation more deeply and to be more faithful to their mission. We are in a place that is associated with the culture of monasticism. Does this still have something to say to us today, or are we merely encountering the world of the past? In order to answer this question, we must consider for a moment the nature of Western monasticism itself. What was it about? From the perspective of monasticism's historical influence we could say that, amid the great cultural upheaval resulting from migrations of peoples and the emerging new political configurations, the monasteries were the places where the treasures of ancient culture survived, and where at the same time a new culture slowly took shape out of the old. But how did it happen? What motivated men to come together to these places? What did they want? How did they live?

First and foremost, it must be frankly admitted straight away that it was not their intention to create a culture, or even to preserve a culture from the past. Their motivation was much more basic. Their goal was *quaerere Deum.* Amid the confusion of the times, in which nothing seemed permanent, they wanted to do the essential—to make an effort to find what was perennially valid and lasting—life itself. They were searching for God. They wanted to go from the inessential to the essential, to the only truly important and reliable thing there is. It is sometimes said that they were "eschatologically" oriented. But this is not to be understood in a temporal sense, as if they were looking ahead to the end of the world or to their own death, but in an existential sense: they were seeking the definitive behind the provisional. *Quaerere Deum:* because they were Christians, this was not an expedition into a trackless wilderness, a search leading them into total darkness. God himself had provided signposts—indeed, he had marked out a path that was theirs to find and to follow. This path was his word, which had been disclosed to men in the books of the sacred scriptures. Thus, by inner necessity, the search for God demands a culture of the word, or,—as Jean Leclercq put it, eschatology and grammar are intimately connected with one another in Western monasticism.[1] The longing for God, the *désir de Dieu,* includes *amour des lettres,* love of the word, exploration of all its dimensions. Because in the biblical word God comes toward us and we toward him, we must learn to penetrate the secret of language, to understand it in its construction and in the manner of its expression. Thus it is through the search for God that the secular sciences take on their importance, sciences that show us the path toward language. Because the search for God required the culture of the word, it was appropriate that the monastery should have a library, pointing out pathways to the word. It was also appropriate to have a school in which these

1. Cf. Jean Leclercq, *L'amour des letters et le désir de Dieu: Initiation aux auteurs monasiques du Moyen Âge* (Paris: Cerf, 2008).

pathways could be opened up. Benedict calls the monastery a *dominici servitii schola.* The monastery serves *eruditio,* the formation and education of man—a formation whose ultimate aim is that man should learn how to serve God. But it also includes the formation of reason—education—through which man learns to perceive, in the midst of words, the Word itself.

Yet in order to have a full vision of the culture of the word, which essentially pertains to the search for God, we must take a further step. The Word, which opens the path of that search, and is to be identified with this path, is a shared word. True, it pierces every individual to the heart (cf. Acts 2:37). Gregory the Great describes this as a sharp stabbing pain, which tears open our sleeping soul and awakens us, making us attentive to the essential reality, to God.[2] But in the process, it also makes us attentive to one another. The word does not lead to a purely individual path of mystical immersion, but to the pilgrim fellowship of faith. And so this word must not only be pondered, but also correctly read. As in the rabbinic schools, so too with the monks, reading by the individual is at the same time a corporate activity. "But if *legere* and *lectio* are used without an explanatory note, then they designate for the most part an activity that, like singing and writing, engages the whole body and the whole spirit," says Jean Leclercq on the subject.[3]

And once again, a further step is needed. We ourselves are brought into conversation with God by the word of God. The God who speaks in the Bible teaches us how to speak with him ourselves. Particularly in the book of Psalms, he gives us the words with which we can address him, with which we can bring our life, with all its high points and low points, into conversation with him, so that life itself thereby becomes a movement toward him. The psalms also contain frequent instructions about how they should be sung and accompanied by instruments. For

2. Cf. Leclercq, *L'amour des letters,* 35.
3. Leclercq, *L'amour des letters,* 21.

prayer that issues from the word of God, speech is not enough: music is required. Two chants from the Christian liturgy come from biblical texts in which they are placed on the lips of angels: the Gloria, which is sung by the angels at the birth of Jesus, and the Sanctus, which, according to *Isaiah 6*, is the cry of the seraphim who stand directly before God. Christian worship is therefore an invitation to sing with the angels, and thus to lead the word to its highest destination. Once again, Jean Leclercq says on this subject, "The monks had to find melodies that translate into music the acceptance by redeemed man of the mysteries that he celebrates. The few surviving *capitula* from Cluny thus show the Christological symbols of the individual modes."[4]

For Benedict the words of the Psalm—*coram angelis psallam Tibi, Domine*—"in the presence of the angels, I will sing your praise" (cf. Ps 138:1)—are the decisive rule governing the prayer and chant of the monks. What this expresses is the awareness that in communal prayer one is singing in the presence of the entire heavenly court and is thereby measured according to the very highest standards; that one is praying and singing in such a way as to harmonize with the music of the noble spirits who were considered the originators of the harmony of the cosmos, the music of the spheres. From this perspective one can understand the seriousness of a remark by St. Bernard of Clairvaux, who used an expression from the Platonic tradition handed down by Augustine, to pass judgment on the poor singing of monks, which for him was evidently very far from being a mishap of only minor importance. He describes the confusion resulting from a poorly executed chant as a falling into the "zone of dissimilarity"—the *regio dissimilitudinis*. Augustine had borrowed this phrase from Platonic philosophy in order to designate his condition prior to conversion: man, who is created in God's likeness, falls in his godforsakenness into the "zone of dissimilarity"—into a remoteness from God, in which he no

---

4. Leclercq, *L'amour des letters*, 229.

longer reflects him, and so has become dissimilar not only to God, but to himself, to what being human truly is.[5] Bernard is certainly putting it strongly when he uses this phrase, which indicates man's falling away from himself, to describe bad singing by monks. But it shows how seriously he viewed the matter. It shows that the culture of singing is also the culture of being, and that the monks have to pray and sing in a manner commensurate with the grandeur of the word handed down to them, with its claim on true beauty. This intrinsic requirement of speaking with God and singing of him with words he himself has given is what gave rise to the great tradition of Western music. It was not a form of private "creativity," in which the individual leaves a memorial to himself and makes self-representation his essential criterion. Rather it is about vigilantly recognizing with the "ears of the heart" the inner laws of the music of creation, the archetypes of music that the Creator built into his world and into men, and thus discovering music that is worthy of God, and at the same time truly worthy of man—music whose worthiness resounds in purity.

In order to understand to some degree the culture of the word, which developed deep within Western monasticism from the search for God, we need to touch at least briefly on the particular character of the book, or rather books, in which the monks encountered this word. The Bible, considered from a purely historical and literary perspective, is not simply a book, but a collection of literary texts that were redacted over the course of more than a thousand years, and in which the inner unity of the individual books is not immediately apparent. On the contrary, there are visible tensions between them. This is already the case within the Bible of Israel, which we Christians call the Old Testament. It is only rectified when we as Christians link the New Testament writings as, so to speak, a hermeneutical key with the Bible of Israel, and so understand the latter as the journey toward Christ.

5. Augustine, *Confessions* VII.10.16.

With good reason, the New Testament generally designates the Bible not as "the Scripture" but as "the Scriptures," which, when taken together, are naturally then regarded as the one word of God to us. But the use of this plural makes it quite clear that the word of God only comes to us through the human word and through human words—that God only speaks to us through the humanity of human agents, through their words and their history. This means again that the divine element in the word and in the words is not self-evident. To say this in a modern way: the unity of the biblical books and the divine character of their words cannot be grasped by purely historical methods. The historical element is seen in the multiplicity and the humanity. From this perspective one can understand the formulation of a medieval couplet that at first sight appears rather disconcerting: *littera gesta docet—quid credas allegoria.*[6] The letter indicates the facts; what you have to believe is indicated by allegory—that is to say, by Christological and pneumatological exegesis.

We may put it even more simply: Scripture requires exegesis, and it requires the context of the community in which it came to birth and in which it is lived. This is where its unity is to be found, and here too its unifying meaning is opened up. To put it yet another way: there are dimensions of meaning in the word and in words that only come to light within the living community of this history-generating word. Through the growing realization of the different layers of meaning, the word is not devalued, but in fact appears in its full grandeur and dignity. Therefore the *Catechism of the Catholic Church* can rightly say that Christianity does not simply represent a religion of the book in the classical sense.[7] It perceives in the words *"the* Word" the *Logos* itself, which spreads its mystery through this multiplicity and the reality of a human history. This particular structure of the Bible issues a constantly new challenge to every generation. It excludes

---

6. Cf. Augustine of Dacia, *Rotulus pugillaris* I.
7. Cf. *Catechism of the Catholic Church* (1993), n. 108.

by its nature everything that today is known as fundamentalism. In effect the word of God can never simply be equated with the letter of the text. To attain to it involves a transcending and a process of understanding, led by the inner movement of the whole, and hence it also has to become a process of living. Only within the dynamic unity of the whole are the many books *one* book. The word of God and his action in the world are revealed only in the word and history of human beings.

The whole drama of this topic is illuminated in the writings of St. Paul. What is meant by transcending the letter and understanding it solely from the perspective of the whole, he forcefully expressed as follows: "The letter kills, but the Spirit gives life" (2 Cor 3:6). And he continues, "Where the Spirit is ... there is freedom" (cf. 2 Cor 3:17). But one can only understand the greatness and breadth of this vision of the biblical word if one listens closely to Paul and then discovers that this liberating Spirit has a name, and hence that freedom has an inner criterion: "The Lord is the Spirit. Where the Spirit is ... there is freedom" (2 Cor 3:17). The liberating Spirit is not simply the exegete's own idea, the exegete's own vision. The Spirit is Christ, and Christ is the Lord who shows us the way. With the word of Spirit and of freedom, a further horizon opens up, but at the same time a clear limit is placed upon arbitrariness and subjectivity, which unequivocally binds both the individual and the community and brings about a new, higher obligation than that of the letter—namely, the obligation of insight and love. This tension between obligation and freedom, which extends far beyond the literary problem of scriptural exegesis, has also determined the thinking and acting of monasticism and has deeply marked Western culture. This tension presents itself anew as a challenge for our own generation as we face two poles: on the one hand, subjective arbitrariness, and on the other, fundamentalist fanaticism. It would be a disaster if today's European culture could only conceive freedom as absence of obligation, which would inevitably play into the hands of fanaticism and arbitrariness. Absence of obligation and arbitrariness do not signify freedom, but its destruction.

Thus far in our consideration of the "school of God's service," as St. Benedict describes monasticism, we have examined only its orientation toward the word—toward the "*ora.*" Indeed, this is the starting point that sets the direction for the entire monastic life. But our consideration would remain incomplete if we did not also at least briefly glance at the second component of monasticism, indicated by the "*labora.*" In the Greek world manual labor was considered something for slaves. Only the wise man, the one who is truly free, devotes himself to the things of the spirit; he views manual labor as somehow beneath him, and leaves it to people who are not suited to this higher existence in the world of the spirit. The Jewish tradition was quite different: all the great rabbis practiced at the same time some form of handcraft. Paul, who as a rabbi and then as a preacher of the gospel to the Gentile world was also a tentmaker and earned his living with the work of his own hands, is no exception here, but stands within the common tradition of the rabbinate. Monasticism took up this tradition; manual work is a constitutive element of Christian monasticism. In his *Regula,* St. Benedict does not speak specifically about schools, although in practice he presupposes teaching and learning, as we have seen. However, in one chapter of his Rule, he does speak explicitly about work.[8] And so does Augustine, who dedicated a book of his own to monastic work. Christians, who thus continued in the tradition previously established by Judaism, must have felt further vindicated by Jesus's saying in St. John's Gospel, in defense of his activity on the Sabbath: "My Father is working still, and I am working" (Jn 5:17). The Graeco-Roman world did not have a creator God; according to its vision, the highest divinity could not, as it were, dirty his hands in the business of creating matter. The "making" of the world was the work of the Demiurge,

8. Cf. Benedict, *Regula,* chap. 48.

a lower deity. The Christian God is different: he, the one, real, and only God, is also the Creator. God is working; he continues working in and on human history. In Christ he enters personally into the laborious work of history. "My Father is working still, and I am working." God himself is the Creator of the world, and creation is not yet finished. God works, *ergázetai!* Thus human work was now seen as a special form of human resemblance to God, as a way in which man can and may share in God's activity as creator of the world. Monasticism involves not only a culture of the word, but also a culture of work, without which the emergence of Europe, its ethos, and its influence on the world would be unthinkable. Naturally this ethos had to include the idea that human work and shaping of history is understood as sharing in the work of the Creator and must be evaluated in those terms. Where such evaluation is lacking, where man arrogates to himself the status of god-like creator, his shaping of the world can quickly turn into destruction of the world.

We set out from the premise that the basic attitude of monks in the face of the collapse of the old order and its certainties was *quaerere Deum*—setting out in search of God. We could describe this as the truly philosophical attitude: looking beyond the penultimate, and setting out in search of the ultimate and the true. By becoming a monk a man set out on a broad and noble path, but he had already found the direction he needed: the word of the Bible, in which he heard God himself speaking. Now he had to try to understand him, so as to be able to approach him. So the monastic journey is indeed a journey into the inner world of the received word, even if an infinite distance is involved. Within the monks' seeking there is already contained, in some respects, a finding. Therefore, if such seeking is to be possible at all, there has to be an initial spur, which not only arouses the will to seek, but also makes it possible to believe that the way is concealed within this word, or rather that in this word, God himself has set out toward men, and hence men can come to God through it.

To put it another way, there must be proclamation, which speaks to man and so creates conviction, which in turn can become life. If a way is to be opened up into the heart of the biblical word as God's word, this word must first of all be proclaimed outwardly. The classic formulation of the Christian faith's intrinsic need to make itself communicable to others is a phrase from the First Letter of Peter, which in medieval theology was regarded as the biblical basis for the work of theologians: "Always have your answer ready for people who ask you the reason (the *logos*) for the hope that you all have" (1 Pet 3:15). (The *Logos,* the reason for hope, must become *apo-logía;* it must become a response). In fact, Christians of the nascent Church did not regard their missionary proclamation as propaganda, designed to enlarge their particular group, but as an inner necessity, consequent upon the nature of their faith: the God in whom they believed was the God of all people, the one, true God, who had revealed himself in the history of Israel and ultimately in his Son, thereby supplying the answer that was of concern to everyone and for which all people, in their innermost hearts, are waiting. The universality of God, and of reason open toward him, is what gave them the motivation—indeed, the obligation—to proclaim the message. They saw their faith as belonging, not to cultural custom that differs from one people to another, but to the domain of truth, which concerns all people equally.

The fundamental structure of Christian proclamation "outward"—toward searching and questioning mankind—is seen in St. Paul's address at the Areopagus. We should remember that the Areopagus was not a form of academy at which the most illustrious minds would meet for discussion of lofty matters, but a court of justice, which was competent in matters of religion and ought to have opposed the import of foreign religions. This is exactly what Paul is reproached for: "he seems to be a preacher of foreign divinities" (Acts 17:18). To this, Paul responds, "I have found an altar of yours with this inscription: 'to an un-

known god.' What therefore you worship as unknown, this I
proclaim to you" (Acts 17:23). Paul is not proclaiming unknown
gods. He is proclaiming him whom men do not know and yet do
know—the unknown-known; the one they are seeking, whom
ultimately they know already, and who yet remains the unknown
and unrecognizable. The deepest layer of human thinking and
feeling somehow knows that he must exist; that at the beginning
of all things, there must be not irrationality, but creative reason—not blind chance, but freedom. Yet even though all men
somehow know this, as Paul expressly says in the Letter to the
Romans (cf. Rom 1:21), this knowledge remains unreal: a God
who is merely imagined and invented is not God at all. If he does
not reveal himself, we cannot gain access to him. The novelty of
Christian proclamation is that it can now say to all peoples: he
has revealed himself. He personally. And now the way to him is
open. The novelty of Christian proclamation does not consist in
a thought, but in a deed: God has revealed himself. Yet this is no
blind deed, but one that is itself *Logos*—the presence of eternal
reason in our flesh. *Verbum caro factum est* (cf. Jn 1:14), just so,
amid what is made (*factum*) there is now *Logos; Logos* is among
us. Creation (*factum*) is rational. Naturally, the humility of reason is always needed, in order to accept it: man's humility, which
responds to God's humility.

Our present situation differs in many respects from the one
that Paul encountered in Athens, yet despite the difference, the
two situations also have much in common. Our cities are no longer filled with altars and with images of multiple deities. God
has truly become for many the great unknown. But just as in the
past, when behind the many images of God the question concerning the unknown God was hidden and present, so too the
present absence of God is silently besieged by the question concerning him. *Quaerere Deum*—to seek God and to let oneself
be found by him—that is today no less necessary than in former
times. A purely positivistic culture that tried to drive the ques-

tion concerning God into the subjective realm as being unscientific would be the capitulation of reason, the renunciation of its highest possibilities, and hence a disaster for humanity, with very grave consequences. What gave Europe's culture its foundation—the search for God and the readiness to listen to him—remains today the basis of any genuine culture.

Universities: "Laboratories of Culture"

From *Address to the Participants in the First European Meeting of University Lecturers,* June 23, 2007

I am particularly pleased to receive you during the first European Meeting of University Lecturers, sponsored by the Council of European Episcopal Conferences and organized by teachers from the Roman universities, coordinated by the Vicariate of Rome's Office for the Pastoral Care of Universities. It is taking place on the fiftieth anniversary of the Treaty of Rome, which gave rise to the present European Union, and its participants include university lecturers from every country on the continent, including those of the Caucasus: Armenia, Georgia, and Azerbaijan.

The theme of your meeting—"A New Humanism for Europe: The Role of the Universities"—invites a disciplined assessment of contemporary culture on the continent. Europe is presently experiencing a certain social instability and diffidence in the face of traditional values, yet its distinguished history and established academic institutions have much to contribute to shaping a future of hope. The "question of man," which is central to your discussions, is essential for a correct understanding of current cultural processes. It also provides a solid point of departure for the effort of universities to create a new cultural presence and activity in the service of a more united Europe. Promoting a new humanism, in fact, requires a clear understanding of what this "newness" actually embodies. Far from being the fruit of a superficial desire for novelty, the quest for a new humanism must take serious account of the fact that Europe today is experiencing a massive cultural shift, one in which men and women are increasingly conscious of their call to be actively engaged in shaping their own history. Historically it was in Europe that humanism developed, thanks to the fruitful interplay among the various cultures of her peoples and the Christian faith. Europe today needs to preserve and reappropriate her authentic tradition if she is to remain faithful to her vocation as the cradle of humanism.

The present cultural shift is often seen as a "challenge" to the culture of the university and Christianity itself, rather than as a "horizon" against which creative solutions can and must be found. As men and women of higher education, you are called to take part in this demanding task, which calls for sustained reflection on a number of foundational issues.

Among these I would mention in the first place the need for a comprehensive study of the crisis of modernity. European culture in recent centuries has been powerfully conditioned by the notion of modernity. The present crisis, however, has less to do with modernity's insistence on the centrality of man and his concerns than with the problems raised by a "humanism" that claims to build a *regnum hominis* detached from its necessary ontological foundation. A false dichotomy between theism and authentic humanism, taken to the extreme of positing an irreconcilable conflict between divine law and human freedom, has led to a situation in which humanity, for all its economic and technical advances, feels deeply threatened. As my predecessor, Pope John Paul II, stated, we need to ask "whether in the context of all this progress, man, as man, is becoming truly better, that is to say, more mature spiritually, more aware of the dignity of his humanity, more responsible and more open to others."[9] The anthropocentrism that characterizes modernity can never be de-

9. John Paul II, Encyclical Letter *Redemptor Hominis* (March 4, 1979), n. 15.

tached from an acknowledgment of the full truth about man, which includes his transcendent vocation.

A second issue involves the broadening of our understanding of rationality. A correct understanding of the challenges posed by contemporary culture and the formulation of meaningful responses to those challenges must take a critical approach toward narrow and ultimately irrational attempts to limit the scope of reason. The concept of reason needs instead to be broadened in order to be able to explore and embrace those aspects of reality that go beyond the purely empirical. This will allow for a more fruitful, complementary approach to the relationship between faith and reason. The rise of the European universities was fostered by the conviction that faith and reason are meant to cooperate in the search for truth, each respecting the nature and legitimate autonomy of the other, yet working together harmoniously and creatively to serve the fulfillment of the human person in truth and love.

A third issue needing to be investigated concerns the nature of the contribution that Christianity can make to the humanism of the future. The question of man, and thus of modernity, challenges the Church to devise effective ways of proclaiming to contemporary culture the realism of her faith in the saving work of Christ. Christianity must not be relegated to the world of myth and emotion, but respected for its claim to shed light on the truth about man, to be able to transform men and women spiritually, and thus to enable them to carry out their vocation in history. In my recent visit to Brazil I voiced my conviction that "unless we do know God in and with Christ, all of reality becomes an indecipherable enigma."[10] Knowledge can never be limited to the purely intellectual realm; it also includes a renewed ability to look at things in a way free of prejudices and preconceptions,

---

10. Benedict XVI, *Address to the Inaugural Session of the Fifth General Conference of the Bishops of Latin America and the Caribbean,* n. 3, Apostolic Journey to Brazil, Aparecida, May 13, 2007.

and to allow ourselves to be amazed by reality, whose truth can be discovered by uniting understanding with love. Only the God who has a human face, revealed in Jesus Christ, can prevent us from truncating reality at the very moment when it demands ever new and more complex levels of understanding. The Church is conscious of her responsibility to offer this contribution to contemporary culture.

In Europe as elsewhere, society urgently needs the service to wisdom that the university community provides. This service extends also to the practical aspects of directing research and activity to the promotion of human dignity and to the daunting task of building the civilization of love. University professors in particular are called to embody the virtue of intellectual charity, recovering their primordial vocation to train future generations not only by imparting knowledge, but by the prophetic witness of their own lives. The university for its part must never lose sight of its particular calling to be a *universitas* in which the various disciplines, each in its own way, are seen as part of a greater *unum*. How urgent is the need to rediscover the unity of knowledge and to counter the tendency to fragmentation and lack of communicability that is all too often the case in our schools! The effort to reconcile the drive to specialization with the need to preserve the unity of knowledge can encourage the growth of European unity and help the continent to rediscover its specific cultural vocation in today's world. Only a Europe conscious of its own cultural identity can make a specific contribution to other cultures while remaining open to the contribution of other peoples.

Dear friends, it is my hope that universities will increasingly become communities committed to the tireless pursuit of truth, "laboratories of culture" where teachers and students join in exploring issues of particular importance for society, employing interdisciplinary methods, and counting on the collaboration of theologians. This can easily be done in Europe, given the presence of so many prestigious Catholic institutions and faculties of theology. I am convinced that greater cooperation and new forms of fellowship between the various academic communities will enable Catholic universities to bear witness to the historical fruitfulness of the encounter between faith and reason. The result will be a concrete contribution to the attainment of the goals of the Bologna process and an incentive for developing a suitable university apostolate in the local Churches. Effective support for these efforts, which have been increasingly a concern of the European Episcopal Conferences,[11] can come from those ecclesial associations and movements already engaged in the university apostolate.

Universitas: A Vocation to Communion

From *Address to the Representatives of the World of Culture*
at the University of Pavia, Pastoral Visit to Vigevano
and Pavia, April 22, 2007

Your university is one of the oldest and most distinguished of the Italian universities, and—I repeat the words of the rector magnificent—among the teachers who have honored it are figures such as Alessandro Volta, Camillo Golgi, and Carlo Forlanini.

I am also eager to recall that teachers and students marked by an eminent spiritual stature have passed through your athenaeum. They were Michele Ghislieri, who later became Pope St. Pius V, St. Charles Borromeo, St. Alessandro Sauli, St. Riccardo Pampuri, St. Gianna Beretta Molla, Bl. Contardo Ferrini, and the servant of God Teresio Olivelli.

Dear friends, every university has an inherent community vocation; indeed, it is precisely a *universitas,* a community of teachers and students committed to seeking the truth and to acquiring superior cultural and professional skills.

---

11. Cf. John Paul II, Apostolic Exhortation *Ecclesia in Europa* (June 28, 2003), nn. 58–59.

The centrality of the person and the community dimension are two coessential poles for an effective structuring of the *universitas studiorum.*

Every university must always preserve the traits of a study center "within man's reach," where the student is preserved from anonymity and can cultivate a fertile dialogue with his teachers from which he draws an incentive for his cultural and human growth.

From this structure derive certain applications that are connected to one another. First of all, it is certain that only by putting the person at the center and making the most of dialogue and interpersonal relations can the specializing fragmentation of disciplines be overcome and the unitive perspective of knowledge be recovered.

Naturally, and also rightly, the disciplines tend to specialization, while what the person needs is unity and synthesis.

Second, it is fundamentally important that the commitment to scientific research be open to the existential question of meaning for the person's life itself. Research seeks knowledge, whereas the person also needs wisdom—that knowledge, as it were, that is expressed in the *"knowing-living."*

Third, only in appreciating the person and interpersonal relationships can the didactic relationship become an educational relationship, a process of human development. Indeed, the structure gives priority to communication while people aspire to sharing.

I know that this attention to the person, his integral experience of life, and his aspiration to communion are very present in the pastoral action of the Church of Pavia in the field of culture. This is witnessed to by the work of university colleges of Christian inspiration.

Among these, I too would like to recall the Collegio Borromeo, desired by St. Charles Borromeo with Pope Pius IV's Bull of foundation, and the Collegio Santa Caterina, founded by the diocese of Pavia to comply with the wishes of the servant of God Paul VI, with a crucial contribution from the Holy See.

In this sense the work of the parishes and ecclesial movements is also important, especially that of the Diocesan University Center and the Italian Catholic University Students' Association (FUCI).

The purpose of their activity is to welcome the person in his totality, to propose harmonious processes of human, cultural, and Christian formation, and to provide spaces for sharing, discussion, and communion.

I would like to take this opportunity to ask both students and teachers not to feel that they are merely the object of pastoral attention, but to participate actively and to make their contribution to the cultural project of Christian inspiration that the Church promotes in Italy and in Europe.

In meeting you, dear friends, the thought of Augustine, co-patron of this university together with St. Catherine of Alexandria, springs spontaneously to mind. Augustine's existential and intellectual development witnesses to the fertile interaction between faith and culture.

St. Augustine was a man driven by a tireless desire to find the truth, to find out what life is, to know how to live, to know man. And precisely because of his passion for the human being, he necessarily sought God, because it is only in the light of God that the greatness of the human being and the beauty of the adventure of being human can fully appear.

At first this God appeared very remote to him. Then Augustine found him: this great and inaccessible God made himself close, one of us. The great God is our God; he is a God with a human face. Thus his faith in Christ did not have its ultimate end in his philosophy or in his intellectual daring, but on the contrary, impelled him further to seek the depths of the human being and to help others to live well, to find life, the art of living.

This was his philosophy: to know how to live with all the

reason and all the depths of our thought, of our will, and to allow ourselves to be guided on the path of truth, which is a path of courage, humility, and permanent purification.

Faith in Christ brought all Augustine's seeking to fulfillment, but fulfillment in the sense that he always remained on the way. Indeed, he tells us, even in eternity our seeking will not be completed; it will be an eternal adventure, the discovery of new greatness, new beauty.

He interpreted the words of the Psalm, "Seek his face continually," and said, this is true for eternity; and the beauty of eternity is that it is not a static reality, but immense progress in the immense beauty of God.

Thus he could discover God as the founding reason, but also as love that embraces us, guides us, and gives meaning to history and to our personal life.

This morning I had the opportunity to say that this love for Christ shaped his personal commitment. From a life patterned on seeking, he moved on to a life given totally to Christ and thus to a life for others.

He discovered—this was his second conversion—that being converted to Christ means not living for oneself, but truly being at the service of all.

May St. Augustine be for us and also for the academic world a model of dialogue between reason and faith, a model of a broad dialogue that alone can seek truth, hence also peace.

As my venerable predecessor, John Paul II, commented in his encyclical *Fides et Ratio,* "The Bishop of Hippo succeeded in producing the first great synthesis of philosophy and theology, embracing currents of thought both Greek and Latin. In him too the great unity of knowledge, grounded in the thought of the Bible, was both confirmed and sustained by a depth of speculative thinking."[12]

12. John Paul II, *Fides et Ratio,* n. 40.

I therefore invoke the intercession of St. Augustine so that the University of Pavia may always be distinguished by special attention to the individual, by an accentuated community dimension in scientific research, and by a fruitful dialogue between faith and culture.

The Question of God Is the *Crucial Question*

From *Address to the Catholic University of the Sacred Heart,* May 21, 2011

Our time is one of intense and rapid change that also reflects on university life; the humanistic culture seems to be affected by a progressive decline, while the so-called "productive" disciplines, such as technological and economic studies, are emphasized. There is a tendency to reduce the human horizon to a measurable level and to eliminate the fundamental question of meaning from systematic and critical knowledge. Contemporary culture tends to exclude religion from rational spaces to the extent that empirical sciences monopolize territories of reason. There does not seem to be room for reasons to believe; therefore the religious dimension is exiled to the realm of opinion and personal choice. In this context the very purpose and characteristics of the university are radically questioned.

Ninety years after its founding, the Catholic University of the Sacred Heart finds itself at a historical turning point, in which it is important to consolidate and increase the reasons for which it was born, bringing with it an ecclesial connotation that is made evident by the adjective "Catholic"; the Church, indeed "expert in humanity," is a promoter of authentic humanism. In this perspective the original vocation of the university emerges, born of the search for the truth, for the whole truth, for the whole truth of our existence. And by its obedience to the truth and to the demands of the knowledge of truth, it becomes a school of *humanitas* where vital understanding is cultivated, where mature character is fashioned, and where valuable knowledge and skills are passed on. The Christian perspective does not set itself against scientific knowledge and the conquests of human intelligence; rather, it considers faith the horizon of meaning, the way to full truth, the guide for authentic development. Without focusing on the truth, without an attitude of humble and ardent research, every culture crumbles, declines into relativism, and loses itself in the ephemeral. Instead, the Christian prospective, pulled from the grip of reductionism that mortifies and circumscribes it, can open itself to an interpretation truly illuminated by what is real, offering an authentic service to life.

Dear friends, faith and culture are permanently connected heights, a manifestation of that *desiderium naturale videndi Deum* that is present in every person. When this union dissolves, humanity tends to fold in on itself and close itself to its own creative capacities. It is then necessary that there should be in the university a genuine passion for the question of the absolute truth itself, and therefore theological knowledge, which is an integral part of the curriculum in your athenaeum. Uniting in itself audacity for research and patience for growth, the theological horizon can and should value all the resources of reason. The question of the Truth and the Absolute—the question of God—is not an abstract investigation divorced from daily life, but is the *crucial question* on which the discovery of the meaning of the world and of life depends. The gospel is the basis for a view of the world and the person that does not cease to emanate cultural, humanistic, and ethical merits. Therefore the knowledge of faith enlightens man's search. This search is rendered human and integrated in works of good, tearing it from the temptation of the calculating thought that exploits knowledge and makes scientific discoveries a means of power and of enslavement to man.

The horizon that invigorates the work of the university can and should be an authentic passion for human beings. Only through service to others is science utilized to till and keep the universe (cf. Gen 2:15). Serving others is living the truth in charity; it is loving life and respecting it, beginning with situations in which it is frail and defenseless. This is our duty, especially in times of crisis; the history of our culture demonstrates how human dignity was truly recognized in its totality to the light of Christian faith. The Catholic university is called to be a place that, par excellence, shapes that openness to knowledge, that passion for truth, that interest in the history of mankind that characterizes authentic Christian spirituality. Indeed, taking on a closed or detached attitude in the face of a perspective of faith means forgetting that throughout history it has been, and still is, a leaven of culture and light for intelligence, stimulus to develop all positive potentials for the authentic good of human beings. As the Second Vatican Council stated, faith is able to give light to existence, affirming, "For faith throws a new light on all things and makes known the full ideal which God has set for man, thus guiding the mind towards solutions that are fully human."[13]

The Catholic university is a place where this should occur with particular efficacy, under the scientific and didactic profile. This particular service to the Truth is a gift of grace and qualifying expression of evangelical charity. The demonstration of faith and the testimony of love are inseparable. The profound nucleus of the truth of God, in fact, is the love with which he bends over man, and in Christ has offered gifts of infinite grace. In Jesus we discover that God is love and that only through love can we know him, as St. John said: "For love is of God, and he who loves is born of God and knows God" (1 Jn 4:7). And as St. Augustine states, "*Non intratur in veritatem nisi per caritatem.*"[14]

The summit of the knowledge of God is reached through love—love that goes to the root and is not satisfied with occasional philanthropic expressions, but illumines the meaning of life with the Truth of Christ, who transforms the heart of man

---

13. Second Vatican Council, *Gaudium et Spes* (December 7, 1965), n. 11.
14. Augustine, *Contra Faustum,* n. 32.

and uproots selfishness that causes misery and death. Humans need love; humans need truth in order to not dispel the frail treasure of freedom and be exposed to the violence of passion and to manipulation, both open and hidden.[15] The Christian faith does not make love a vague, sympathetic, merciful feeling, but a force able to illuminate the paths of life in all its expressions. Without this vision, without this primal and profound theological dimension, love is satisfied with occasional help and renounces its prophetic duty to transform the life of the person and the very structures of society. It is this specific task that the mission of the university calls you to fulfill as passionate protagonists, convinced that the power of the gospel is capable of renewing human relations and penetrating hearts with reality.

Dear young university students of the "Cattolica," you are a living example of that quality of faith that changes life and saves the world with its problems and hopes, questions and certainties, aspirations and involvement that the desire for a better life produce and that prayer nourishes. Dear representatives of the technical and administrative staff, be proud of the duties that are assigned to you in the context of the large university family in supporting the multifaceted formative and professional activities. And to you, dear faculty, a decisive role is entrusted to you: to demonstrate how the Christian faith is a leaven of culture and light for intelligence, a stimulus to develop every positive potential for the authentic good of all. That which reason loses sight of, faith enlightens and manifests.

Contemplation of God's work reveals to knowledge the demand for rational, systematic, and critical investigation; the search for God strengthens love for secular arts and sciences: "*Fides ratione adiuvatur et ratio fide perficitur,*" as Hugh of St. Victor stated.[16]

From this perspective the beating heart and constant nourishment of university life is the chapel, to which the pastoral center

---

15. Cf. John Paul II, Encyclical *Centesimus Annus* (January 5, 1991), n. 46.
16. Hugh of St. Victor, *De Sacramentis* I.III.30, *PL* 176, 232.

is united where the spiritual assistants of the various campuses are called to perform their precious priestly mission, which is essential to the Catholic University's identity. As Bl. John Paul II taught, the chapel "is *a place of the spirit,* where believers in Christ, involved in different ways in academic study, can pause for prayer and find nourishment and direction. It is a *training-ground for the Christian virtues,* where the life received in Baptism grows and systematically develops. It is a *welcoming and open home* for all those who, heeding the voice of the Teacher within, become seekers of the truth and serve mankind by their daily commitment to a knowledge which goes beyond merely narrow and pragmatic goals. In the setting of a modernity in decline, the university chapel is called to be a *vital center for promoting the Christian renewal of culture,* in respectful and frank dialogue, in a clear and well-grounded viewpoint (cf. 1 Pet 3:15), in a witness which open to questioning and capable of convincing."[17] Thus said John Paul II in 1998.

Dear friends, may the Catholic University of the Sacred Heart, in tune with the goals of the Toniolo Institute, continue on its path with renewed faith, effectively demonstrating that the light of the gospel is a source of true culture able to spark energies of a new, integral, and transcendent humanism.

Revealing God in Everything that Exists

From *Address to Artists in the Sistine Chapel,* November 21, 2009

Today's event is focused on you, dear and illustrious artists, from different countries, cultures, and religions, some of you perhaps remote from the practice of religion, but interested nevertheless in maintaining communication with the Catholic Church, in not reducing the horizons of existence to mere material realities, to a reductive and trivializing vision. You represent the varied

17. John Paul II, *Address to European University Chaplains,* May 1, 1998.

world of the arts and so, through you, I would like to convey to all artists my invitation to friendship, dialogue, and cooperation.

Some significant anniversaries occur around this time. It is ten years since the *Letter to Artists* by my venerable predecessor, the servant of God Pope John Paul II. For the first time, on the eve of the Great Jubilee of the Year 2000, the pope, who was an artist himself, wrote a letter to artists combining the solemnity of a pontifical document with the friendly tone of a conversation among all who, as we read in the initial salutation, "are passionately dedicated to the search for new 'epiphanies' of beauty." Twenty-five years ago the same pope proclaimed Blessed Fra Angelico the patron of artists, presenting him as a model of perfect harmony between faith and art. I also recall how on May 7, 1964, forty-five years ago, in this very place, a historic event took place, at the express wish of Pope Paul VI, to confirm the friendship between the Church and the arts. The words that he spoke on that occasion resound once more today under the vault of the Sistine Chapel and touch our hearts and our minds. "We need you," he said. "We need your collaboration in order to carry out our ministry, which consists, as you know, in preaching and rendering accessible and comprehensible to the minds and hearts of our people the things of the spirit, the invisible, the ineffable, the things of God himself. And in this activity … you are masters. It is your task, your mission, and your art consists in grasping treasures from the heavenly realm of the spirit and clothing them in words, colors, forms—making them accessible." So great was Paul VI's esteem for artists that he was moved to use daring expressions. "And if we were deprived of your assistance," he added, "our ministry would become faltering and uncertain, and a special effort would be needed, one might say, to make it artistic, even prophetic. In order to scale the heights of lyrical expression of intuitive beauty, priesthood would have to coincide with art." On that occasion Paul VI made a commitment to "re-establish the friendship between the Church and artists," and he invited artists to make a similar, shared commitment, analyzing seriously and objectively the factors that disturbed this relationship and assuming individual responsibility, courageously and passionately, for a newer and deeper journey in mutual acquaintance and dialogue in order to arrive at an authentic "renaissance" of art in the context of a new humanism.

That historic encounter, as I mentioned, took place here in this sanctuary of faith and human creativity. So it is not by chance that we come together in this place, esteemed for its architecture and its symbolism, and above all for the frescoes that make it unique, from the masterpieces of Perugino and Botticelli, Ghirlandaio and Cosimo Rosselli, Luca Signorelli and others, to the Genesis scenes and the Last Judgment of Michelangelo Buonarroti, who has given us here one of the most extraordinary creations in the entire history of art. The universal language of music has often been heard here, thanks to the genius of great musicians who have placed their art at the service of the liturgy, assisting the spirit in its ascent toward God. At the same time, the Sistine Chapel is remarkably vibrant with history, since it is the solemn and austere setting of events that mark the history of the Church and of mankind. Here, as you know, the College of Cardinals elects the pope; here it was that I myself, with trepidation but also with absolute trust in the Lord, experienced the privileged moment of my election as successor of the Apostle Peter.

Dear friends, let us allow these frescoes to speak to us today, drawing us toward the ultimate goal of human history. The Last Judgment, which you see behind me, reminds us that human history is movement and ascent, a continuing tension toward fullness, toward human happiness, toward a horizon that always transcends the present moment, even as the two coincide. Yet the dramatic scene portrayed in this fresco also places before our eyes the risk of man's definitive fall, a risk that threatens to engulf him whenever he allows himself to be led astray by the forces of evil. So the fresco issues a strong prophetic cry against evil, against every form of injustice. For believers, though, the risen Christ is the Way, the Truth, and the Life. For his faithful followers, he is the Door through which we are brought to that "face-to-face" vision of God from which limitless, full, and definitive happiness flows. Thus Michelangelo presents to our gaze the alpha and the omega, the beginning and the end of history, and he invites us to walk the path of life with joy, courage, and hope. The dramatic beauty of Michelangelo's painting, its colors and forms, becomes a proclamation of hope, an invitation to raise our gaze to the ultimate horizon. The profound bond between beauty and hope was the essential content of the evocative message that Paul VI addressed to artists at the conclusion of the Second Vatican Ecumenical Council on December 8, 1965: "To all of you," he proclaimed solemnly, "the Church of the Council declares through our lips: if you are friends of true art, you are our friends!" And he added, "This world in which we live needs beauty in order not to sink into despair. Beauty, like truth, brings joy to the human heart, and is that precious fruit which resists the erosion of time, which unites generations and enables them to be one in admiration. And all this through the work of your hands.... Remember that you are the custodians of beauty in the world."

Unfortunately, the present time is marked not only by negative elements in the social and economic sphere, but also by a weakening of hope, by a certain lack of confidence in human relationships, which gives rise to increasing signs of resignation, aggression, and despair. The world in which we live runs the risk of being altered beyond recognition because of unwise human actions that, instead of cultivating its beauty, unscrupulously exploit its resources for the advantage of a few and not infrequently disfigure the marvels of nature. What is capable of restoring enthusiasm and confidence, what can encourage the human spirit to rediscover its path, to raise its eyes to the horizon, to dream of a life worthy of its vocation—if not beauty? Dear friends, as artists you know well that the experience of beauty, beauty that is authentic, not merely transient or artificial, is by no means a supplementary or secondary factor in our search for meaning and happiness; the experience of beauty does not remove us from reality—on the contrary, it leads to a direct encounter with the daily reality of our lives, liberating it from darkness, transfiguring it, making it radiant and beautiful.

Indeed, an essential function of genuine beauty, as emphasized by Plato, is that it gives man a healthy "shock"; it draws him out of himself, wrenches him away from resignation and from being content with the humdrum—it even makes him suffer, piercing him like a dart, but in so doing it "reawakens" him, opening afresh the eyes of his heart and mind, giving him wings, carrying him aloft. Dostoevsky's words that I am about to quote are bold and paradoxical, but they invite reflection. He says this: "Man can live without science, he can live without bread, but without beauty he could no longer live, because there would no longer be anything to do to the world. The whole secret is here, the whole of history is here." The painter Georges Braque echoes this sentiment: "Art is meant to disturb, science reassures." Beauty pulls us up short, but in so doing it reminds us of our final destiny; it sets us back on our path, fills us with new hope, gives us the courage to live to the full the unique gift of life. The quest for beauty that I am describing here is clearly not about escaping into the irrational or into mere aestheticism.

Too often, though, the beauty that is thrust upon us is illusory and deceitful, superficial and blinding, leaving the onlooker dazed; instead of bringing him out of himself and opening him up to horizons of true freedom as it draws him aloft, it imprisons him within himself and further enslaves him, depriving him of hope and joy. It is a seductive, but hypocritical beauty that rekindles desire, the will to power, to possess, and to dominate others; it is a beauty that soon turns into its opposite, taking on the guise of indecency, transgression, or gratuitous provocation.

Authentic beauty, however, unlocks the yearning of the human heart, the profound desire to know, to love, to go toward the Other, to reach for the Beyond. If we acknowledge that beauty touches us intimately, that it wounds us, that it opens our eyes, then we rediscover the joy of seeing, of being able to grasp the profound meaning of our existence, the mystery of which we are part; from this mystery we can draw fullness, happiness, the passion to engage with it every day. In this regard Pope John Paul II, in his *Letter to Artists,* quotes the following verse from a Polish poet, Cyprian Norwid: "Beauty is to enthuse us for work, and work is to raise us up."[18] And later he adds, "In so far as it seeks the beautiful, fruit of an imagination which rises above the everyday, art is by its nature a kind of appeal to the mystery. Even when they explore the darkest depths of the soul or the most unsettling aspects of evil, the artist gives voice in a way to the universal desire for redemption."[19] And in conclusion he states, "Beauty is a key to the mystery and a call to transcendence."[20]

These ideas impel us to take a further step in our reflection. Beauty, whether that of the natural universe or that expressed in art, precisely because it opens up and broadens the horizons of human awareness, pointing us beyond ourselves, bringing us face to face with the abyss of infinity, can become a path toward the transcendent, toward the ultimate mystery, toward God. Art, in all its forms, at the point where it encounters the great questions of our existence, the fundamental themes that give life its meaning, can take on a religious quality, thereby turning into a path of profound inner reflection and spirituality. This close proximity, this harmony between the journey of faith and the artist's path, is attested by countless artworks that are based upon the personalities, the stories, the symbols of that immense deposit of "figures"—in the broad sense—namely the Bible, the sacred

18. John Paul II, *Letter to Artists* (April 4, 1999), n. 3.
19. John Paul II, *Letter to Artists,* n. 10.
20. John Paul II, *Letter to Artists,* n. 16.

scriptures. The great biblical narratives, themes, images, and parables have inspired innumerable masterpieces in every sector of the arts, just as they have spoken to the hearts of believers in every generation through the works of craftsmanship and folk art, which are no less eloquent and evocative.

In this regard one may speak of a *via pulchritudinis,* a path of beauty that is at the same time an artistic and aesthetic journey, a journey of faith, of theological inquiry. The theologian Hans Urs von Balthasar begins his great work entitled *The Glory of the Lord: A Theological Aesthetics* with these telling observations: "Beauty is the word with which we shall begin. Beauty is the last word that the thinking intellect dares to speak, because it simply forms a halo, an untouchable crown around the double constellation of the true and the good and their inseparable relation to one another." He then adds, "Beauty is the disinterested one, without which the ancient world refused to understand itself, a word that both imperceptibly and yet unmistakably has bid farewell to our new world, a world of interests, leaving it to its own avarice and sadness. It is no longer loved or fostered even by religion." And he concludes, "We can be sure that whoever sneers at her name as if she were the ornament of a bourgeois past— whether he admits it or not—can no longer pray and soon will no longer be able to love." The way of beauty leads us, then, to grasp the whole in the fragment, the infinite in the finite, God in the history of humanity. Simone Weil wrote in this regard, "In all that awakens within us the pure and authentic sentiment of beauty, there, truly, is the presence of God. There is a kind of incarnation of God in the world, of which beauty is the sign. Beauty is the experimental proof that incarnation is possible. For this reason all art of the first order is, by its nature, religious."

Hermann Hesse makes the point even more graphically: "Art means: revealing God in everything that exists." Echoing the words of Pope Paul VI, servant of God Pope John Paul II restated the Church's desire to renew dialogue and cooperation with artists: "In order to communicate the message entrusted to her by Christ, *the Church needs art*";[21] but he immediately went on to ask, "Does art need the Church?"—thereby inviting artists to rediscover a source of fresh and well-founded inspiration in religious experience, in Christian revelation, and in the "great codex" that is the Bible.

Dear artists, as I draw to a conclusion, I too would like to make a cordial, friendly, and impassioned appeal to you, as did my predecessor. You are the custodians of beauty: thanks to your talent, you have the opportunity to speak to the heart of humanity, to touch individual and collective sensibilities, to call forth dreams and hopes, to broaden the horizons of knowledge and of human engagement. Be grateful, then, for the gifts you have received and be fully conscious of your great responsibility to communicate beauty, to communicate in and through beauty! Through your art, you yourselves are to be heralds and witnesses of hope for humanity! And do not be afraid to approach the first and last source of beauty, to enter into dialogue with believers, with those who, like yourselves, consider that they are pilgrims in this world and in history toward infinite Beauty! Faith takes nothing away from your genius or your art; on the contrary, it exalts them and nourishes them, it encourages them to cross the threshold and to contemplate with fascination and emotion the ultimate and definitive goal, the sun that does not set, the sun that illumines this present moment and makes it beautiful.

St. Augustine, who fell in love with beauty and sang its praises, wrote these words as he reflected on man's ultimate destiny, commenting almost *ante litteram* on the Judgment scene before your eyes today: "Therefore we are to see a certain vision, my brethren, that no eye has seen, nor ear heard, nor the heart of man conceived: a vision surpassing all earthly beauty, whether it be that of gold and silver, woods and fields, sea and sky, sun and moon, or stars and angels. The reason is this: it is the source

21. John Paul II, *Letter to Artists,* n. 12.

of all other beauty."²² My wish for all of you, dear artists, is that you may carry this vision in your eyes, in your hands, and in your heart, that it may bring you joy and continue to inspire your fine works.

A Work of Beauty Is Pure Gratuity

From *Homily for Holy Mass with Dedication of the Church of the Sagrada Familia and of the Altar,* Apostolic Journey to Santiago de Compostela and Barcelona, November 7, 2010

"This day is holy to the Lord your God; do not mourn or weep.... The joy of the Lord is your strength" (Neh 8:9–11). With these words from the first reading that we have proclaimed, I wish to greet all of you taking part in this celebration.

Today marks an important step in a long history of hope, work, and generosity that has gone on for more than a century. At this time I would like to mention each and every one of those who have made possible the joy that fills us today, from the promoters to the executors of this work, the architects and the workers, all who in one way or another have given their priceless contribution to the building of this edifice. We remember of course the man who was the soul and the artisan of this project, Antoni Gaudí, a creative architect and a practicing Christian who kept the torch of his faith alight to the end of his life, a life lived in dignity and absolute austerity. This event is also in a certain sense the high point of the history of this land of Catalonia, which, especially since the end of the nineteenth century, has given an abundance of saints and founders, martyrs and Christian poets. It is a history of holiness, artistic and poetic creation, born from the faith, which we gather and present to God today as an offering in this Eucharist.

The joy that I feel at presiding at this ceremony became all the greater when I learned that this shrine, since its beginnings,

22. Augustine, *In 1 Ioannis* 4.5.

has had a special relationship with St. Joseph. I have been moved above all by Gaudí's confidence when, in the face of many difficulties, filled with trust in divine Providence, he would exclaim, "Saint Joseph will finish this church." So it is significant that it is also being dedicated by a pope whose baptismal name is Joseph.

What do we do when we dedicate this church? In the heart of the world, placed before God and mankind, with a humble and joyful act of faith, we raise up this massive material structure, fruit of nature and an immense achievement of human intelligence that gave birth to this work of art. It stands as a visible sign of the invisible God, to whose glory these spires rise like arrows pointing toward absolute light and to the One who is Light, Height, and Beauty itself.

In this place Gaudí desired to unify that inspiration that came to him from the three books that nourished him as a man, as a believer, and as an architect: the book of nature, the book of sacred scripture, and the book of the liturgy. In this way he brought together the reality of the world and the history of salvation, as recounted in the Bible and made present in the liturgy. He made stones, trees, and human life part of the church so that all creation might come together in praise of God, but at the same time he brought the sacred images outside so as to place before people the mystery of God revealed in the birth, passion, death, and resurrection of Jesus Christ. In this way he brilliantly helped to build our human consciousness, anchored in the world yet open to God, enlightened and sanctified by Christ. In this he accomplished one of the most important tasks of our times: overcoming the division between human consciousness and Christian consciousness, between living in this temporal world and being open to eternal life, between the beauty of things and God as beauty. Antoni Gaudí did this not with words, but with stones, lines, planes, and points. Indeed, beauty is one of mankind's greatest needs; it is the root from which the branches of our peace and the fruits of our hope come forth. Beauty also reveals God because, like him, a work of beauty is pure gratuity; it calls us to freedom and draws us away from selfishness.

We have dedicated this sacred space to God, who revealed and gave himself to us in Christ so as to be definitively God among men. The revealed Word, the humanity of Christ, and his Church are the three supreme expressions of his self-manifestation and self-giving to mankind. As says St. Paul in the second reading, "Let each man take care how he builds. For no other foundation can anyone lay than that which is laid, which is Jesus Christ" (1 Cor 3:10–11). The Lord Jesus is the stone that supports the weight of the world, which maintains the cohesion of the Church and brings together in ultimate unity all the achievements of mankind. In him we have God's word and presence and from him the Church receives her life, her teaching, and her mission. The Church of herself is nothing; she is called to be the sign and instrument of Christ, in pure docility to his authority and in total service to his mandate. The one Christ is the foundation of the one Church. He is the rock on which our faith is built. Building on this faith, let us strive together to show the world the face of God who is love and the only one who can respond to our yearning for fulfillment. This is the great task before us: to show everyone that God is a God of peace, not of violence; of freedom, not of coercion; of harmony, not of discord. In this sense I consider that the dedication of this church of the Sagrada Familia is an event of great importance at a time in which man claims to be able to build his life without God, as if God had nothing to say to him. In this masterpiece Gaudí shows us that God is the true measure of man; that the secret of authentic originality consists, as he himself said, in returning to one's origin that is God. Gaudí, by opening his spirit to God, was capable of creating in this city a space of beauty, faith, and hope that leads man to an encounter with him who is truth and beauty itself. The architect expressed his sentiments in the following words: "A church [is] the only thing worthy of representing the soul of a people, for religion is the most elevated reality in man."

This affirmation of God brings with it the supreme affirmation and protection of the dignity of each and every man and woman: "Do you not know that you are God's temple? ... God's temple is holy, and you are that temple" (1 Cor 3:16–17). Here we find joined together the truth and dignity of God and the truth and dignity of man. As we consecrate the altar of this church, which has Christ as its foundation, we are presenting to the world a God who is the friend of man, and we invite men and women to become friends of God. This is what we are taught in the case of Zacchaeus, of whom today's gospel speaks (Lk 19:1–10); if we allow God into our hearts and into our world, if we allow Christ to live in our hearts, we will not regret it: we will experience the joy of sharing his very life, as the object of his infinite love.

This church began as an initiative of the Association of the Friends of Saint Joseph, who wanted to dedicate it to the Holy Family of Nazareth. The home formed by Jesus, Mary, and Joseph has always been regarded as a school of love, prayer, and work. The promoters of this church wanted to set before the world love, work, and service lived in the presence of God, as the Holy Family lived them. Life has changed greatly, and with it enormous progress has been made in the technical, social, and cultural spheres. We cannot simply remain content with these advances. Alongside them there also need to be moral advances, such as in care, protection, and assistance to families, inasmuch as the generous and indissoluble love of a man and a woman is the effective context and foundation of human life in its gestation, birth, growth, and natural end. Only where love and faithfulness are present can true freedom come to birth and endure. For this reason the Church advocates adequate economic and social means so that women may find in the home and at work their full development, that men and women who contract marriage and form a family receive decisive support from the state, that the life of children may be defended as sacred and inviolable from the moment of their conception, that the reality of birth be given due respect and receive juridical, social, and legislative support. For this reason the Church resists every form of denial of human life and gives its support to everything that would promote the natural order in the sphere of the institution of the family.

As I contemplate with admiration this sacred space of marvelous beauty, of so much faith-filled history, I ask God that in the land of Catalonia new witnesses of holiness may rise up and flourish and present to the world the great service that the Church can and must offer to humanity: to be an icon of divine beauty, a burning flame of charity, a path so that the world may believe in the One whom God has sent (cf. Jn 6:29).

Dear brothers and sisters, as I dedicate this splendid church, I implore the Lord of our lives that, from this altar, which will now be anointed with holy oil and upon which the sacrifice of the love of Christ will be consumed, there may be a flood of grace and charity upon the city of Barcelona and its people, and upon the whole world. May these fruitful waters fill with faith and apostolic vitality this archdiocesan Church, its pastors, and its faithful.

7. SCIENCE, TECHNOLOGY, AND THEOLOGY

Love Alone Guarantees the Humanity of Research

From *Address to The Catholic University of the Sacred Heart on the Occasion of the 50th Anniversary of the Faculty of Medicine and Surgery of the Agostino Gemelli Polyclinic,* Rome, May 3, 2012

On this occasion I would like to contribute a few thoughts. Our time is one in which the experimental sciences have transformed the vision of the world and even man's understanding of himself. The many discoveries and the rapid succession of innovative technologies are a well-founded reason for pride, but they are frequently not without disturbing implications. Indeed, against the background of the widespread optimism in scientific knowledge extends the shadow of a crisis in thought. Rich in means but less so in their aims, the men and women of our time are often conditioned by reductionism and relativism, which lead to the loss of meaning of things; blinded, as it were, by technical efficiency, they forget the fundamental horizon of the need for meaning, thereby relegating the transcendent dimension to irrelevance. Against this background thought is weakened and an ethical impoverishment that blurs valuable norms of reference gains ground.

What was the fertile root of European culture and progress seems to have been forgotten. In it the search for the Absolute—the *quaerere Deum*—included the need to deepen the knowledge of the profane sciences, the entire world of knowledge.[1] Scientific research and the question of meaning, even with their specific epistemological and methodological features, in fact flow from one source, the *Logos,* that presides over creative work and guides the sense of history. A fundamentally technological and practical mindset generates a perilous imbalance between what is technologically possible and what is morally sound, with unforeseeable consequences.

Thus it is important for culture to rediscover the vigor of the meaning and dynamism of transcendence—in a word, to present the horizon of the *quaerere Deum* decisively. St. Augustine's famous sentence springs to mind: "you have made us for yourself [O Lord] and our heart is restless until it rests in you."[2]

It may be said that the impulse of scientific research itself stems from the longing for God that dwells in the human heart: basically, scientists, even unconsciously, strive to attain that truth which can give meaning to life. Yet, however enthusiastic and tenacious human research is, it is incapable merely with its own efforts of reaching a safe landing place, for "man is incapable of fully explaining the strange semi-darkness that overshadows the question of the eternal realities.... God must take the initiative of reaching out and speaking to man."[3]

To restore reason to its native, integral dimension, one must rediscover the source that scientific research shares with the quest for faith, *fides quaerens intellectum,* according to Anselm's intuition. Science and faith have a fruitful reciprocity, an almost complementary need for understanding the real. Paradoxical-

1. Cf. Benedict XVI, *Address to Representatives from the World of Culture at the "Collège des Bernardins" in Paris,* Apostolic Journey to France, Paris, September 12, 2008.

2. Augustine, *Confessions* Bk. i, 1.

3. Joseph Ratzinger, *Christianity and the Crisis of Cultures,* translated by Brian McNeil (San Francisco: Ignatius Press, 2006), 100.

ly, however, the positivist culture itself, excluding the question on God from scientific discussion, determines the decline of thought and the enfeeblement of the ability to understand this reality.

Yet the human quest for *quaerere Deum* would lose itself in a maze if it were not to meet illumination and reliable orientation, which is the way of God himself who, with immense love, makes himself close to man: "In Jesus Christ God not only speaks to man but also seeks him out.... It is a search which begins in the heart of God and culminates in the Incarnation of the Word."[4]

As the religion of the *Logos,* Christianity does not relegate faith to the sphere of the irrational, but attributes the origin and sense of reality to creative Reason, which, in the crucified God, is expressed as love and invites us to take the way of the *quaerere Deum:* "I am the way, the truth, and the life." Here St. Thomas Aquinas comments, "For the destination of this way is the end of human desire. Now human beings especially desire two things: first, a knowledge of the truth, and this is characteristic of them; secondly, that they continue to exist, and this is common to all things. These two were already applied to Christ.... If then, you ask which way to go, accept Christ, for he is the way."[5]

The gospel of life thus illuminates man's uphill journey, and when he faces the temptation of absolute autonomy, reminds him, "man's life comes from God; it is his gift, his image, his imprint, a sharing in his breath of life."[6] And it is precisely by taking the path of faith that man is enabled to discern in the very realities of suffering and death, which pass through his life, an authentic possibility for the good and for life. In the Cross of Christ he perceives the Tree of Life, a revelation of God's passionate love for man. The cure of those who are suffering is thus a daily encounter with the Face of Christ, and the dedication of

4. John Paul II, *Tertio Millennio Adveniente* (November 10, 1994), n. 7.
5. Thomas Aquinas, *Commentary on the Gospel of John,* chapter 14, lecture 2.
6. John Paul II, *Evangelium Vitae* (March 25, 1995), n. 39.

the mind and the heart become a sign of God's mercy and of his victory over death.

Experienced fully, the search is enlightened by science and faith, and from these two "wings" draws dynamism and an impetus, without ever losing its proper humility, the sense of its own limitations. In this way the quest for God becomes fertile for the mind, a leaven of culture, a champion of true humanism, a search that does not stop at the surface.

Dear friends, always let yourselves be guided by the knowledge that comes from on high, by knowledge illuminated by faith, recalling that wisdom demands the passion and effort of seeking.

The indispensable task of the Catholic university fits in here. It is a place in which the educational relationship is placed at the service of the person in the construction of a qualified scientific skill, rooted in a patrimony of the different branches of knowledge that the evolution of generations has distilled into wisdom of life; a place in which the relationship of treatment is not a profession, but a mission; where the charity of the Good Samaritan is the first seat of learning and the face of suffering man is Christ's own Face: "you did it to me" (Mt 25:40).

The Catholic University of the Sacred Heart, in the daily work of research, teaching, and study, lives in this *traditio* that expresses its own potential for innovation: no progress, less still at the cultural level, is nourished by mere repetition, but demands an ever new beginning. Further, it requires the availability for exchange and dialogue that opens the mind and witnesses to the rich fruitfulness of the patrimony of faith. In this way the personality is endowed with a solid structure in which the Christian identity penetrates daily life and from within expresses an excellent professionalism.

Today the Catholic university, which has a special relationship with the See of Peter, is called to be an exemplary institution that does not limit learning to economic question, but rather broadens its scope to the ability to plan. In this the gift of intelligence investigates and develops the gifts of the created world, surmounting a utilitarian vision of existence geared solely to production, because "the human being is made for gift, which expresses and makes present his transcendent dimension."[7]

Precisely this combination of scientific research and unconditional service to life outlines the Catholic features of the Agostino Gemelli Faculty of Medicine and Surgery, because the perspective of faith is found within—neither superimposed nor juxtaposed—the keen and tenacious search for knowledge.

A Catholic faculty of medicine is a place where transcendent humanism is not a rhetorical slogan, but a rule of daily devotion put into practice. Dreaming of an authentically Catholic faculty of medicine and surgery, Fr. Gemelli—and many others with him, such as Prof. Brasca—brought back to the center of attention the human person in his frailty and greatness, in the ever new resources of passionate research and likewise in the awareness of both the limitation and the mystery of life. For this reason you wished to set up a new university center for life to support other institutions already in existence, such, as for example, the Paul VI International Scientific Institute. I therefore encourage attention to life in all its phases.

I would now like to address in particular all the patients present here at the Gemelli, to assure them of my prayers and affection and to tell them that here they will always be lovingly cared for because the face of the suffering Christ is reflected in their own faces.

It is truly God's love that shines out in Christ, that renders the researcher's gaze acute and penetrating and grasps what no investigation can perceive. Blessed Giuseppe Toniolo had this clearly in mind when he asserted that it is in man's nature to read in others the image of God who is Love and his imprint on cre-

7. Benedict XVI, *Caritas in Veritate*, n. 34.

ation. Without love even science loses its nobility. Love alone guarantees the humanity of research.

The Ambiguity of Technological Progress

From *Address to Rome's University Students,* December 13, 2007

Dear young university students, at this familiar encounter, permit me to bring to your attention two brief reflections. The first regards the journey of your spiritual formation. The diocese of Rome wanted to give greater emphasis to young university students' preparation for confirmation; therefore, your pilgrimage to Assisi last November 10 represented the "summons," and this evening your attendance has been the "response." In fact, about 150 of you were presented as candidates for the sacrament of confirmation, which you will receive at the next Pentecost vigil. This is a worthy initiative that fits well into the itinerary of preparation for the World Youth Day scheduled to take place in Sydney in July 2008.

To the candidates for the sacrament of confirmation and to all of you, dear young friends, I would like to say, direct your gaze to the Virgin Mary, and from her "yes," learn also to pronounce your "yes" to the divine call. The Holy Spirit enters into our lives in the measure in which we open our hearts with our "yes": the fuller the "yes," the fuller is the gift of his presence. To understand better, we can refer to a very simple reality: light. If a window's shutters are hermetically sealed, although the light is shining it cannot illuminate the house. If there is a little fissure, a ray of light enters; if the shutters are opened a little more, the room begins to lighten up, but only when completely opened do the sun's rays illuminate and warm the environment. Dear friends, Mary is greeted by the angel as "full of grace," which means exactly this: her heart and her life are totally open to God, and this is why she is completely pervaded by his grace. May she help you to make yourselves a free and full "yes" to God, so that you can be renewed, indeed, transformed by the light and joy of the Holy Spirit.

The second reflection that I wish to propose to you concerns the recent encyclical on Christian hope entitled *Spe Salvi,* "In hope we were saved," words taken from St. Paul's Letter to the Romans (8:24). Ideally I consign it to you, dear university students of Rome, and through you to the whole university, scholastic, cultural, and educational world. Is not the theme of hope particularly suited to young people? In particular I suggest you make the part of the encyclical that concerns the hope of the modern age an object of your reflection and discussion, even in groups. In the seventeenth century Europe experienced an authentic epochal turning point, and from then on it has increasingly confirmed a mentality that views human progress as the work of science and technology alone, while faith concerns only the salvation of the soul, a purely individual salvation. The two great idea-powers of modernity, reason and freedom, are, as it were, separated from God in order to become autonomous and to cooperate in the construction of the "kingdom of man," practically in opposition to the kingdom of God. From here a materialistic concept spread, nourished by the hope that, by changing the economic and political structures, one could finally bring about a just society where peace, freedom, and equality reign. This process, which is not deprived of values and historical motivations, contains, however, a fundamental error: man, in fact, is not only the product of determined economic and social conditions. Technical progress does not necessarily coincide with the moral growth of the person; rather, without ethical principles, science, technology, and politics can be used, as has happened and unfortunately still happens, not for the good, but for the harm of individuals and of humanity.

Dear friends, it is such current themes that stimulate your reflection and favor even more the positive comparison and collaboration that already exist among all state, private, and pontifical universities.

"The Objective Structure of the Universe and the Intellectual Structure of the Human Being Coincide"

From *Message to Archbishop Rino Fisichella, Rector Magnificent of the Pontifical Lateran University, on the Occasion of the International Congress "From Galileo's Telescope to Evolutionary Cosmology, Science, Philosophy and Theology in Dialogue,"* November 30–December 2, 2009

When one opens the *Sidereus Nuncius* and reads Galileo's first words, one is immediately struck by the Pisan scientist's wonder at all that he himself had achieved: "I propose great things in this brief treatise for the observation and contemplation of scholars of nature," he wrote. "Great, I say, because of the excellence of the subject in itself, for its newness, unknown in past centuries, and also for the instrument through which these same things are manifested to our sight."[8] It was the year 1609 when Galileo first pointed skyward an instrument that "I myself devised," he wrote, "enlightened at the outset by divine grace": the telescope. It is easy to imagine what he saw; his awe became excitement and enthusiasm that prompted him to write, "Without any doubt it is a great thing to add innumerable other stars to the immense multitude of fixed stars that until today it has been possible to discern with the natural faculty of sight, and that exceed by more than ten times the number of ancient stars already recorded."[9] The scientist was able to observe with his own eyes what, until that moment, had been no more than controversial hypotheses. It would not be wrong to presume that at this sight, Galileo's profoundly believing mind must have been opened, as it were quite naturally, to prayerful praise, making his own the feelings expressed by the Psalmist: "O Lord, our Lord, how majestic is your name in all the earth! ... When I look at your heavens, the work of your fingers, the moon and the stars that you have estab-

8. Galileo Galilei, *Sidereus Nuncius* [1610], translated [into Italian] by P. A. Giustini (Rome: Lateran University Press, 2009), 89.

9. Galileo, *Sidereus Nuncius,* 89.

lished; what is man that you are mindful of him, and the son of man that you care for him? Yet … you have given him dominion over all the works of your hands; you have put all things under his feet" (cf. Ps 8:1, 3–7).

With this discovery the cultural awareness of facing a crucial point in the history of humanity increased. Science was becoming something different from what the ancients had always thought it to be. Aristotle had made it possible to arrive at the certain knowledge of phenomena, starting with evident and universal principles; Galileo then showed in practice how to approach and observe the phenomena themselves in order to understand their secret causes. The method of deduction gave way to that of induction and prepared the ground for experimentation. The concept of science that had remained the same for centuries was now changing, entering into a modern conception of the world and of humankind. Galileo had delved into unknown paths of the universe; he was opening the door wide to observe ever more immense expanses in space. It is probable that over and above his intentions, the Pisan scientist's discovery also made it possible to go back in time, prompting questions about the very origins of the cosmos and making it clear that after emerging from the Creator's hands, the universe also has a history of its own; "groaning in travail," to borrow the Apostle Paul's words, in the hope that it would be "set free from its bondage to decay and obtain the glorious liberty of the children of God" (Rom 8:21–22).

Today too the universe continues to give rise to questions to which mere observation does not succeed in giving satisfactory answers; the natural and physical sciences alone do not suffice. Indeed, if the analysis of the phenomena remains closed in on itself, it risks making the cosmos seem an insoluble enigma. Matter has an intelligibility that can speak to the human mind and point out a way that goes beyond the mere phenomenon. It is Galileo's lesson that led to this thought.

Was it not the Pisan scientist who maintained that God wrote the book of nature in the language of mathematics? Yet the human mind invented mathematics in order to understand creation; but if nature is really structured with a mathematical language, and mathematics invented by man can manage to understand it, this demonstrates something extraordinary. The objective structure of the universe and the intellectual structure of the human being coincide; the subjective reason and the objectified reason in nature are identical. In the end it is "one" reason that links both and invites us to look to a unique creative Intelligence.[10]

Questions on the immensity of the universe, its origins, and its end, as well as on understanding it, do not admit of a scientific answer alone. Those who look at the cosmos, following Galileo's lesson, will not be able to stop at merely what is observed with the telescope; they will be impelled to go beyond it and wonder about the meaning and end to which all creation is ordered. At this stage philosophy and technology have an important role in smoothing out the way toward further knowledge. Philosophy, confronting the phenomena and beauty of creation, seeks with its reasoning to understand the nature and finality of the cosmos. Theology, founded on the revealed word, examines the beauty and wisdom of the love of God who has left his imprint on created nature.[11] Both reason and faith are involved in this gnoseological act; both offer their light. The greater the knowledge of the complexity of the cosmos, the greater the number of instruments that can satisfy it will be required. There is no conflict on the horizon between the various branches of scientific knowledge and of philosophy and theology. On the contrary, only to the extent that they succeed in entering into dialogue and in exchanging their respective competencies will they be able to present truly effective results to people today.

Galileo's discovery was a crucial landmark in the history of

10. Cf. Benedict XVI, *Address to the Young People of the Diocese of Rome,* April 6, 2006.
11. Cf. Thomas Aquinas, *Summa Theologiae* Ia, q. 45, a. 6.

humanity. It led to other great discoveries with the invention of instruments that have made the technological progress achieved precious.

From the satellites that observe the various phases of the universe, which has paradoxically become smaller, to the highly sophisticated machines used by biomedical engineering, everything shows the greatness of the human mind that, according to the biblical commandment, is called to "subdue" the whole of creation (cf. Gn 1:28), to "till" it and "keep" it (Gn 2:15). Nevertheless, a subtle risk is always involved in so many breakthroughs—namely, that human beings may trust only in science and forget to lift their gaze to the transcendent Being, the Creator of all, who in Jesus Christ revealed his Face of love. I am sure that this Congress's interdisciplinary approach will enable the importance of a unitive vision—the result of a common effort for real scientific progress in the contemplation of the cosmos to be grasped.

Theological Study Is at the Service of the University and Humanity

From *Address to a Delegation of the Theological Faculty of the University of Tübingen in Germany,* March 21, 2007

I thank you for this visit, and I can say that it makes me deeply happy.

On the one hand, an encounter with one's past is always beautiful, because there is something rejuvenating about it. On the other, however, it is something more than a nostalgic meeting.

You yourself, Your Excellency, said that it is also a sign: a sign on the one hand of how dear to me theology is—and how could it be otherwise?—because I had considered teaching to be my true vocation, even if the Good Lord suddenly wanted something else.

At the same time, however, it is also a sign on your part; that is, that you see the interior unity between theological research, doctrine and theological work, and pastoral service in the Church, and thus the total ecclesial commitment for the human being, for the world, and for our future.

Yesterday evening, of course, I started rummaging among my memories with a view to this meeting. So it was that a memory came to mind that fits in with what you have just said, Mr. Dean: in other words, the memory of the Grand Senate. I do not know today whether all the appointments still pass through the Grand Senate.

It was very interesting that when, for example, a chair of mathematics or Assyriology or the physics of solid bodies or any other subject was to be assigned, the contribution from the other faculties was minimal, and everything was resolved quite quickly because almost no one dared to speak out. The situation in the humanistic disciplines was rather different, and when the chairs of theology came up in both faculties, in the end, all had their say.

Thus it was evident that all the professors of the university felt in some way competent in theology; they had the feeling that they could and should participate in the decision. Theology was obviously very dear to them.

Consequently, on the one hand it could be perceived that their colleagues in the other faculties in a certain way considered that theology was the heart of the university, and on the other that theology was precisely something that concerned everyone, in which all felt involved and somehow also knew that they were competent.

In other words, come to think of it, this means that precisely in the debate concerning the chairs of theology, the university could be experienced as a university. I am pleased to learn that these cooptations exist today, more than in the past, although Tübingen has always striven for this.

I do not know whether the *Leibniz-Kolleg* of which I was a member still exists; in any case, the modern university runs a considerable risk of becoming, as it were, a complex of advanced study institutes externally and institutionally united, rather than being able to create the interior unity of *universitas*.

Theology was evidently something in which the universitas was present and in which it was demonstrated that the whole forms a unit, and that precisely at its root are a common questioning, a common task, a common purpose.

I think, moreover, that one can see in this a deep appreciation of theology. I consider this a particularly important fact.

It reveals that in our time—at least in the Latin countries, where the secularity of the state and state institutions is emphasized to the extreme, and therefore the omission of all that has to do with the Church, Christianity, and faith is demanded—interconnections exist from which it is impossible to separate that complex reality that we call theology (which is also fundamentally linked with the Church, faith, and Christianity).

It thus becomes evident in our collection of European situations—however secular, in a certain perspective, they are and must be—that Christian thought, with its questions and answers, is present and accompanies them.

I maintain, on the one hand, that this fact shows that theology itself continues in a certain way to make its contribution and to constitute what the university is.

But on the other, it naturally also implies an immense challenge to theology to satisfy this expectation, to be equal to it, and to carry out the service entrusted to it and expected of it.

I am pleased that through the cooptations that have now become visible in a rather practical way—far more than they used to be—the intra-university debate makes the university truly what it is, involving it in a collective self-questioning and responding.

However, I think that this is also a reason to reflect on how far we are able—not only in Tübingen, but also elsewhere—to satisfy this need. The university and society, humanity, in fact, need questions, but they also need answers. And I hold that in this regard there emerges for theology—and not only for theology—a certain dialectic between scientific rigor and the greatest question that transcends it and constantly emerges from it: the question about truth.

I would like to make this clearer with an example. An exegete, an interpreter of sacred scripture, must explain it as a historical work "secundum artem"—that is, with the scientific rigor that we know in accordance with all the historical elements that require it and with the necessary methodology.

This alone, however, does not suffice for him to be a theologian. If he were to limit himself to doing this, then theology, or at any rate the interpretation of the Bible, would be something similar to Egyptology or Assyriology, or any other specialization.

To be a theologian and to carry out this service for the university, and I dare to say for humanity—hence, the service that is expected of him—he must go further and ask, but is what is said there true? And if it is true, does it concern us? And how does it concern us? And how can we recognize that it is true and concerns us?

In my opinion, in this regard, even in the scientific context, theology is always also requested and called into question over and above the scientific perspective.

The university and humanity are in need of questions. Whenever questions are no longer asked, even those that concern the essential and go beyond any specialization, we no longer receive answers, either.

Only if we ask, and if with our questions we are radical, as radical as theology must be radical over and above any specialization, can we hope to obtain answers to these fundamental questions that concern us all.

First of all, we have to ask questions. Those who do not ask do not get a reply.

But I would add that for theology, in addition to the courage to ask, we also need the humility to listen to the answers that the Christian faith gives us—the humility to perceive in these answers their reasonableness and thus to make them newly accessible to our time and to ourselves.

Thus, not only is the university built up, but humanity also is helped to live.

Theology: Science of Faith

From *Address During Conferral of the First "Ratzinger Prize,"*
June 30, 2011

[Yet] the conferral of the prize can perhaps afford us an opportunity to concentrate for a moment on the fundamental question of what "theology" actually is. Tradition tells us that theology is the science of faith. Here, however, the question immediately arises: is this truly possible? Or is it not in itself a contradiction? Is not science perhaps the opposite of faith? Does not faith cease to be faith when it becomes science? And does not science cease to be science when it is ordered or even subordinated to faith?

These questions, which already posed a serious problem to medieval theology, have become even more impelling with the modern concept of science, and at first sight even seem to have no solution. We understand theology in this way because, in the modern epoch, it has withdrawn from vast sectors, primarily to the area of history, in order to demonstrate here its serious scientific character. It must be recognized with gratitude that this has led to the achievement of grandiose works, and the Christian message has received a new light that is able to reveal its profound riches. Yet, if theology is totally relegated to the past, today it leaves faith in darkness.

Then, at a second stage, the focus was on practice, to show how theology, in connection with psychology and sociology, could be a useful branch of knowledge that provides concrete instructions for life. This is important, too, but if faith, the foundation of theology, were not at the same time to become the object of thought, if praxis were to refer only to itself or to exist only by what it borrows from the human sciences, it would then be emptied and deprived of a foundation.

These approaches are therefore insufficient. However useful and important they may be, they would become an expedient if the true question were to remain unanswered. Briefly: is what we believe in true or not? The question about the truth is at stake in theology—its ultimate and essential foundation. Here a saying of Tertullian can help us take a step forward. He wrote, "Christ has surnamed himself Truth, not Custom"—*non consuetudo sed veritas.*[12]

Christian Gnilka has shown that the concept of "custom" can mean the pagan religions that, in accordance with their nature, were not faith, but rather "custom": one does what one has always done. Traditional forms of worship are observed, and it is hoped thereby to maintain the correct relationship with the mysterious environment of the divine. The revolutionary aspect of Christianity in antiquity was precisely its break with "custom" out of love for the truth. Here Tertullian was speaking above all on the basis of the Gospel according to St. John, in which is found the other fundamental interpretation of the Christian faith that is expressed in the designation of Christ as *Logos.*

If Christ is the *Logos,* the truth, human beings must respond to him with their own *logos,* with their reason. To arrive at Christ they must be on the path of the truth. They must open themselves to the *Logos,* to creative Reason, from which their own reason derives and to which it refers them. From this it may be understood that Christian faith, by its very nature, must bring theology into being, must question itself on the reasonableness of faith—although of course the concept of reason and that of science embrace many dimensions—and in this way the con-

12. Tertullian, *On the Veiling of Virgins* 1.1.

crete nature of the connection between faith and reason must be fathomed ever anew.

Although in Christianity the fundamental connection between *Logos,* truth, and faith is clearly presented, the concrete form of this connection has given rise and is giving rise to ever new questions. It is clear that, today, this question that occupied and will occupy every generation can be addressed neither in detail nor broadly. I would like to try to make one small suggestion.

In the prologue to his Commentary on the *Sentences,* St. Bonaventure spoke of a double use of reason. He spoke of a use that is irreconcilable with the nature of faith and a use that instead belongs to the very nature of faith. *Violentia rationis* therefore exists—the despotism of reason that makes itself the supreme and ultimate judge of all things. This kind of use of reason is certainly impossible in the context of faith. What did Bonaventure mean by this?

A sentence of Psalm 95 can reveal its meaning to us. Here God says to his people, "In the wilderness, when your fathers tested me, and put me to the proof, though they had seen my work" (Ps 95:8–9). A reference is made here to a dual encounter with God: they have "seen." Yet for them this did not suffice. They "tested" God. They wished to subject him to experimentation. He was, so to speak, subjected to an interrogatory and had to submit to an experimental procedure of testing. This use of reason in the modern age has reached the climax of its development in the context of the natural sciences.

Experimental reason largely appears today as the sole form of rationality that is declared scientific. What cannot be scientifically proven or disproven falls outside the scientific sphere. Within this framework great works have been achieved as we know; that this is right and necessary in the context of the knowledge of nature and of its laws no one would seriously question. Yet there is a limit to such a use of reason: God is not an object for human experimentation. He is the Subject and manifests himself solely in the relationship of person to person: this is part of the person's essence.

In this perspective Bonaventure mentions a second use of reason that applies to the context of the "personal," to the important questions implied by actually being human. Love desires to know better what it loves. Love, true love, does not make people blind, but seeing. The thirst for knowledge, for a true knowledge of the other person, is part of love. For this reason the fathers of the Church found the precursors and forerunners of Christianity—outside the world of the revelation of Israel—not in the context of formal religion, but on the contrary in human beings in search of God, in search of the truth, in the "philosophers": in people who were thirsting for truth and were therefore on their way toward God.

When this type of reason is not used, the great questions of humanity fall outside the context of reason and are left to irrationality. This is why an authentic theology is so important. Right faith directs reason to open itself to the divine so that, guided by love for the truth, it may know God more closely. The initiative for this journey is with God, who has placed in human hearts the desire to seek his Face. On the one hand, humility, which lets itself be "touched" by God, and on the other, the discipline bound to the order of reason that keeps love from blindness and helps to develop its visual power, are both part of theology.

I am well aware that all this has not provided an answer to the question on the possibility and duty of right theology, and that light has been shed only on the greatness of the challenge inherent in the nature of theology. Yet it is this very challenge that we human beings need, because it impels us to open our reason by questioning ourselves on the truth itself, on the Face of God. We are therefore grateful to the prizewinners who have shown in their work that reason, progressing on the path marked out by faith, is not an alienated reason, but a reason that corresponds with its most exalted vocation.

Universities: Knowledge and Action

From *Address to the Participants of a Seminar on European Higher Education,* April 10, 2006

I am pleased to welcome you and cordially greet all of you who are taking part in the seminar on the theme, "The Cultural Heritage and Academic Values of the European University and the Attractiveness of the European Higher Education Area." You come from about fifty European countries that adhere to the so-called "Bologna Process," to which the Holy See has also made its own contribution.

In these days your reflection has focused on the contribution that European universities, enriched by their long tradition, can offer to building the Europe of the third millennium, taking into account the fact that every cultural reality is both a memory of the past and a project for the future.

The Church intends to make her own contribution to this reflection as she has done over the centuries. She has taken a constant interest in the study centers and universities of Europe that, together with "the service of thought," have passed on to the young generations the values of a special cultural patrimony, enriched by two millenniums of humanist and Christian experience.[13]

At first monasticism exercised considerable influence. Its merits, both in the spiritual and religious context, also extend to the economic and intellectual spheres. In Charlemagne's time, real schools were founded with the Church's contribution, and the emperor wanted as many people as possible to benefit from them.

A few centuries later the university came into being, receiving an essential impetus from the Church. Numerous European universities, from the University of Bologna to those of Paris, Krakow, Salamanca, Cologne, Oxford, and Prague, to mention

13. Cf. John Paul II, *Ecclesia in Europa,* n. 59.

but a few, rapidly developed and played an important role in consolidating the European identity and building up its cultural heritage.

University institutions have always been distinguished by love of wisdom and the quest for truth, as the true purpose of universities, with constant reference to the Christian vision that recognizes the human being as the masterpiece of creation, since he is formed in the image and likeness of God (cf. Gn 1:26–27).

The conviction that there is a profound unity between truth and good, between the eyes of the mind and those of the heart —"*Ubi amor, ibi oculos,*" as Riccardo di San Vittore said[14]—has always been typical of this vision: love makes one see. Universities came into being from the love of knowledge and from the curiosity of knowing, of knowing what the world is, what man is, but also from a knowledge that leads to action, that leads ultimately to love.

Distinguished ladies and gentlemen, with a quick glance at the "old" continent it is easy to see the cultural challenges that Europe faces today, since it is committed to rediscovering its own identity, which is not exclusively economic or political. The basic question today, as in the past, remains the anthropological question: What is man? Where does he come from? Where must he go? How must he go?

In other words, it is a matter of clarifying the conception of the human being on which new projects are based.

And you are rightly asking yourselves which human being, which image of man, does the university intend to serve: an individual withdrawn into the defense of his own interests, a single perspective of interests, a materialistic perspective, or a person who is open to solidarity with others in the search for the true meaning of existence, which must be a common meaning that transcends the individual?

We also wonder what the relationship between the human

14. Cf. Riccardo di San Vittore, *Beniamin Minor* c. 13.

person, science, and technology is. If, in the nineteenth and twentieth centuries, technology made amazing progress, at the beginning of the twenty-first century further steps were taken: technology also took charge, thanks to computer science, of part of our mental processes, with consequences that involve our way of thinking and can condition our very freedom.

It must be forcefully stated that the human being cannot and must not ever be sacrificed to the success of science and technology; this is why the so-called "anthropological question" assumes its full importance.

For us, the heirs of the humanist tradition founded on Christian values, this question should be faced in the light of the inspiring principles of our civilization, which found in European universities authentic laboratories for research and for deepening knowledge.

"From the biblical conception of man Europe drew the best of its humanistic culture," John Paul II noted in his post-synodal exhortation *Ecclesia in Europa,* "and, not least, advanced the dignity of the person as a subject of inalienable rights."[15] Thus, "the Church," my venerable predecessor added, "helped to spread and consolidate those values that have made European culture universal."[16]

But man cannot understand himself fully if he ignores God. This is the reason that, at the time when the Europe of the third millennium is being built, the religious dimension of human existence cannot be neglected.

Here the special role of the university emerges as a scientific universe that is not merely limited to various specializations; in the current situation the university is required not to stop at teaching or imparting technical and professional knowledge, which are very important disciplines but do not suffice, for it must also undertake to play an attentive educational role at the

15. John Paul II, *Ecclesia in Europa,* n. 25.
16. John Paul II, *Ecclesia in Europa,* n. 25.

service of the new generations, making use of the legacy of ideals and values that marked the past millennia.

Thus universities will be able to help Europe to preserve and rediscover its "soul," revitalizing the Christian roots that brought it into being.

The Accuracy and Limitations of Science

From *Address to the Members of the Pontifical Academy of Sciences,* November 6, 2006

I am pleased to greet the members of the Pontifical Academy of Sciences on the occasion of this plenary assembly, and I thank Professor Nicola Cabibbo for his kind words of greeting in your name. The theme of your meeting—"Predictability in Science: Accuracy and Limitations"—deals with a distinctive attribute of modern science. Predictability, in fact, is one of the chief reasons for science's prestige in contemporary society. The establishment of the scientific method has given the sciences the ability to predict phenomena, to study their development, and thus to control the environment in which man lives.

This increasing "advance" of science, and especially its capacity to master nature through technology, has at times been linked to a corresponding "retreat" of philosophy, of religion, and even of the Christian faith. Indeed, some have seen in the progress of modern science and technology one of the main causes of secularization and materialism: why invoke God's control over these phenomena when science has shown itself capable of doing the same thing? Certainly the Church acknowledges that "with the help of science and technology…, man has extended his mastery over almost the whole of nature," and thus "he now produces by his own enterprise benefits once looked for from heavenly powers."[17] At the same time Christianity does not posit an inevitable conflict between supernatural faith and scientific progress. The

17. Second Vatican Council, *Gaudium et Spes,* n. 33.

very starting point of biblical revelation is the affirmation that God created human beings, endowed them with reason, and set them over all the creatures of the earth. In this way man has become the steward of creation and God's "helper." If we think, for example, of how modern science, by predicting natural phenomena, has contributed to the protection of the environment, the progress of developing nations, the fight against epidemics, and an increase in life expectancy, it becomes clear that there is no conflict between God's providence and human enterprise. Indeed, we could say that the work of predicting, controlling, and governing nature, which science today renders more practicable than in the past, is itself a part of the Creator's plan.

Science, however, while giving generously, gives only what it is meant to give. Man cannot place in science and technology so radical and unconditional a trust as to believe that scientific and technological progress can explain everything and completely fulfill all his existential and spiritual needs. Science cannot replace philosophy and revelation by giving an exhaustive answer to man's most radical questions—questions about the meaning of living and dying, about ultimate values, and about the nature of progress itself. For this reason, the Second Vatican Council, after acknowledging the benefits gained by scientific advances, pointed out that the "scientific methods of investigation can be unjustifiably taken as the supreme norm for arriving at truth," and added that "there is a danger that man, trusting too much in the discoveries of today, may think that he is sufficient unto himself and no longer seek the higher values."[18]

Scientific predictability also raises the question of the scientist's ethical responsibilities. His conclusions must be guided by respect for truth and an honest acknowledgment of both the accuracy and the inevitable limitations of the scientific method. Certainly this means avoiding needlessly alarming predictions when these are not supported by sufficient data or exceed sci-

18. Second Vatican Council, *Gaudium et Spes,* n. 57.

ence's actual ability to predict. But it also means avoiding the opposite—namely a silence, born of fear, in the face of genuine problems. The influence of scientists in shaping public opinion on the basis of their knowledge is too important to be undermined by undue haste or the pursuit of superficial publicity. As my predecessor, Pope John Paul II, once observed, "Scientists, precisely because they 'know more,' are called to 'serve more.' Since the freedom they enjoy in research gives them access to specialized knowledge, they have the responsibility of using that knowledge wisely for the benefit of the entire human family."[19]

Dear academicians, our world continues to look to you and your colleagues for a clear understanding of the possible consequences of many important natural phenomena. I think, for example, of the continuing threats to the environment that are affecting whole peoples and the urgent need to discover safe, alternative energy sources available to all. Scientists will find support from the Church in their efforts to confront these issues, since the Church has received from her divine founder the task of guiding people's consciences toward goodness, solidarity, and peace. Precisely for this reason she feels duty-bound to insist that science's ability to predict and control must never be employed against human life and its dignity, but always placed at its service, at the service of this and future generations.

There is one final reflection that the subject of your assembly can suggest to us today. As some of the papers presented in the last few days have emphasized, the scientific method itself, in its gathering of data and in the processing and use of those data in projections, has inherent limitations that necessarily restrict scientific predictability to specific contexts and approaches. Science cannot, therefore, presume to provide a complete, deterministic representation of our future and of the development of every phenomenon that it studies. Philosophy and theology might make an important contribution to this fundamentally

19. John Paul II, *Address to the Pontifical Academy of Sciences,* November 11, 2002.

epistemological question by, for example, helping the empirical sciences to recognize a difference between the mathematical inability to predict certain events and the validity of the principle of causality, or between scientific indeterminism or contingency (randomness) and causality on the philosophical level, or, more radically, between evolution as the origin of a succession in space and time and creation as the ultimate origin of participated being in essential Being.

At the same time there is a higher level that necessarily transcends all scientific predictions—namely, the human world of freedom and history. Whereas the physical cosmos can have its own spatial-temporal development, only humanity, strictly speaking, has a history, the history of its freedom. Freedom, like reason, is a precious part of God's image within us, and it can never be reduced to a deterministic analysis. Its transcendence vis-à-vis the material world must be acknowledged and respected, since it is a sign of our human dignity. Denying that transcendence in the name of a supposed absolute ability of the scientific method to predict and condition the human world would involve the loss of what is human in man and, by failing to recognize his uniqueness and transcendence, could dangerously open the door to his exploitation.

Study Theology With Every Discipline

From *Address to Students and Teachers of the Ecclesiastical Universities of Rome,* October 30, 2008

In this year, in which we celebrate the bi-millennial jubilee of the birth of the Apostle Paul, I would like to pause briefly together with you on one aspect of his message that seems to me particularly suitable for you, students and academics, and on which I also spoke yesterday in the catechesis during the General Audience. I am referring, then, to what St. Paul writes on Christian wisdom, in particular in his First Letter to the Corinthians, a community in which rivalries had broken out among the disciples. The apostle confronts the problem of these divisions within the community, pointing out a sign of false wisdom among them, or of a mentality that is still immature because it is carnal and not spiritual (cf. 1 Cor 3:1–3). Referring next to his own experience, Paul reminds the Corinthians that Christ sent him to preach the gospel "not with worldly 'wisdom,' however, lest the cross of Christ be rendered void of its meaning" (1 Cor 1:17).

From here he takes up a reflection on the "wisdom of the Cross" or, it is worth saying, the wisdom of God, which opposes the wisdom of this world. The apostle insists on the existent contrast between the two wisdoms, only one of which is true—the divine, while the other is in reality "foolishness." Now the stupefying news, which must always be rediscovered and received, is the fact that divine wisdom, in Christ, has been given to us, has made us participants. At the end of the second chapter of the aforementioned Letter, there is an expression that summarizes this news and for just this reason never ceases to surprise. St. Paul writes, "But we have the mind of Christ" (1 Cor 2:16).

This contrast of the two wisdoms is not to be identified with the difference between theology to one side and philosophy and science to the other. It actually concerns two fundamental attitudes. The "wisdom of this world" is a way of living and of viewing things apart from God and following dominant opinions, according to the criteria of success and power. "Divine wisdom" consists in following the mind of Christ; it is Christ who opens the eyes of our heart to follow the path of truth and love.

Dear students, you have come to Rome to deepen your knowledge in the theological field, and even if you study other material different from theology, for example law, history, humanities, art, etc., still, spiritual formation according to the mind of Christ remains fundamental for you, and this is the prospect of your studies. Therefore these words of the Apostle Paul and those that we read immediately after, still in the First Letter to the Corinthians, are important for you: "Who, for example, knows a man's innermost self but the man's own spirit within him? Similarly no one knows what lies at the depths of God but the Spirit of God. The Spirit we have received is not the world's spirit but God's Spirit, helping us to recognize the gifts he has given us" (1 Cor 2:11–12). Here we are still within the sphere of contrast between human wisdom and that which is divine. In order to know and understand spiritual things, it is necessary to be spiritual men and women, because if one is of the flesh one inevitably falls into foolishness, even if one studies much and becomes "scholarly" and a "master of worldly argument" (cf. 1 Cor 1:20).

In this Pauline text we can see an approach as meaningful as the gospel verses that tell of Jesus's blessing of God the Father, because the Lord says, "you have hidden these things from the wise and clever and revealed them to babes" (Mt 11:25). The "wise" of which Jesus speaks are those whom Paul calls the "wise of this world." Meanwhile, the "babes" are those whom the apostle calls "foolish," "weak," "low and despised" (1 Cor 1:27–28), but who in reality, if they accept "the word of the Cross" (1 Cor 1:18), become truly wise. This is why Paul exhorts those who consider themselves wise according to worldly criteria to "become a fool," to become truly wise before God (1 Cor 3:18). This is not an anti-intellectual attitude; it is not in opposition to *recta ratio*. Paul following Jesus is opposed to the type of arrogant intellectualism in which a man, even if he knows a great deal, loses sensitivity to truth and the freedom to open himself to the newness of divine action.

Thus, dear friends, this Pauline reflection does not at all wish to lead to an undervaluing of the human effort necessary for knowledge, but instead places it on another level: Paul cared to emphasize, and he does so without compromise, what it is that truly counts for salvation and what instead can bring division and ruin. The apostle thus denounces the poison of false wisdom—

that is, human pride. It is not in fact knowledge in itself that can do harm, but the presumption, the "bragging" over what one has come or presumes to have come to know. It is precisely here that divisions and disagreements originate in the Church and, analogously, in society. Thus it entails a cultivation of wisdom not according to the flesh, but rather according to the Spirit. We know well that St. Paul, with the words "flesh, carnal" does not refer to the body, but to a way of living only for oneself and according to worldly standards. Therefore, according to Paul, it is always necessary to purify one's own body of the poison of pride present in each one of us. We too, with St. Paul, must raise the cry, "Who will free us?" (cf. Rom 7:24). And we too can receive with him the response: the grace of Jesus Christ, that the Father has given us through the Holy Spirit (cf. Rom 7:25). The "mind of Christ," which through grace we have received, purifies us of false wisdom. And this "mind of Christ" welcomes us through the Church and into the Church, taking us to the river of her living tradition. The iconography that depicts Jesus-Wisdom in the womb of Mother Mary, symbol of the Church, expresses this very well: *In gremio Matris sedet Sapientia Patris;* in Mary's womb sits the Wisdom of the Father—that is, Christ. Remaining faithful to that Jesus whom Mary offers us, to the Christ whom the Church presents to us, we can commit ourselves intensely to intellectual work, internally free from the temptation of pride and boasting always and only in the Lord.

The Mutual Enrichment of Science and Theology

From *Address to Members of the Pontifical Academy of Sciences on the Occasion of Their Plenary Assembly,* October 31, 2008

In choosing the topic "Scientific Insight into the Evolution of the Universe and of Life," you seek to focus on an area of inquiry that elicits much interest. In fact, many of our contemporaries today wish to reflect upon the ultimate origin of beings, their cause, and their end, and the meaning of human history and the universe.

In this context questions concerning the relationship between science's reading of the world and the reading offered by Christian revelation naturally arise. My predecessors Pope Pius XII and Pope John Paul II noted that there is no opposition between faith's understanding of creation and the evidence of the empirical sciences. Philosophy in its early stages had proposed images to explain the origin of the cosmos on the basis of one or more elements of the material world. This genesis was not seen as a creation, but rather a mutation or transformation; it involved a somewhat horizontal interpretation of the origin of the world. A decisive advance in understanding the origin of the cosmos was the consideration of being *qua* being and the concern of metaphysics with the most basic question of the first or transcendent origin of participated being. In order to develop and evolve, the world must first *be,* and thus have come from nothing into being. It must be created, in other words, by the first Being, who is such by essence.

To state that the foundation of the cosmos and its developments is the provident wisdom of the Creator is not to say that creation has only to do with the beginning of the history of the world and of life. It implies, rather, that the Creator founds these developments and supports them, underpins them and sustains them continuously. Thomas Aquinas taught that the notion of creation must transcend the horizontal origin of the unfolding of events, which is history, and consequently all our purely naturalistic ways of thinking and speaking about the evolution of the world. Thomas observed that creation is neither a movement nor a mutation. It is instead the foundational and continuing relationship that links the creature to the Creator, for he is the cause of every being and all becoming.[20]

To "evolve" literally means "to unroll a scroll"—that is, to

20. Cf. Thomas Aquinas, *Summa Theologiae* I, q. 45, a. 3.

read a book. The imagery of nature as a book has its roots in Christianity and has been held dear by many scientists. Galileo saw nature as a book whose author is God in the same way that scripture has God as its author. It is a book whose history, whose evolution, whose "writing" and meaning, we "read" according to the different approaches of the sciences, while all the time presupposing the foundational presence of the author who has wished to reveal himself therein. This image also helps us to understand that the world, far from originating out of chaos, resembles an ordered book; it is a cosmos. Notwithstanding elements of the irrational, chaotic, and the destructive in the long processes of change in the cosmos, matter as such is "legible." It has an inbuilt "mathematics." The human mind therefore can engage not only in a "cosmography" studying measurable phenomena, but also in a "cosmology" discerning the visible inner logic of the cosmos. We may not at first be able to see the harmony both of the whole and of the relations of the individual parts or their relationship to the whole. Yet there always remains a broad range of intelligible events, and the process is rational in that it reveals an order of evident correspondences and undeniable finalities: in the inorganic world, between microstructure and macrostructure; in the organic and animal world, between structure and function; and in the spiritual world, between knowledge of the truth and the aspiration to freedom. Experimental and philosophical inquiry gradually discovers these orders; it perceives them working to maintain themselves in being, defending themselves against imbalances, and overcoming obstacles. And thanks to the natural sciences we have greatly increased our understanding of the uniqueness of humanity's place in the cosmos.

The distinction between a simple living being and a spiritual being that is *capax Dei* points to the existence of the intellective soul of a free transcendent subject. Thus the magisterium of the Church has constantly affirmed that "every spiritual soul is created immediately by God—it is not 'produced' by the parents—and also that it is immortal."[21] This points to the distinctiveness of anthropology and invites exploration of it by modern thought.

Distinguished academicians, I wish to conclude by recalling the words addressed to you by my predecessor, Pope John Paul II, in November 2003: "scientific truth, which is itself a participation in divine Truth, can help philosophy and theology to understand ever more fully the human person and God's Revelation about man, a Revelation that is completed and perfected in Jesus Christ. For this important mutual enrichment in the search for the truth and the benefit of mankind, I am, with the whole Church, profoundly grateful."[22]

Pius XII: Science and Morality

From *Address to Participants at a Congress on "The Heritage of the Magisterium of Pius XII and the Second Vatican Council,"* Promoted by the Pontifical Lateran University and the Pontifical Gregorian University, November 8, 2008

I have admired the demanding theme on which you have concentrated your attention. In the last years, when one spoke of Pius XII, the attention was drawn in an excessive way to only one issue, considered, moreover, in a rather unilateral manner. Every other consideration aside, this has impeded an adequate approach to the figure of great historical-theological depth that Pope Pius XII has been. The convergence of the impressive activity that took place during this pontificate and, in a singular way, his magisterium, on what you have considered in these days is an eloquent proof of what I just affirmed. Indeed, his magisterium is characterized for the vast and beneficent breadth and for his exceptional quality, such that one cannot fail to say that

21. *Catechism of the Catholic Church* (1993), n. 366.
22. John Paul II, *Address to the Members of the Pontifical Academy of Sciences,* November 10, 2003.

it constitutes a precious heritage of which the Church has and continues to treasure.

I have spoken of "the vast and beneficent breadth" of this magisterium. It suffices to recall, in this regard, the encyclicals and the many addresses and radio messages contained in the twenty volumes of his *Teachings.* There are more than forty encyclicals published by him. Among them *Mystici Corporis* stands out, in which the pope deals with the theme of the true and intimate nature of the Church. On the scale of research he sheds light on our profound ontological union with Christ and in him, through him, and with him with all the other faithful moved by his Spirit, who are nourished by his body and, transformed in him, are able to continue to extend his salvific work in the world.

Intimately linked to *Mystici Corporis* are two other encyclicals: *Divino Afflante Spiritu,* on the sacred scripture, and *Mediator Dei,* on the sacred liturgy. These present two sources from which those who belong to Christ Head of that mystical body, the Church, must draw. In this wide-ranging context Pius XII has considered the various categories of persons: priests, religious, and laity who, by the will of the Lord, partake in the Church, although with different vocations and duties. Thus he has pronounced wise norms on the formation of priests, who must distinguish themselves for personal love for Christ, simplicity and sobriety of life, loyalty to their bishop, and openness to those who are entrusted to their pastoral care. Then in the encyclical *Sacra Virginitas* and in other documents on religious life, Pius XII has put in clear light the excellence of the "gift" that God grants to certain persons, inviting them to consecrate themselves totally to his service and to their neighbor in the Church.

In this perspective the pope strongly insists on the return to the gospel and to the authentic charism of the founders and foundresses of the various religious orders and congregations, foreseeing also the necessity of some healthy reforms. There have also been numerous occasions in which Pius XII has treated the responsibility of laity in the Church, in particular taking advantage of the large international congresses dedicated to this theme. He willingly faced problems of specific professions, indicating, for example, the duty of judges, of lawyers, of social workers, of doctors; to the latter, the supreme pontiff dedicated numerous discourses illustrating the deontological norms that must be respected in their work. In the encyclical *Miranda Prorsus,* the pope dwelt on the great importance of the modern means of communication, which in an ever more incisive way are influencing public opinion. This is exactly why the supreme pontiff, who utilized the new invention of the radio maximally, emphasized the duty of journalists to supply truthful information respectful of the moral norms.

Pius XII also addressed his attention to science and to the extraordinary progress that it achieved. While admiring the conquests reached in these fields, the pope did not fail to warn about the risks that research that disregards moral values could bring. It suffices to recall one example: the famous discourse he pronounced when the atom was split. With extraordinary foresight, the pope admonished about the need to impede at whatever cost that these ingenious scientific progresses would be used to build deadly arms that would be able to provoke dreadful catastrophes and even the total destruction of humanity. How can one not recall the long and inspiring discourses concerning the hoped-for reordering of civil society, national and international, for which he indicates justice as a necessary foundation, true supposition for coexistence among peoples: *"opus iustitiae pax!"*? Equally worthy of special mention is the mariological teaching of Pius XII, which would reach its culmination in the proclamation of the Dogma of the Assumption of Mary Most Holy, through whom the holy father intended to emphasize the eschatological dimension of our existence and exalt the dignity of the woman, as well.

What can be said of the quality of Pius XII's teaching? He

was contrary to improvisations; he wrote each discourse with the maximum care, weighing each phrase and each word before pronouncing it in public. He attentively studied the various questions, and he had the habit of asking council from renowned specialists when he treated themes requiring a particular competence. By nature and temperament Pius XII was a realistic and measured man, disinclined to easy optimism, but he was likewise immune from the danger of pessimism that is not suitable for believers. He abhorred sterile polemics and was deeply distrustful in regard to fanaticism and sentimentalism.

These interior attitudes of his justify the value and depth, as well as the trustworthiness of his teaching, and explain the confident adhesion that not only the faithful reserve for them, but also many people who do not belong to the Church. Considering the lofty and widespread quality of Pius XII's magisterium, one must consider how he was able to do so much, although he had to dedicate himself to many other duties connected to his office as supreme pontiff: the daily governing of the Church, the nomination and the visits of bishops, the visits of the heads of state and of diplomats, the countless audiences granted to private persons and many diverse groups.

Everyone acknowledges Pius XII's uncommon intelligence, iron memory, singular familiarity with foreign languages, and a noteworthy sensitivity. It is said that he was an accomplished diplomat, an outstanding jurist, an excellent theologian. All this is true, but it does not explain everything; in him there was also the continuous effort and the firm will to give himself to God without regard for his delicate health. This was the true driving force of his behavior: all was born from love for his Lord Jesus Christ and from love for the Church and for humanity. Indeed, before all else he was a priest in constant and intimate union with God, a priest who found the strength for his enormous work in long periods of prayer before the blessed sacrament, in silent colloquy with his Creator and Redeemer. From there sprang the origin and impulse of his magisterium as, on the other hand, it was for his every other activity.

Therefore it must not be surprising that his teaching continues even today to shed light in the Church. Already fifty years have passed since his death, but his multifaceted and fruitful magisterium remains even for Christians today one of priceless value. Certainly the Church, mystical body of Christ, is a living and vital organism, not steadfastly defending what was fifty years ago. But development occurs in coherency. This is why the heritage of the magisterium of Pius XII has been gathered by the Second Vatican Council and reproposed to the later Christian generations. It is well-known that of the oral interventions and writings presented by the Second Vatican Council Fathers, over one thousand references cite the magisterium of Pius XII. Not all the documents of the Council have an array of notes, but in those documents that do have them, the name of Pius XII recurs more than two hundred times. This means that, with the exception of sacred scripture, this pope is the most authoritative and frequently cited source. It is also well-known that the special notes of these documents are not generally simple explicative references, but often constitute true and proper integral parts of conciliar texts. They do not furnish only justifications to support what the text affirms, but offer an interpretive key.

Therefore we can rightly say that in the person of the supreme pontiff Pius XII the Lord has made an exceptional gift to his Church, for which we must all be thankful. Therefore I renew the expression of my appreciation for the important work you undertook in preparing and carrying out this international symposium on the magisterium of Pius XII, and I hope that the precious inheritance that the immortal pontiff left to the Church continues to be reflected upon to draw useful application to the problems emerging today.

Scientific Research as Christian Inspiration

From *Address to the Students and Teachers of the "Libera Università Maria Santissima Assunta" (Lumsa)*, November 12, 2009

The contemporary context is marked by a disturbing educational emergency, on which I have been able to reflect on various occasions, and in which the task of those called to the teaching profession acquires a quite special importance. It is primarily a question of the role of university teachers, but also of the actual educational curriculum of students training to be teachers in the different kinds and grades of school or as professionals in the various social milieus. In fact every profession becomes an opportunity for the witness and practical expression of values personally internalized during the academic period. The profound economic crisis that has spread across the whole world, together with its root causes, has brought to the fore the need for a more decisive and courageous investment in the field of knowledge and education as a way to respond to the numerous open-ended challenges and to prepare the young generations to build a better future.[23] Thus the need is being felt to make connections in thought, to teach interdisciplinary collaboration and reciprocal learning. Moreover, in the face of the profound changes that are taking place, it is ever more urgently necessary to refer to the fundamental values that must be passed on as an indispensable patrimony to the young generations and, consequently, to question oneself on what these values are. Academic institutions are therefore being confronted by pressing ethical questions.

In this context, faithful to their specific identity and in the effort to render a qualified service in the Church and in society, Catholic universities are entrusted with an important role. In this regard the instructions given by my venerable predecessor John Paul II in the apostolic constitution *Ex Corde Ecclesiae* are more timely than ever. He invited the Catholic university

23. Cf. Benedict XVI, *Caritas in Veritate,* nn. 30–31, 66.

to assure in an institutional manner a Christian presence in the university world. In the complex social and cultural reality, the Catholic university is expected to act with a Christian inspiration, not only of individuals, but of the university community as a whole; with a continuing sapiential reflection, illumined by faith, and scientific research; in fidelity to the Christian message as it comes to us through the Church; with an institutional commitment to the service of the people of God and of the human family in their pilgrimage to the transcendent destination.[24]

Dear friends, LUMSA is a Catholic university; this Christian inspiration is a specific element of its identity. As may be read in its *Magna Carta,* it proposes scientific work oriented to the search for truth in a dialogue between faith and reason, striving for the ideal spiritual integration of knowledge and values. At the same time a formative activity is established, to be carried out with constant attention to ethics, elaborating positive syntheses between faith and culture and between science and knowledge, for the full and harmonious development of the human person. This structure, dear teachers, is both stimulating and demanding for you. Indeed, while you strive to be ever better qualified in teaching and in research, you also propose to cultivate the educational mission. Today, as in the past, the university stands in need of true teachers who transmit, together with scientific content and knowledge, a strict method of research and profound values and motivation. Immersed in a fragmented and relativistic society, dear students, always keep your minds and hearts open to the truth. Devote yourselves to acquiring a profound knowledge that contributes to the integral formation of your personality, to refining your ability to seek the true and the good throughout your life, to train professionally in order to become builders of a society in which there is greater justice and solidarity. May Mother Tincani's example nurture in you all the commitment to accompany your rigorous academic work with an intense inner life sustained by prayer.

24. Cf. Benedict XVI, *Caritas in Veritate,* n. 13.

CONCLUSION

CARITAS AND MISSION

University Life: A Missionary Commitment

Pope Benedict XVI, *Address to the Participants of the*
First European Meeting of University Students Promoted by the
University Section of the Catechesis School University (CSU)
Commission of the Council of European Bishops'
Conferences (CCEE), July 11, 2009

What does the Church expect of you? It is the very theme on which you are reflecting that suggests the appropriate response: *"New Disciples of Emmaus: Being Christians in the University."* After the meeting of European professors that took place two years ago, now you students are also coming together to offer the Bishops' Conferences of Europe your willingness to continue on the path of cultural elaboration that St. Benedict intuited would be necessary for the human and Christian maturation of the European peoples. This can happen if, like the disciples of Emmaus, you encounter the risen Lord in a practical experience of Church and, in particular, in the eucharistic celebration. As I reminded your peers a year ago during the World Youth Day held in Sydney, "At each Mass, in fact, the Holy Spirit descends anew, invoked by the solemn prayer of the Church, not only to transform our gifts of bread and wine into the Lord's body and blood but also to transform our lives, to make us, in his power, 'one body, one spirit in Christ.'"[1] Your missionary commitment in the university context therefore consists in witnessing to the personal encounter you have had with Jesus Christ, the Truth that illuminates the path of every person. That "newness of heart" capable of giving a new sense of direction to personal existence originates from the encounter with him; and it is only in this way that one becomes a ferment and leaven of a society enlivened by evangelical love.

Therefore it is easy to understand why pastoral ministry within the university must be expressed with its full theological and spiritual value, helping young people to ensure that communion with Christ leads them to perceive the deepest mystery of mankind and of history. And, precisely because of their specific evangelizing action, the ecclesial communities involved in this missionary action, such as, for example, the university chaplaincies, can be the place for the formation of mature believers, men and women aware of being loved by God and called, in Christ, to become animators of university ministry. The Christian presence within universities becomes increasingly demanding and at the same time fascinating, because faith, as in past centuries, is called to offer its irreplaceable service to knowledge, which in contemporary society is the true driving force behind development. It is on knowledge, enriched with the contribution of faith, that a people's ability to know how to look to the future with hope, overcoming the temptations of a purely materialistic vision of our essence and of history, depends.

Dear young people, you are the future of Europe. Immersed in these years of study in the world of knowledge, you are called to make use of your best resources—not only intellectual—in order to build your characters and to contribute to the common good. Working for the development of knowledge is the specific vocation of universities and, in the face of the vastness and com-

---

1. Pope Benedict XVI, *Homily at World Youth Day Mass,* Apostolic Journey to Sydney (Australia) on the Occasion of the 23rd World Youth Day, Sydney, July 20, 2008.

plexity of knowledge available to humanity, it requires a higher and higher moral and spiritual quality. The new cultural synthesis being formed in our time in Europe and the globalized world needs the contribution of intellectuals who can present the subject of God anew in academic lecture halls, or rather regenerate that human desire to seek God *"quaerere Deum"* that I have mentioned on other occasions....

Dear young people, together with your teachers you help to create laboratories of faith and culture, sharing the efforts of study and research with all the friends whom you meet at the university. Love your universities, which are training grounds for virtue and service. The Church in Europe places deep trust in all of your generous apostolic commitment, aware of the challenges and difficulties, but also of the great potential of pastoral action in the university sphere.

INDEX

A Reason Open to God: On Universities, Education, and Culture
was designed in Garamond by Kachergis Book Design of Pittsboro,
North Carolina. It was printed on 60-pound Natures Natural
and bound by Thomson-Shore of Dexter, Michigan.